Health Policy Management

A Case Study Approach

Rachel Ellison, PhD
Assistant Professor
Health Services Administration Program Coordinator
University of Louisiana at Lafayette

Lesley Clack, ScD
Assistant Professor
Master of Health Administration Program Coordinator
University of Georgia

JONES & BARTLETT
LEARNING

World Headquarters
Jones & Bartlett Learning
5 Wall Street
Burlington, MA 01803
978-443-5000
info@jblearning.com
www.jblearning.com

Jones & Bartlett Learning books and products are available through most bookstores and online booksellers. To contact Jones & Bartlett Learning directly, call 800-832-0034, fax 978-443-8000, or visit our website, www.jblearning.com.

Production Credits
VP, Product Management: Amanda Martin
Director of Product Management: Matthew Kane
Product Specialist: Christina Freitas
Manager, Project Management: Lori Mortimer
Project Specialist: John Coakley
Digital Project Specialist: Rachel DiMaggio
Senior Marketing Manager: Jennifer Scherzay
Production Services Manager: Colleen Lamy
Product Fulfillment Manager: Wendy Kilborn
Composition: S4Carlisle Publishing Services
Project Management: S4Carlisle Publishing Services
Cover Design: Theresa Manley
Text Design: Kristin E. Parker
Senior Media Development Editor: Troy Liston
Rights & Permissions Manager: John Rusk
Cover Image (Title Page, Part Opener, Chapter Opener):
   © exdez/Getty Images
Printing and Binding: McNaughton & Gunn

Library of Congress Cataloging-in-Publication Data
Names: Ellison, Rachel, PhD, author. | Clack, Lesley, author.
Title: Health policy management : a case approach / by Rachel Ellison, Lesley
   Clack.
Description: Burlington, MA : Jones & Bartlett Learning, [2020] | Includes
   bibliographical references.
Identifiers: LCCN 2019018810 | ISBN 9781284154276 (paperback)
Subjects: | MESH: Health Policy | Guideline Adherence | Ethics, Medical |
   United States
Classification: LCC RA418 | NLM WA 540 AA1 | DDC 362.1--dc23
LC record available at https://lccn.loc.gov/2019018810

6048

Printed in the United States of America
24 23 22 21 20   10 9 8 7 6 5 4 3 2 1

Contents

Foreword

Tell me and I forget. Teach me and I remember. Involve me and I learn.

Quote by Benjamin Franklin

Health policy management is a subject to be learned by health administration students and employed by health administration graduates. Several years ago, we had a faculty debate over the relative emphasis of health policy and health management in the health administration curriculum. Many of us were fascinated to learn about the health policy challenges facing senior managers in health systems, and the management challenges facing senior health policy analysts and policymakers. Clearly, our health administration students need to learn health policy management. This new book provides both content and a foundation for pedagogy to assure that health policy management is remembered and learned.

The editors of this book, Rachel Ellison and Lesley Clack, have solicited and obtained policy descriptions and cases from nearly 30 authors who are well-known in the health policy and management field. The book opens with a policy introduction and presentation of the legislative process. In each section, there is a good balance of material that establishes a framework to think about issues that require thoughtful policy-making. Some cases highlight the framework (e.g., Case 1-2: How Policy is Made: A Process Model). Most cases highlight the policy itself (e.g., Case 1-3: Policymaking for a Better Tomorrow: Stop the Bullying). For each case, there is a manageable number of questions to guide the learning process.

Following the introduction, one-third of this text discusses cases concerning the financing of health care. This is appropriate given the critical role of financing as a policy tool. The rest of the book covers a range of health policy issues from quality and safety to rights and ethics. These topics are substantive enough for any one of the policy issues addressed to warrant a book and a course all to itself. The keys to this book, and the course that it would serve, are to first recognize the policy-making process that underlies so many issues affecting health administration, and to then develop responses that are thoughtful and responsive to the many parties affected by policy.

Tailoring a book to a clear audience is very important. There are already health policy books designed for nurses (Porche, 2019), other clinical professionals (Bodenheimer & Grumbach, 2018), and graduate health administration students and public policy students. The *Journal of Health Administration Education* occasionally publishes cases, though most are aimed at graduate students. The editors here have sought out cases specifically to address health policy management for undergraduates who are unlikely to have substantial administrative, clinical, or policy experience. These cases offer a good balance of substantive-yet-approachable health policy management foundations and issues.

In most circumstances, we cannot do the first best thing and directly involve students in health policy development, response, or analysis. There are too many financial, logistical, and time-related constraints. Consequently, studying cases is the next best option. Beyond reading prescriptions for results, cases involve students in understanding issues and exploring responses. This book provides a solid foundation upon which students will develop their knowledge of health policy management.

Dean G. Smith, PhD

Dean and Richard A. Culbertson Professor of Health Policy & Systems Management, School of Public Health, Louisiana State University Health Sciences Center – New Orleans

Professor Emeritus of Health Management & Policy, School of Public Health, University of Michigan – Ann Arbor

Editor, *Journal of Health Administration Education*

▶ References

Bodenheimer, T. S., & Grumbach, K. (2018). *Understanding health policy: A clinic approach* (7th ed.). New York, NY: McGraw-Hill.

Porche, D. J. (2019). *Heath policy: Application for nurses and other healthcare* (2nd ed.). Burlington, MA: Jones & Bartlett Learning.

Preface

Health Policy Management: A Case Study Approach is intended to provide both instructors and students with didactic content that is supported by case studies that allow for critical thinking and analysis of different health policy concepts. This book came about due to both editors' experiences with teaching health policy courses, and their recognition of the need for textbooks that stand the test of time. In an ever-changing health policy landscape, this text is needed more than ever. The core of this book is its case study approach. The didactic content is intended to be limited in scope in order to allow instructors to add current health policy context through their teaching, while the case studies offer a way for students to apply current health policy concepts and ideology in their analyses.

The 42 cases included in this book represent a wide diversity of situations and experiences within the health policy context. Analysis of each case study will help readers uncover a deeper understanding of each topic. We hope that you find this text to be a valuable teaching tool that enhances students' experience in health policy management and related courses.

Best,
Rachel Ellison, PhD & Lesley Clack, ScD

© exdez/Getty Images

Acknowledgments

We would like to thank the 25+ contributing authors for their efforts, and for sharing their wealth of experience and knowledge through the case studies. The contributors range from faculty to practitioners, with backgrounds across the healthcare spectrum from policy, management, law, nursing, informatics, and beyond. It is through their contributions that we are able to provide such diverse and immersive cases.

In addition, we would like to thank our team at Jones & Bartlett Learning for this opportunity, and for their assistance and guidance through this process. And finally, we appreciate the encouragement and support from friends, family, and colleagues throughout this journey.

▶ About the Editors

Rachel Ellison, PhD
Rachel Ellison is currently an assistant professor in the department of Allied Health at the University of Louisiana at Lafayette in Lafayette, Louisiana. She is the program coordinator of the Health Services Administration program and her focus lies in the areas of health policy, healthcare leadership, and healthcare finance. She earned a Bachelor of Science in Health Care Systems Administration from Ferris State University, a Master of Science in Health Care Management from Kaplan University, and a PhD in Human Services from Capella University.

Lesley Clack, ScD
Lesley Clack is currently an assistant professor and corrdinator of the Master of Health Administration Program in the Department of Health Policy and Management at the University of Georgia, College of Public Health in Athens, GA. She has expertise across the healthcare management spectrum, focusing in the areas of organizational behavior, strategic management, and quality improvement. She earned a Bachelor of Science in Biological Science from the University of Georgia, a Master of Science in Counseling Psychology from the University of West Alabama, and a Doctor of Science in Health Systems Management from Tulane University.

© exdez/Getty Images

Contributors

Christina Juris Bennett, JD
Assistant Professor
University of Oklahoma
Oklahoma City, OK

Erik L. Carlton, DrPH, MS
Assistant Professor
University of Memphis
Memphis, TN

Gregory A. Cline, PhD
Assistant Professor
Grand Valley State University, School
   of Public, Nonprofit, & Health
   Administration
Grand Rapids, MI

Barbara Cohen, PhD, JD, RN
Faculty, Health Services Management,
   Larry L. Luing School of Business
Berkeley College
New York, NY

**Cathy Coleman, DNP, MSN, PHN, CNL,
   CPHQ, OCN**
Assistant Professor
University of San Francisco, School of
   Nursing & Health Professions
San Francisco, CA

Alice Colwell, MSN, RNC-NIC
Assistant Professor
Kent State University
Kent, Ohio

**Kelly L. Colwell, EdD, MRC, RRT, NPS,
   CPFT, AE-C**
Assistant Professor
Youngstown State University
Youngstown, OH

**Shirley K. Comer, DNP, RN, JD, CNE,
   ACNS-BC, APN**
Senior Lecturer
Governors State University
University Park, IL

Kristy Courville, MHA, RHIA
Senior Instructor, College of Nursing
   and Allied Health Professions
University of Louisiana at Lafayette
Lafayette, LA

Marsha Davenport, MD, MS, MPH, FACPM
Clinical Associate Professor
Towson University
Towson, MD

Donald Haney, CMA, LNHA, MBA
Administrator
Thornapple Manor
Hastings, MI

Cassandra R. Henson, DrPA, MBA
Assistant Professor
Towson University
Towson, MD

Raymond J. Higbea, PhD
Associate Professor
Grand Valley State University, School
   of Public, Nonprofit, & Health
   Administration
Grand Rapids, MI

Lara J. Jaskiewicz, PhD, MPH, MBA
Associate Professor
Grand Valley State University, School
   of Public, Nonprofit, & Health
   Administration
Grand Rapids, MI

Kim Johnson, PMHNP-BC, FNP-C, RN
Assistant Professor
Middle Georgia State University
Macon, GA

Kathy J. Keister, PhD, RN, CNE
Associate Professor
Wright State University
Dayton, OH

Yen Vi Khuu-Eickhoff, MHSA
Instructor, Health Information
   Technology
Centura College
Norfolk, VA

Sharyl Kinney, DrPH, RN, CPH
Assistant Professor
University of Oklahoma Health
   Sciences Center, College of Public
   Health
Oklahoma City, OK

Alyssa Luboff, PhD
Adjunct Assistant Professor
Portland State University
Portland, OR

Steven A. Marzolf, MSA, BS, RN, FACHE
Regional Chief Nursing Officer
Spectrum Health
Hastings, MI

Mary McGinty, RT(R)(M)(ARRT)
Imaging Supervisor
Zuckerberg San Francisco General
   Hospital & Trauma Center
Department of Radiology, Avon Breast
   Center & Mobile Mammography
   Outreach Program
San Francisco, CA

Mary D. Mites-Campbell, PhD, MSN-Adm., RN, CTTS, CCHP
Assistant Professor
Nova Southeastern University
Hollywood, FL

Jeffery Skinner, MHA, BSN, RN, CEN
Nurse Manager
Spectrum Health
Grand Rapids, MI

Catherine E. Tymkow, EdD, DNP, MS(N), RN, APN, WHNP-BC
Associate Professor
Governors State University
University Park, IL

Lynne J. Walker, MSN, RNC-NIC, CNE
Lecturer
Kent State University
Kent, OH

Ramona Wallace, DO, PhD
Medical Director
Muskegon Family Care
Muskegon, MI

Wendy Whitner, PhD, MPH
Clinical Assistant Professor
Towson University
Towson, MD

Jacqueline Woeppel, ScD, MBA, RHIA, CCS
Epidemiologist
TennCare
Nashville, TN

▶ Reviewers

Kimberly A. Cleveland, JD, MSN, RN, C-MBC
Nurse Attorney
Fulton, OH

Lenore H. Cortez, MSN, RNC
Clinical Instructor of Nursing
Angelo State University
San Angelo, TX

Donna Dellalacono, NP, PhD
Adjunct Professor
Curry College
Milton, MA

Julie E. Grady, MSN, RN, CNL
Assistant Professor
Curry College School of Nursing
Milton, MA

Rosemary Hathaway, PhD, RN
Associate Professor
Goodwin College
Hartford, CT

Judith McLeod, DNP, CPNP
Dean
California Southern University
Costa Mesa, CA

Deborah Morrill, MSN, RN, CMSRN
Lecturer
University of Bridgeport School of
    Nursing
Bridgeport, CT

Deborah Ulmer, PhD, Med, BSN, RN
Associate Professor
Longwood University
Farmville, VA

Charlotte Ward, PhD, CNE, RN
Adjunct Professor
Kaplan University School of Nursing
Mt. Juliet, TN

Deborah S. Wiltshire, EdD, MSN, RN
Associate Professor
Mars Hill University
Mars Hill, NC

SECTION 1

Introduction to Health Policy Management

CHAPTER 1

The Basics of the Policymaking Process

Rachel Ellison, PhD

▶ Introduction

Policymaking in the United States is complex. Policymakers are key stakeholders in the process and aim to solve problems and improve the quality of life for their fellow citizens. Before anyone can understand the policymaking process, it is imperative to define the term *policy*. Scholars have defined the term *policy* in many different ways. For the sake of consistency in this textbook, "a policy is a rule to guide decisions based on good intent and societal values when dealing with a matter of public concern" (Hyde, 2017, p. 3).

▶ Who Makes a Policy?

Policies are made by private actors, government entities, and authoritative decision-makers. Government entities play a large role in the policymaking process, but they are not the only key players. For example, private actors, such as an insurance company that decides to cover certain health prevention measures or the Gates Foundation, which provides grants to improve the nutrition of people in developing countries, all make health policy decisions (Teitelbaum & Wilensky, 2017). Whether the person making the policy is a private or government entity, the decision being made must be authoritative (Teitelbaum & Wilensky, 2017). Policymakers have the power to motivate others, create plans for the future, and implement decisions, which is essential in the policymaking process.

▶ Why Do Policies Get Made?

The main reason to create a healthcare policy is to address a problem, need, and/or public concern. If the problem goes beyond a singular person or entity and affects the larger community, a policy might be needed (Teitelbaum & Wilensky, 2017). For example, states are enforcing policies that ban e-cigarettes because they have become a problem and public concern. However, just because there is a problem affecting the public does not mean that the federal legislative branch needs to start the policymaking process. For example, demand for flu vaccines sometimes exceeds supply. Although there are government solutions to this problem, such as CDC-oriented interventions, other avenues are also available. Private research institutes can use their own funding and grants to help with the shortage of flu vaccines. Ultimately, private actors and government entities are both key players in the policymaking process.

▶ The Policymaking Process

All policies are authoritative decisions made through a complex process (Longest, 2016). Various branches of government play a role in the public policymaking process by setting the agenda and implementing the policy decisions that deal with matters of public concern. At the federal, state, and local levels of government, policymaking occurs in three interrelated and cyclical phases: policy formulation, policy implementation, and policy modification (Longest, 2016). Policy formulation includes agenda setting and development of legislation; policy implementation consists of designing, rulemaking, operating, and evaluating procedures; and policy modification involves revisiting and modifying prior decisions (Longest, 2016).

The cyclical phases of the policymaking process run on a consistent basis. Once a policy is implemented, the task of maintaining it and ensuring the law is relevant and efficient becomes a task in itself. Termination of policies does occur often due to policymakers' shifting goals, values, beliefs, and priorities (Bernstein, 2017). When new issues arise, the policymaking process begins again with policy formation and agenda setting. The cyclical phases help governing bodies successfully address new and important challenges (Bernstein, 2017).

▶ Federal Policymaking

The federal government comprises three branches: the executive, legislative, and judicial branches. There are main policymakers in each branch of government, and each is tasked with different duties in order to implement policy.

The president is the main policymaker of the executive branch (Porche, 2019). The president and his or her staff, which includes advisors and cabinet members, identify issues of public concern. The advisors and cabinet members transform the public concerns into policy options for the president to consider.

The legislative branch of the federal government is responsible for enacting "necessary and proper laws" (Teitelbaum & Wilensky, 2017). Congress, which is part of the legislative branch, is granted all legislative powers, meaning Congress decides which laws are passed. Congressional responsibilities are completed by two chambers: the House of Representatives and the Senate. Legislators from the House of Representatives and the Senate are elected officials. Legislators have the responsibility of voting for policies that are in the best interest of the people they serve. Not only do they vote for the policies, but these officials are the primary drafters of policy and legislation.

The Supreme Court is in charge of the judicial branch of the federal government. The main duty of the judicial branch when it comes to policymaking is to interpret the law and determine its constitutionality (Porche, 2019). This sets a precedent for policy development. Judicial policies are established through the interpretation of laws, the Constitution, and the rules of executive agencies (Porche, 2019). Supreme Court justices often use the intent and meaning of policy during judicial hearings and discussions, which in turn impact future policy implementation.

▶ State Policymaking

Important policy decisions are made at the state level. Each state's government is similar to the federal government when it comes to policymaking duties. Each state has three branches of government. Legislatures pass laws, and the judiciary system has trial and appellate courts (Teitelbaum & Wilensky, 2017). The governor is the head of the state executive branch. One of the governor's duties is to set policies, including health policies that are a matter of public concern. The governor also has the responsibility of appointing members of the cabinet and state administrative agencies to regulate and implement state laws.

Unlike the federal government, most states are required to have a balanced budget (Teitelbaum & Wilensky, 2017). If the budget is not balanced, states will raise revenue or cut programs. Money can be shifted and allocated to other programs to help balance the budget. States try to prevent cutting programs and shifting money due to decreased funding and negative public turmoil, but oftentimes, it is unavoidable.

In terms of health care, states do oversee professional licensure. For example, states regulate nursing and medical licenses. Each state has their own requirements and regulatory boards that oversee these medical professionals. However, state-level policymaking is an in-depth process; there are limits to a state's power to enforce health policies. Making substantial change to and also initiating, implementing, and enforcing a health policy is a profound process in a state government.

▶ Summary

As you read in this chapter, the policymaking process is extensive. Various people are active players and key stakeholders. In the United States, policies are implemented to alleviate a problem, fill a need, and/or address a public concern. The federal and state governments play a large role in enacting health policies. The case study scenarios accompanying this chapter explain policymaking from different standpoints. These case studies show the diversity of policymakers, legislation, and the time it takes for policies to be implemented. Below are important terms relating to this chapter's content to assist in analyzing the case studies.

Key Terms

Agenda Setting is the longest and most complex aspect of the policymaking process. The series of actions include defining the problem, germinating a policy, and developing ideas toward legislative development.

Executive Branch is responsible for implementing and enforcing the laws.

Judicial Branch interprets the law and determines its constitutionality.

Legislative Branch consists of the two houses of Congress: the Senate and the House of Representatives.

Legislative Process includes the development and submission of legislation to one of the legislative chambers by a policy entrepreneur.

Modification Process is the last phase of the policy process. This is the review and refinement phase.

Office for Civil Rights (OCR) enforces laws against discrimination based on race, color, national origin, disability, age, sex, and religion.

Operations Process begins once the bill is signed into law by the executive and becomes the duty of the executive.

Policy is a rule to guide decisions based on good intent and societal values dealing with a matter of public concern.

Policymakers are private actors, government entities, and authoritative decision-makers.

Policymaking Process is a decision-making process that includes policy formulation, policy implementation, and policy modification.

References

Bernstein, R. (2017). An introduction to the public policy-making cycle. https://online.pointpark .edu/public-administration/policy-making-cycle

Birkland, T. (2016). *An introduction to the policy process: Theories, concepts, and models of public policy making* (4th ed.). New York: Taylor & Francis.

Hyde, P. S. (2017). The patience for policy—Building networks to make a difference. *Kinesiology Review, 6*(1), 3–11.

Longest, B. B. (2016). *Health policymaking in the United States* (6th ed.). Chicago, IL: Health Administration Press.

Porche, D. (2019). *Health policy: Application for nurses and other healthcare professionals* (2nd ed.). Burlington, MA: Jones & Bartlett Learning.

Teitelbaum, J. B., & Wilensky, S. E. (2017). *Essentials of health policy and law* (3rd ed.). Burlington, MA: Jones & Bartlett Learning.

🔍 CASE 1-1

Renaming Streets: Influencing Political Change

Mary Mites-Campbell, PhD, MSN-Adm., RN, CTTS, CCHP

Since 2016, the push to officially remove Confederate monuments, flags, street names, and symbols from the public environment has been a matter of increasing political debate. According to Strother, Piston, and Ogorzalek (2017), the symbolic representation of Confederate leaders has fomented a debate on "heritage verse hatred" or "pride versus prejudice." In an effort to explore the concepts, Strother, Piston, et al. (2017) employed various facets that analyzed the situation, in addition to historical ramifications affiliated with Confederate leaders.

In 2016, a municipality in South Florida became entangled in the nationwide debate when the city mayor and commissioners received appeals from Mr. Jones, a community activist and think tank leader, to rename Confederate streets that ran throughout the city, especially in African American communities. Because those names represented physiological and psychological suppression of a minority population, residents wanted them renamed.

Specifically, in May 2016, these South Florida community residents, including Mr. Jones, requested the city rename Nathan Bedford Forrest, John Bell Hood, and Robert E. Lee Streets, which honored Confederate leaders responsible for the death of African Americans, Whites, and others during the American Civil War. The request was presented to the city's Minority Advisory Council (MAC) in June 2016 by the mayor, city commissioners, Mr. Jones,. The MAC's task was to provide recommendations on two points: (1) Should the city commission rename Forrest, Hood, and Lee Streets? (2) What steps should the city commission take concerning the matter? The MAC chair, a PhD healthcare professional, led the opine request with the support of the city staff liaison. Although this was a city matter, national attention meant that the issue had to be handled with dignity and respect for the residents.

The Minority Advisory Council (MAC) and Local Process

The following items were provided to the MAC to assist with the decision-making process: (1) a copy of an interoffice memorandum dated December 2015 from the chief civic affairs officer to the mayor and commissioners concerning the matter, and (2) the political process presentation on street renaming by the city's staff liaison. The presentation included (a) the importance of street names; (b) the controversy concerning Forrest, Hood, and Lee Streets; (c) the standard criteria for street renaming; (d) flexibilities that could be recommended to the city commission on street renaming; (e) the impact that street renaming would have on residents and businesses, especially those with abutting streets; and (f) finally, examples that outlined the standard cost of the applicant/petitioner process for pursuing street renaming.

To understand the street renaming process, the MAC chair, council, and city staff liaison reviewed the city's standardized process intensely. The council understood that in order to prevent further conflict, standardized policies on street naming were paramount for setting the street naming criteria. Examining various explanations on what constituted a street name was vital to the advisory council opening. Two naming conventions were considered by the MAC for the renaming process: (1) grid systems—in a grid plan the streets are named to indicate their location on a coordinate plane such as numbers or letters, and (2) distinguished or famous individuals—to commemorate a person who lived or worked in that area or a major historical figure. The African American communities that Forrest, Lee, and Hood Streets ran through included young, impressionable children striving for educational and social advancement. These children and their parents wanted the streets named after positive role models who were familiar to residents and promoted upward mobility in the community (Strother, Ogorzalek, & Piston, 2017).

CASE STUDIES

In this city, streets that ran east to west were named after U.S. presidents and famous military figures. There was no definitive rationale for the naming order except that the city's engineering department may have had draftsmen decide in the early 1920s. Forrest Street ran from the beach through three African American communities, in which the street name was used as an identifiable icon in the community.

Further, it was paramount that the MAC chair, council, and city staff liaison understand the financial impact associated with the street name change(s). Each name change would include (1) an application fee, (2) the required mailing cost for resident and business notifications, (3) the city recording cost, and (4) the cost of changing road signs, in addition to other administrative fees.

There are five (5) steps in completing the application fee and approval process for street naming:

1. *Valid signatures of two-thirds of the property owners* abutting the streets were required, although African Americans represented 17% of the property-owning residents (United States Census Bureau, 2016). Renting or leasing residents were not permitted to vote in the renaming process. If residential voting occurred, businesses and residents residing on Forrest, Hill, and Lee Streets would be given the opportunity to vote.
2. *Application fee of $2,000 per street* (i.e., totaling $6,000). Changing the street names would impact street signs and mailing. If the city commissioners and mayor approved the street renaming change at a 5/7 vote, the city would absolve the cost. If the city officials did not approve the street renaming by a 5/7 vote, the groups who submitted the application would inherit the cost. The total cost for the street renaming would be $21,849.50.
3. *Submitted application to be reviewed by the city's naming committee.* Residents residing on Forrest, Hood, and Lee Streets received a city notice announcing an informational seminar on the process for renaming streets and the city's renaming committee role. The MAC and city commissioners/mayor received the training.
4. *City commission approval or disapproval.* The approval of the city commission required a 5/7 vote in favor of street renaming. The disapproval would be reflected by the non-5/7 approval vote. All fees could be waived by the city commission if they voted 5/7 in favor of the street renaming. This process would negate the need for valid signatures from two-thirds of property owners abutting the streets.
5. *The notification process to all city residents.* Residents will be notified during a special city council session of the new street names.

Because the MAC functioned as an advisory council to the city mayor, the city commissioners, and the city residents, it was imperative that the MAC allowed residents an opportunity to deliberate on the matter. The community provided various points for and against street renaming. The street renaming effort received support from several state and county officials, state representatives, the head of the sheriff's department, a public defender, the county property appraiser, and local clergy. The two-thirds property owner's nonvoters caused resident unrest and caused further deliberation at city meetings and with individual district commissioners and the mayor.

What Were the Next Steps?

Ultimately, the city commission voted 5-2 on the renaming of the street names, waiving the city's need to notify property owners of street name changes and the need for a ballot measure. A public renaming ad hoc committee was established for identifying suitable street names. The MAC chair established positive relationships that led to a change in the public policy process and interprofessional collaboration at all levels of city political processes. Political change is a paradigm shift relying on integrated relationships among stakeholders, including healthcare professionals, to build the best political outcomes.

Discussion Questions

1. What impact do street names have on residents residing on the them? Is this a concern for healthcare professionals?
2. Should healthcare professionals act as advocates in community political endeavors? Why or why not?
3. How can healthcare professionals influence political change at the local level?
4. What steps should the MAC chair (as a healthcare professional) take to ensure a continuous positive relationship with the city commissioner?

References

Strother, L., Ogorzalek, T., & Piston, S. (2017). The Confederate flag largely disappeared after the Civil War. The fight against civil rights brought it back. *The Washington Post.* https://www.washingtonpost .com/news/monkey-cage/wp/2017/06/12/confederate-symbols-largely-disappeared-after -the-civil-war-the-fight-against-civil-rights-brought-them-back/?noredirect=on&utm_term =.2c1aaffb2447

Strother, L., Piston, S., & Ogorzalek, T. (2017). Pride or prejudice?: Racial prejudice, Southern heritage, and white support for the Confederate battle flag. *Du Bois Review: Social Science Research on Race, 14*(1), 295–323.

United States Census Bureau. (2016). Quick facts, Hollywood City, Florida. https://www.census.gov /quickfacts/fact/table/hollywoodcityflorida,US/PST045216.

ZipAtlas. (2017). Percentage of Blacks and Whites in Hollywood, Florida by zip code. http://zipatlas.com /us/fl/hollywood/zip-code-comparison/percentage-white-population.htm.

🔍 CASE 1-2

How Policy Is Made: A Process Model

Raymond J. Higbea & Gregory A. Cline, PhD

This case study examines the policymaking process through the use of a process model (see **FIGURE 1-1**). Although this model divides the policy process up into four categories of actions, which include agenda setting, legislative development, operations, and modification, one has to be cognizant that this is a very dynamic process with constantly moving actions within and among the four categories. The policymaking process is best understood within the context of the four categories of action coupled with an example to explain how the process works. For this case study, the health insurance exchanges in the Patient Protection and Affordable Care Act are provided to illustrate the actions in each of the four categories.

Agenda setting is the longest and most complex of the policy process categories, encompassing the time from the definition of a problem and germination of a policy idea to legislation development (Longest, 2016). In total, this process may span 10 to 50 years, with a mean time of 20 years. First, a problem is socially constructed and raised to the level of a public problem when there appears to be no reasonable private solution. Next, a series of interest groups, individuals of interest, and political leaders develop public solutions and state experiments addressing the problem that are aligned with their political philosophy. Finally, when the political situation is conducive (due to an actual or orchestrated event and/or alignment of a political party in the legislative and executive branches), the political solution progresses from a political proposal to legislation.

The *legislative process* includes the development and submission of legislation to one of the legislative chambers by a policy entrepreneur. Once the legislation has been submitted, the chamber leader can choose to either not advance the legislation or forward it to the appropriate committee(s). During the committee process, the legislation is thoroughly

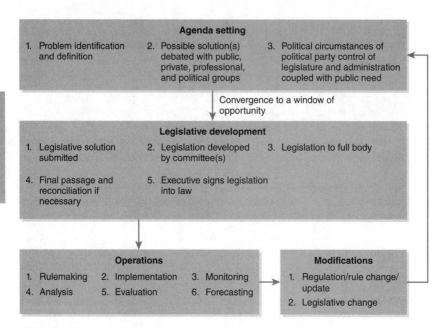

Agenda setting

1. Problem identification and definition
2. Possible solution(s) debated with public, private, professional, and political groups
3. Political circumstances of political party control of legislature and administration coupled with public need

Convergence to a window of opportunity

Legislative development

1. Legislative solution submitted
2. Legislation developed by committee(s)
3. Legislation to full body
4. Final passage and reconciliation if necessary
5. Executive signs legislation into law

Operations

1. Rulemaking
2. Implementation
3. Monitoring
4. Analysis
5. Evaluation
6. Forecasting

Modifications

1. Regulation/rule change/update
2. Legislative change

FIGURE 1-1 The Policy Process Model

read, marked up, and voted on. If a majority of the committee does not vote in favor of the legislation, it normally dies there. However, if the leadership has a strong favorable opinion of the bill, it can pass to the full chamber. When the committee votes in favor of the legislation, it passes back to the chamber leadership that will then proceed to whip up sufficient votes to support the legislation before returning it to the full chamber. If the legislation does not pass by the margin set by the full chamber, the bill dies. However, if the bill does pass by the margin set by one chamber, it moves to the other chamber that must agree, write new legislation, or ignore the bill. Once both chambers agree and pass the bill, it moves to an executive who either vetoes or signs the bill.

The *operations process* begins once the bill is signed into law by the executive branch and becomes the duty of the executive to "take care [to] faithfully execute the laws" (U.S. Const., Article 2, Section 3). Laws are "faithfully executed" by the executive branch through processes that include rulemaking, implementation, monitoring, analysis, evaluation, and forecasting. While these are all very detailed and sequential steps, they also add to the dynamism of legislation; no law is static but rather is always undergoing review and refinement.

The dynamism of review and refinement results in *modifications*, the last and final stage of the policy process. As laws are "operationalized," consequences—intended and unintended—surface that need to be addressed if the law is to continue to be successfully executed. Depending upon what evaluation and analytic results show, problematic concerns may be addressed by rule and regulatory change. If so, the executive goes through the process of notification and consent through the *Federal Register* to ensure all parties have the opportunity to comment prior to implementing any changes. If the necessary changes require new legislation, the problems or concerns head back through the policy process with the executive branch working with congressional leaders to develop legislation to address the concerns.

FIGURE 1-2 provides a summary of how the health insurance exchange idea has moved through the policy process. As discussed above, agenda setting was the longest phase (20 years); the legislative process was the shortest at 9 months; implementation took 2 years;

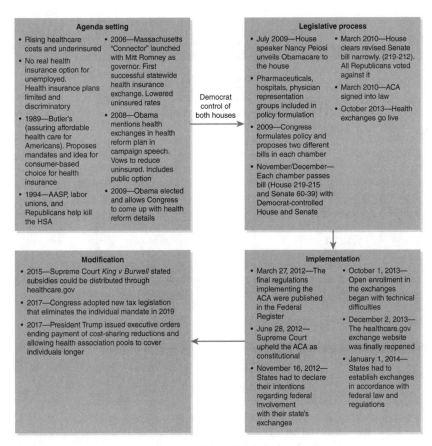

FIGURE 1-2 Health Insurance Exchange and the Policy Process

and modification, 2 years. This figure also illustrates how a multitude of political and nonpolitical actors influence the development and implementation of the health insurance exchange. A final salient observation illustrated by this figure is how all branches of government have been involved with health insurance exchanges at various stages of the policy process.

Discussion Questions

1. Based upon the above description of the policy process, how long should health leaders expect to work on a public problem before it becomes law?
2. Describe how health leaders were involved in the policy process that led to the passage and implementation of the health insurance exchange.
3. Were the modifications to the health insurance exchange regulatory or legislative? Explain.
4. Upon gaining an understanding of the policy process and through the example of how the health insurance exchanges work, what are the lessons for health leaders?

References

Longest, B. B. (2016). *Health policymaking in the United States* (6th ed.). Chicago, IL: Health Administration Press.

U.S. Const., Article 2, Section 3.

$\mathcal{P}$ *CASE 1-3*

Policymaking for a Better Tomorrow: Stop the Bullying

Rachel Ellison, PhD

Susie Smith, a mother of three, lives in the suburbs of Orlando near the happiest place on earth, Walt Disney World. She has two sons and a daughter, ages 17, 14, and 9. They have moved around frequently, but they currently attend school in the Orlando area and have grown to love the city that they now call home. They know Orlando to be more than just a tourist city filled with mouse ears and never-ending traffic.

Susie's two older children go to the same high school, but her daughter attends a different school. Over the past few weeks, Susie has noticed her middle son is very withdrawn, emotional, and won't eat. She asks her oldest son if there is something going on at school that she should know about. He tells her that her middle son is being bullied by a group of kids at school. They steal his lunch, throw food at him, kick him, and say derogatory words, among many other terrible things. Susie is appalled by this and immediately goes to her son. Her son says that he is afraid to tell anyone about the bullying because of potential repercussions.

The next day, Susie takes her son to school and demands a meeting with the administration. Her son tells them everything that has been going on. To Susie's surprise, this has been going on for months. The bullies have been tormenting her son online as well as at school and at after-school activities. He has proof of all the interactions from emails and text messages. Susie's son drops a bombshell and tells her and the school administration that he has thought about committing suicide because he can't take it anymore. Susie is so devastated by this she decides it's time to take this problem to Washington, D.C.

Susie's first plan of action is to research policies and laws. She assumes there is already a federal policy on bullying, but what she finds shocks her. There is no federal law that is specific to bullying (HHS, 2018). When bullying is based on race, color, national origin, sex, disability, or religion, the U.S. Department of Education's Office for Civil Rights can get involved, but only in some cases (HHS, 2018). Research has been conducted both federally and on a state level regarding bullying. The statistics are alarming:

- 28% of U.S. students in grades 6–12 experience bullying
- 20% of U.S. students in grades 9–12 experience bullying
- 30% of young people have admitted to bullying others
- 70.6% of young people said they have witnessed bullying in their school
- 70.4% of school staff have seen bullying
- 62% have witnessed bullying two or more times in the last month
- 41% witnesses bullying at least once a week
- Only 20–30% of young people notify adults about bullying (HHS, 2018)

Many states have already taken action against bullying by getting policies signed into law. States have anti-bullying campaigns that run throughout the year to bring awareness to the cause. After doing much research into the state policies and laws, Susie decides to bring awareness to her own community. She finds that bullying is a major issue at her son's school. One out of four teens are bullied (Stomp Out Bullying, 2018). More students came forward after her son described the bullying he had endured. Susie sets up a support group for parents and students. She invites a congressman to one of the meetings, and because of that meeting, he decides to take the issue of bullying head-on. He agrees with Susie and all the others who have been affected by bullying that this is a public policy concern. This issue goes beyond the individual and affects the greater community (Teitelbaum & Wilensky, 2017).

Policies at the state level are thorough, but they must be taken to the federal level if more protection is to be promised. Susie predicts that because state policies have been passed and laws were enacted, then federal policies and laws can be enacted as well. There is a lot of work to be done to get a policy created, but Susie has successfully passed the first hurdle, which is getting a politician to agree with her.

Discussion Questions

1. Why should a federal policy be made about bullying?
2. Choose two states and research their policies on bullying. Compare and contrast these policies. Are students protected? See https://www.stopbullying.gov/laws/index .html
3. Which branch of government will vote for the anti-bullying policy?
4. Are Susie and the congresspeople the best people to make the anti-bullying policy? Why or why not?

References

Stomp Out Bullying. (2018). Get help now. http://www.stompoutbullying.org/information-and-resources /about-bullying-and-cyberbullying/issue-bullying

Teitelbaum, J. B., & Wilensky, S. E. (2017). *Essentials of health policy and law* (3rd ed.). Burlington, MA: Jones & Bartlett Learning.

U.S. Department of Health and Human Services (HHS). (2018). Facts About bullying. https://www .stopbullying.gov/media/facts/index.html#stats

CHAPTER 2
Federal Legislation Governing Medical Care

Rachel Ellison, PhD & Lesley Clack, ScD

▶ Introduction

Health care is not considered a fundamental constitutional right in the United States, but there is federal legislation to ensure that individuals are protected and provided medical care. Some of the healthcare policies discussed in this text that are specifically focused on protecting the rights of medical patients are the Emergency Medical Treatment and Labor Act (EMTALA), Stark Law, and the Genetic Information Nondiscrimination Act (GINA). They are all equally important in protecting the best interest of the people living in the United States.

▶ Emergency Medical Treatment and Labor Act (EMTALA)

The Emergency Medical Treatment and Labor Act (EMTALA) is a federal law that prevents patients from being "dumped" from hospitals for not having the necessary coverage to pay for services rendered (Teitelbaum & Wilensky, 2017). Hospitals lose money when patients don't pay for their hospital or doctor bills; therefore, they turn them away (i.e., "dump" them). This unethical act occurred on a very consistent basis in private hospitals in the late 70s and early 80s. EMTALA, known as the "anti-dumping" statute, was quickly enacted in 1986 to deter hospitals and physicians from turning away patients. Before 1986, patients were showing up to emergency departments in crisis and being turned away because they did not have the funds to pay for their care. Women in labor were also denied care when the hospital found out they did not have health insurance or finances to pay for health services. These actions put many lives in danger, and unfortunately lives were lost.

Congress enacted the EMTALA law to eliminate the no-duty-to-treat principle, which states that a person has no legal right to health services (Teitelbaum & Wilensky, 2017). EMTALA ensures patients are granted health services in any emergent situation in a hospital setting. Hospitals who participate in the Medicare program are required to follow the EMTALA law. For those hospitals that receive Medicare reimbursements, there are two EMTALA compliance requirements:

1. Provide an appropriate, nondiscriminatory medical screening examination (adhering to the hospital's established emergency care guidelines) to all individuals who present at a hospital's emergency department seeking care for an emergency medical condition (Teitelbaum & Wilensky, 2017); and

2. Stabilize the emergent medical condition and/or pregnant woman before a proper transfer can take place. A successful transfer has taken place when the transferring hospital has minimized the risks to the patient's health by providing treatment as within its capability, and the accepting hospital has received the patient and the medical records (Teitelbaum & Wilensky, 2017).

Hospitals that do not follow EMTALA guidelines are breaking the law and should understand that patients have legal rights. Hospitals that violate this policy can face heavy penalties. EMTALA enforcement is complaint driven, and the investigations are conducted by the Centers for Medicare and Medicaid Services (CMS) or the state agency (American College of Emergency Physicians, 2018). Most hospitals are fined $50,000 per EMTALA violation.

▶ EMTALA & Ethics

EMTALA exists because of the atrocious, unethical behavior of physicians and hospitals (Bitterman, 2006). Physicians and hospitals both refused indigent patients because they could not afford to pay for medical services. Whether someone believes this practice to be ethical depends on how a person defines ethical and unethical behavior (Bitterman, 2006).

The Hippocratic oath is one of the oldest medical codes of ethics and has stood the test of time because of what it represents: "the fundamental truth that a sick person requires and is entitled to have trust in a caregiver" (Clark, 2004). The Hippocratic oath is recited at medical school graduations, making it meaningful to generations of practitioners. Ethically, should a physician withhold care from a patient because they don't have money to pay? Does this go against the Hippocratic oath that was taken by all medical students on graduation day? Depending on your definition of ethical behavior, these are questions that can only be answered individually.

▶ Contrary Views of EMTALA

EMTALA has been a controversial health policy since its inception in the 80s. Some studies believe that EMTALA has caused many emergency departments to become saturated, which in turn causes huge financial shortfalls and physician and staff shortages (Monico, 2010). These factors lead to emergency department and hospital closings, which impact care for all patients. Others claim EMTALA has made the emergency room the "go-to walk-in clinic" for the uninsured and underinsured population. Emergency departments are being used inappropriately by those who can't obtain care otherwise (Monico, 2010).

A positive take on EMTALA comes from the school of thought that the policy provides care to the millions of people in the United States who are uninsured—a population that is growing. Those who are uninsured may not have other access to healthcare services (Monico, 2010). EMTALA helps bridge that gap.

▶ Healthcare Professionals and EMTALA

Physicians and nursing staff are at the greatest risk of violating EMTALA. Since its inception in 1986, hospital emergency departments have seen consistent violations by physicians, nurses, and medical staff. Experts say there are a variety of reasons violations are still occurring. Factors include pressure on hospitals to improve their finances, poor staff training, flawed systems and processes, communication mishaps, challenges in getting specialty physicians to be on-call to the ED, and a lack of community resources for serving mentally ill patients (Meyer, 2016).

Nurses can't be held individually liable under EMTALA, but they can be held liable under their state's Nurse Practice Act and may be named in medical malpractice lawsuits. It is unlikely criminal lawsuits will be filed against the violating nurse, but an error could jeopardize a nurse's career. Just like nurses, other healthcare providers and practitioners can't be held liable but can be named in lawsuits. In most cases, the hospital that violated EMTALA will pay a monetary penalty.

The EMTALA monetary penalty has been adjusted only once since 1986 (Bitterman, 2017). In 2017, the Office of Inspector General (OIG) doubled the monetary fines, added a new physician decision-making scenario, and modified factors determining the amount of a penalty. These changes have a large impact on hospitals but also have a huge impact on physicians. One of the biggest changes is the maximum penalty may be imposed for each violation, not on a per patient basis (Bitterman, 2017). The care of any one individual patient can, and often does, result in multiple violations.

▶ Stark Law

Stark Law was enacted in 1989 through Section 1877 of the Social Security Act and was expanded by Congress in 1993 and 1994 into the law as we know it today (CMS, 2015). Stark Law refers to a set of federal laws that govern physician self-referral in the United States. This is the practice of physicians referring patients to certain medical facilities where they have financial interests, such as ownership, investment, or a structured compensation arrangement (Stark Law, 2013). Three provisions to Stark Law govern financial fraud and abuse (CMS, 2015):

1. Prohibits a physician from making referrals for certain designated health services (DHS) payable by Medicare to an entity with which he or she (or an immediate family member) has a financial relationship (ownership, investment, or compensation), unless an exception applies.

2. Prohibits the entity from presenting or causing to be presented claims to Medicare (or billing another individual, entity, or third-party payer) for those referred services.
3. Establishes a number of specific exceptions and grants the Secretary of Health and Human Services the authority to create regulatory exceptions for financial relationships that do not pose a risk of program or patient abuse.

▶ Genetic Information Nondiscrimination Act (GINA)

The Genetic Information Nondiscrimination Act (GINA) was enacted by Congress in 2008 as an amendment to the Employee Retirement Income Security Act of 1974 (ERISA), the Public Health Service Act, and the Internal Revenue Code. GINA was enacted to prohibit genetic discrimination, such as prohibiting a group health plan from adjusting contribution amounts or premiums for a group of individuals on the basis of genetic information (Longest, 2016). GINA also prohibits a group health plan from requiring individuals to undergo genetic testing and prohibits an issuer of a Medicare supplemental policy from: 1) requesting or requiring an individual or a family member to undergo a genetic test; or 2) requesting, requiring, or purchasing genetic information for underwriting purposes or for any individual prior to enrollment (Longest, 2016). GINA is designed to protect the civil rights of patients regarding their genetic information.

▶ Summary

Health care is not a right granted by the Constitution of the United States, which makes governing medical care even more important. Federal laws such as EMTALA, Stark Law, and GINA are examples of laws that protect and provide security for many. EMTALA in particular ensures hospitals and physicians treat patients regardless of their ability to pay for medical services. In the case studies below, ethical questions are addressed as well as legislative questions. The content from the chapter and the key terms below will guide critical thinking about these concepts.

Key Terms

Emergency Medical Treatment and Labor Act (EMTALA) is a federal law that protects patients from being "dumped" from hospitals for not having the necessary coverage to pay for services rendered.

Emergency Preparedness Plan is a course of action developed to mitigate the damage of potential events that could endanger an organization's ability to function.

Office of Inspector General (OIG) develops and distributes resources to assist the healthcare industry in its efforts to comply with the nation's fraud and abuse laws and to educate the public about fraudulent schemes so they can protect themselves and report suspicious activities.

Social Security Act (SSA) America's foremost social welfare law, is designed to counteract the dangers of old age, poverty, disability, and unemployment through a range of government programs and benefits.

Stark Law is a federal regulation that governs physicians referring patients to medical facilities in which there is a financial interest, be it ownership, investment, or a structured compensation arrangement.

References

American College of Emergency Physicians. (2018). EMTALA. https://www.acep.org/life-as-a
-physician/ethics--legal/emtala/emtala-fact-sheet/

Bitterman, R. (2006). EMTALA and the ethical delivery of hospital emergency services. *Emergency Medicine Clinics, 24*(3): 557–577.

Bitterman, R. (2017). Feds increase EMTALA penalties against physicians and hospitals. http://epmonthly.com/article/feds-increase-emtala-penalties-physicians-hospitals/

Clark, J. (2004). Hippocratic oath. *JAMA, 292*(9), 1083–1084.

Centers for Medicare & Medicaid Services (CMS). (2015). Physician self referral. https://www.cms
.gov/Medicare/Fraud-and-Abuse/PhysicianSelfReferral/index.html

Longest, B. B. (2016). *Health policymaking in the United States* (6th ed.). Chicago, IL: Health Administration Press.

Meyer, H. (2016). Why patients still need EMTALA. https://www.modernhealthcare.com/article
/20160326/MAGAZINE/303289881

Monico, E. (2010). Is EMTALA that bad? *AMA Journal of Ethics, Virtual Mentor, 12*(6), 435–516.

Stark Law. (2013). About Stark Law. http://starklaw.org/stark_law.htm

Teitelbaum, J. B., & Wilensky, S. E. (2017). *Essentials of health policy and law* (3rd ed.). Burlington, MA: Jones & Bartlett.

🔍 *CASE 2-1*

Emergency Medical Treatment and Labor Act (EMTALA): Ready or Not?

Marsha Davenport, MD, MS, MPH, FACPM, Wendy M. Whitner, PhD, MPH, &
Cassandra Henson, Dr. P.A., MBA

A Category 5 hurricane is expected to make landfall in 2 days, and the city is bracing for a direct hit. This coastal city is accustomed to preparing for severe weather between June and November. However, resources are often limited, and the poorer areas of the city are at risk for flooding and increased damage from the storm.

Beach River Hospital is a community teaching hospital and considered a key part of the city's infrastructure. The hospital is located on the outskirts of the city bordering one of the poorer counties in the state. Beach River Hospital works closely with the county's public health department and other emergency experts in the city, county, and in other parts of the state to care for residents living in this area. Although Beach River Hospital is not a Level I Trauma Center, it has an agreement with the university hospital, which is a Level I Trauma Center, to transfer trauma patients who may need a higher level of care to that hospital. However, the university hospital is almost 25 miles from Beach River Hospital, even using the main highway.

There are 235 beds and over 425 active medical staff at Beach River Hospital. The hospital has a very busy emergency department (ED) that provides care to a diverse and vulnerable population, primarily comprising poor and older residents living in this community and surrounding areas. Unfortunately, for many of these residents, the Beach River Hospital ED is their primary source of care.

The hospital works with the primary care practices in the area to help engage providers in working more closely with their patients. The goal is to help patients seen in the ED find a primary care doctor if they do not already have one in the area. The hospital also provides educational sessions for patients about the importance of having a primary care provider to ensure that they receive comprehensive coordinated care. These approaches are helping; however, there are still too many patients who come to the ED for their routine care.

Now, in addition to the usual volume of ED patients, the hospital must prepare for a potential increase of patients in all departments. Beach River Hospital leadership is meeting to review the disaster procedures. As the director of patient relations, you have been involved in the disaster planning process to ensure that patients are not forgotten during a crisis. You are comfortable participating on the disaster planning team thanks to your training and experiences. You had emergency preparedness lectures as part of both your undergraduate and graduate healthcare management programs (McSweeney-Feld, Nelson, Whitner, & Engineer, 2017).

Furthermore, in your role as the director of patient relations, you are very knowledgeable about patients' rights and hospital policies, especially compliance with the Emergency Medical Treatment and Labor Act (EMTALA). Hospitals that have an emergency department must implement and comply with EMTALA (CMS, 2012). EMTALA has a number of requirements; however, several key mandates that the hospital ED must cover are: (1) providing a medical screening for patients; (2) stabilizing patients; and (3) providing treatment to decrease risks during transfer (CMS, 2012).

You are aware that complying with the EMTALA regulations is hard for many hospitals. This hospital has worked hard to improve the quality of care for its patients and to find ways to implement and comply with EMTALA despite the increased financial burden (Hsuan, Horwitz, Ponce, Hsia, & Needleman, 2017).

As a result of your input, the disaster plan includes training for staff that emphasizes procedures to protect patients as well as themselves. Beach River Hospital now provides ongoing training and conducts at least one drill annually. So, the hospital leadership feels that the staff is trained, prepared, and ready for emergencies of any type. Although the hospital feels confident in its emergency preparedness plan and staff capabilities, the current plan has not been used for a drill yet this year. Moreover, it has been several years since a hurricane hit this state, and it was a Category 3. This looming hurricane is predicted to be a Category 5. It will be the first time that the new disaster plan will be used by the hospital staff.

In preparation for the emergencies that may result from the hurricane, the director of the emergency department, Dr. Diamond, holds a staff meeting. Dr. Diamond makes it clear that she wants to try to keep the ED available for only the most severe cases. She is concerned that her staff will be overwhelmed when the storm hits. She has already mentioned to the staff that they should begin preparing for a large influx of patients. Dr. Diamond also announces that some of the staff may not be able to go home and will have to stay here at the hospital during the storm to provide care. She asks for volunteers; however, if not enough staff volunteer, then other staff will be required to stay. Many of the healthcare workers are already overwhelmed because they want to be available to fulfill their duties but are also concerned about their families. Many of the staff may not have personal or family preparedness plans (Abbasi, Fadavi, & Bazmi, 2017).

Dr. Diamond has not been very engaged in the hospital's emergency preparedness activities. She did not attend any of the meetings or EMTALA trainings and limited the number of staff from the ED who participated in the trainings. Previously, when you discussed the lack of participation in the EMTALA and disaster trainings, Dr. Diamond responded by saying that her staff already knows how to deal with a crisis: "After all, they are working in an emergency department."

After the ED staff meeting, some of the staff in the ED start turning away patients who do not have insurance and who they know will not be able to pay for services. They send these patients to other hospitals that are further away from their homes or to urgent care centers. None of the staff seems to question the implications of denying services to patients or transferring them without at least conducting a brief physical or screening.

You are troubled to hear that this situation is occurring. As the director of patient relations, you are concerned that the staff may find themselves unprepared for the hurricane and unaware of the hospital's EMTALA policies that protect them and the patients. In addition, it is possible that the ED staff is not only unprepared but also stressed because of the potential for a large number of hurricane-related casualties to arrive at the hospital. Furthermore, you are also concerned that patients are not receiving appropriate care that could put the patients, the staff, and the hospital at risk (CMS, 2012).

You approach Dr. Diamond and discuss this situation with her. You recommend that the ED follows its usual EMTALA policies and that the staff continue to see every patient who comes through the door. Dr. Diamond notes that she did not know that the staff is turning patients away and not following the EMTALA policy. She promises to discuss this issue with her staff.

When Dr. Diamond meets with her staff later in the day, she learns that there are several new members of the triage staff. The new members of the staff thought that they were being helpful in preparing for the hurricane. They reported to Dr. Diamond that patients were sent to other sites only if that patient had something minor that was not considered a true emergency. Dr. Diamond is now faced with some critical decisions to make.

Discussion Questions

1. What are the ethical concerns for Dr. Diamond and her staff?
2. How does the Emergency Medical Treatment and Labor Act (EMTALA) impact the hospital in a disaster?

3. What is the role for the healthcare managers in helping a healthcare facility prepare and respond to a disaster?
4. What new policies might Beach River Hospital develop and implement?

References

Abbasi, M., Fadavi, M., & Bazmi, S. (2017). The underlying factors affecting the ethical performance of health service providers when faced with disasters: A qualitative study. *Journal of Medical Ethics and History of Medicine, 10*(14), 1–9.

Centers for Medicare & Medicaid Services (CMS) (2012). Emergency Medical Treatment and Labor Act (EMTALA). https://www.cms.gov/Regulations-and-Guidance/Legislation/EMTALA/

Hsuan, C., Horwitz, J. R., Ponce, N. A., Hsia, R. Y., and Needleman, J. (2017). Complying with the Emergency Medical Treatment and Labor Act (EMTALA): Challenges and solutions. *American Society for Healthcare Risk Management, 37*(3), 31–41.

McSweeney-Feld, M. H., Nelson, H. W., Whitner, W., & Engineer, C. Y. (2017). Emergency preparedness content in health administration programs: A decade later. *Journal of Health Administration Education, 34*(1), 85–102.

🔎 CASE 2-2

Legislating Improvements for Health Care

Kelly L. Colwell EdD, RRT, MRC, NPS, CPFT, AE-C, Alice Colwell MSN, RNC-NIC, & Lynne Walker MSN, RNC-NIC, CNE

Breward Hospital is part of a large nationwide conglomerate and a fully integrated national health service organization that is committed to serving the needs of a tri-county community in Southwest Ohio. However, the past decade has plagued the healthcare system, and financial hardships have forced Breward Hospital to decrease some services. These financial difficulties resulted in staff reductions and a loss of services rendered. In particular, the Labor and Delivery (L&D) department experienced a subjugation of services, including less nurse staffing and the elimination of an in-house physician "on call" 24 hours a day.

However, regardless of services available, ability to pay, or insurance status, all patients who seek help at a Medicaid-participating hospital are entitled to medical screening examination when a request is made for such an examination or treatment. In 1985, Congress enacted the Emergency Medical Treatment and Labor Act (EMTALA), which specifies these obligations (CMS, 2018).

It is a typical Tuesday afternoon on the L&D unit at Breward Hospital. Cindy, a pregnant woman, gets off the elevator and approaches the charge nurse, saying that she thinks she is in labor. The charge nurse accompanies the pregnant woman and her mother to a labor suite. Mary, the charge nurse, documents a history and performs a physical assessment on the woman. The exchange of information reveals that Cindy is only 23 weeks pregnant. Cindy's signs and symptoms for seeking treatment are mild abdominal cramping and moderate pain radiating down her right leg. Mary asks Cindy if there is any evidence of bleeding, regular uterine contractions, or rupture of membranes, but Cindy denies all of these signs of impending labor. At the time she entered the hospital, Cindy did not appear in any significant pain, appeared joyful, and emotionally stable. Her mother voiced no additional concerns.

Mary has decades of L&D experience and is near certain that Cindy is not in labor at all. Mary's assessment is that Cindy is merely experiencing ligament stretching and that this visit to the hospital does not necessitate notifying a doctor. In addition, the L&D department is not equipped or permitted, by policy, to handle an extremely premature infant delivery should Cindy truly be in labor. Mary tells Cindy that based on the signs and symptoms and

Mary's assessment, Cindy is not in labor but should go to another hospital facility seven miles away. The referral hospital has a physician on call 24 hours a day, staff that will pay closer attention to her, and, most importantly, a neonatal intensive care unit (NICU) that can take care of the premature baby should Cindy deliver. Cindy is given verbal instructions about how to proceed and is wheeled out the door for discharge.

Discussion Questions

1. Did Mary, the nurse, violate the EMTALA statute? Why or why not?
2. What steps should Mary have taken to protect Cindy?
3. Is the hospital liable for this incident, or is Mary the only person who was at fault? Defend your answer.
4. How might Mary's decision affect the health outcomes of Cindy or her unborn fetus?

Reference

Centers for Medicare & Medicaid Services (CMS). (2018). Emergency Medical Treatment and Labor Act. https://www.cms.gov/Regulations-and-Guidance/Legislation/EMTALA/

A Hospital's Lesson on "Dumping" Patients

Rachel Ellison, PhD

Jersey General Medical Center is a large healthcare facility that admits many patients on a daily basis. The emergency department sees approximately 500 patients daily. Dr. Samuel Smothers is the chief operating officer and has the enormous responsibility of ensuring the hospital is operating at the highest potential and following all governmental policies and standards.

Recently a neighboring health system was reported for "dumping" a patient on the street before she was stabilized. The newspaper went on to say the patient came into the hospital complaining of lower right abdominal pain. The patient was homeless and had no health insurance. She was taken back to a room, and her vital signs were checked. Her blood pressure was elevated, and she had a fever of 101.5. Once it was determined that she had no way of paying for her hospital bill, she was taken out of the hospital in a wheelchair and dumped on the sidewalk. This was all captured on security cameras. The patient was found on the sidewalk by a patron who called an ambulance. The patient was transferred to another local hospital where she was admitted and taken to surgery immediately for a ruptured appendix.

This violated the Emergency Medical Treatment and Labor Act (EMTALA). The healthcare system is likely to be fined for wrongdoing. Most fines are on average $50,000 (American College of Emergency Physicians, 2018). Unfortunately, these events happen far too often. Mr. Smothers is concerned that Jersey General Medical Center needs to be better equipped and trained on EMTALA so that everyone working in the emergency department is educated on the law.

Mr. Smothers contacts the director of the clinical education department, Melissa Janes, and they strategize on how to conduct an in-service training on EMTALA. They decide to preside over two in-service trainings so all staff can attend. The morning in-service will run from 8 a.m.–12 p.m., and the afternoon in-service will run from 1 p.m.–5 p.m. It is mandatory for all emergency department staff, clinical and nonclinical, to attend.

Mr. Smothers and Mrs. Janes will each lead topics throughout the in-service. Below is a draft of their outline:

What is EMTALA?

- Emergency Medical Treatment & Labor Act
- Enacted in 1986 in response to widespread concerns that private hospitals were denying emergent care to the indigent and uninsured population.
- Private hospitals were "dumping" them without proving adequate medical care.

Who must comply with EMTALA?

- Medicare participating hospitals that have emergency departments (the majority of all hospitals in the United States accept Medicare funding, which means all of these hospitals participate in EMTALA and must follow the law).

Who does EMTALA protect?

- Any person who comes to an emergency department must be given an appropriate medical examination within the proficiency of the hospital's emergency department to determine if an emergency medical condition exists. This includes providing specialty doctors, running tests, etc.
- If it is determined that there is an emergency condition, the hospital must provide treatment to stabilize or transfer the patient. The hospital must follow the rules of transferring unstable patients. A hospital can transfer an unstable patient only if the transfer is an "appropriate transfer" under the statute.
- EMTALA enforcement is complaint driven. An investigation is conducted by the Centers for Medicare and Medicaid Services or the state agency (American College of Emergency Physicians, 2018).

Another integral part to the in-service training is a role-playing scenario. Mr. Smothers wants to role-play an active EMTALA situation and have the emergency department staff evaluate the scenario. Mr. Smothers is reminded of an EMTALA case where a young, uninsured women in her 30s went to the emergency department because she had difficulty breathing and swelling in her mouth. Tests were conducted, and providers found an abscess at the base of her tongue. This patient needed to see a specialist. An ear, nose, and throat surgeon was called, but he refused to see the patient because she was uninsured. The patient was transferred to another hospital for care. The original hospital was cited for an EMTALA violation and fined $50,000. Mr. Smothers and Mrs. Janes planned to gather hospital staff to act out the scenario.

The emergency department staff will have a half-day filled with educational information regarding the importance of EMTALA and how it affects them on a daily basis in their work environment. Mr. Smothers wants every patient who walks into the emergency department to receive the best quality care regardless of their ability to pay. Jersey General Medical Center has and always will put patients first.

Discussion Questions

1. List three questions that should be asked of the emergency department staff after the scenario is acted out to them.
2. Why would a healthcare system "dump" a patient? How does EMTALA protect the patient?
3. What is the common theme in both scenarios mentioned in the case study?
4. Is the in-service that Mr. Smothers and Mrs. Janes hold enough to ensure that an EMTALA violation will not happen at Jersey General Medical Center? Please explain.

References

American College of Emergency Physicians. (2018). EMTALA. http://newsroom.acep.org /2009-01-04-emtala-fact-sheet

Teitelbaum, J. B., & Wilensky, S. E. (2017). *Essentials of Health Policy and Law* (3rd ed.). Burlington, MA: Jones & Bartlett Learning.

CHAPTER 3

Patient Protection Policies and Regulations

Rachel Ellison, PhD

▶ Introduction

The Health Insurance Portability and Accountability Act (HIPAA) of 1996 was created to keep individuals' medical information safe and private. Before this health policy was adopted, there were no regulations or laws from keeping patients' private medical records and health information secure. Because of this new health policy, the federal government had to decide who could have access to the information and how it could be shared. Recent technological changes in the healthcare landscape, such as the implementation of electronic health records (EHRs), have changed the way medical professionals deal with transferring protected health information (PHI) and electronic protected health information (ePHI) (HHS, 2018a). PHI and ePHI are safeguarded by the Privacy and Security Rules of the HIPAA.

▶ Privacy and Security Rules

The HIPAA Privacy Rule establishes national standards to protect medical records and other personal health information (HHS, 2018a). The rule requires safeguards to protect privacy of personal health information and sets limits and conditions on the uses and disclosures that may be made of such information without patient authorization (HHS, 2018a). Another benefit of the Privacy Rule is that it gives patients control over their health information, including the right to examine and obtain a copy of their health records and to request corrections if needed.

A major goal of the Privacy Rule is to ensure that individuals' health information is properly protected while still allowing the flow of health information necessary to provide and promote high quality health care (HHS, 2018a). Overseeing this objective is a top priority and concern of the U.S. Department of Health and Human Services (DHHS). The rule strives to strike a balance that allows the use of important facts while protecting the confidentiality of people who seek medical care.

According to the U.S. DHHS (2018c), individually identifiable health information, whether electronic, paper, or oral, in any form or media, held or transmitted, is considered protected health information (PHI). This includes:

- the person's past, present, or future physical or mental health or condition;
- the provision of health care to the individual person;
- the past, present, or future payment for the provision of health care to the individual; and
- identifying information—common identifiers can include name, address, birth date, and Social Security number.

The purpose of the Security Rule is to ensure that every covered entity has implemented safeguards to protect the confidentiality, integrity, and availability of ePHI (HHS, 2018c). The Centers for Medicare and Medicaid Services (CMS) have determined the definition of a *covered entity* under both the HIPAA Security and Privacy Rules (CMS, 2018a).

Covered Entities	
Health Plans	■ Health insurance companies ■ Employer-sponsored health plans ■ Health maintenance organizations ■ Government programs (Medicare, Medicaid, and military and veterans' health programs)
Providers	Providers who submit electronic claims: ■ Doctors ■ Dentists ■ Chiropractors ■ Clinics ■ Psychologists ■ Pharmacies ■ Nursing homes
Clearinghouses	Clearinghouses include organizations that process nonstandard health information to match standards for data on behalf of other organizations (CMS, 2018a).
Business Associates	■ Third-party administrators ■ Consultants ■ Healthcare clearinghouses ■ Independent medical transcriptionists (CMS, 2018a).

It is possible for a covered healthcare provider, health plan, or healthcare clearinghouse to be a business associate of another covered entity.

According to the U.S. DHHS, one of the major goals of the Security Rule is to protect the privacy of individuals' health information while allowing covered entities to adopt new technologies to improve the quality and efficiency of patient care (HHS, 2018c). It is equally important to provide quality care and keep individuals' health information secure.

The HIPAA Security Rule protects a subset of information covered by the Privacy Rule (HHS, 2018c). Both the Privacy and Security Rules have common goals. Their purpose is where the differences lie. The purpose of the Privacy Rule is to establish minimum Federal standards for safeguarding the privacy of individually identifiable health information (CMS, 2018b). The Security Rule establishes national standards for electronic protected health information (HHS, 2018c). One other distinction is that the Security Rule does not apply to PHI transmitted orally or in writing.

▶ Individual Rights Provided under HIPAA

The HIPAA is a health policy enacted in 1996 to not only keep individuals PHI secure but also to give individuals the rights to their own information. Those rights come in a variety of ways. The Privacy Rule gives you the right to:

- have corrections added to your health information,
- ask to view your medical records,
- request a copy of your medical records,
- receive a notice of how your health information may be used and shared,
- get a report on when and why your health information was shared for certain purposes,
- decide if you want to give your permission before your health information can be shared or used, and
- file a complaint with your provider or with the U.S. DHHS if your rights are denied (HHS, 2018b).

Any covered entity is required to safeguard and password protect all medical records and EHRs; this should be done regardless of who holds the information. Information in the medical record is sensitive and confidential. Only you and your personal representative have the right to access your medical record. Naming a personal representative can vary by state law, but normally it includes anyone with the power of attorney, a child's parent and/or legal guardian, and the executor of a deceased person's estate (HHS, 2018b).

▶ Compliance

The federal government established the Office for Civil Rights (OCR) to examine and enforce civil rights laws, conscience and religious freedom laws, HIPAA Privacy, Security, and Breach Notification Rules, and the Patient Safety Act Rule and to investigate confidentiality complaints to identify discrimination or violation of the law. The OCR protects individuals by educating communities and teaching social workers and healthcare professionals about civil rights, conscience and religious freedom rights, and health information privacy rights (HHS, 2018b). Their focus is to take action to correct problems.

In most situations, those actions are first taken by those who file a complaint with OCR; anyone can file a complaint within 180 days of the violation. It can be filed by phone, mail, fax, or through the OCR online complaint portal. The complaint must be clear and concise including the business entity, the person or persons involved, and how the acts violated the HIPAA law (HHS, 2018b). Under the Breach Notification Rule, covered entities are required to notify individuals of a breach of PHI. A breach is an event where information is shared and compromises the privacy and security of the PHI (HHS, 2018b). The breach notification must be reported to the OCR. The impermissible use or disclosure of PHI is presumed to be a breach unless covered entities demonstrate there is a low probability the PHI has been compromised based on:

- the nature and extent of the PHI involved, including the types of identifiers and the likelihood of re-identification;
- the unauthorized person who used the PHI or to whom the disclosure was made;
- whether the PHI was actually acquired or viewed; and
- the extent to which the risk to the PHI has been mitigated (CMS, 2018b).

The OCR will investigate health information and privacy complaints only if rights were violated by a covered entity and the complaint was submitted within 180 days. After the investigation is concluded, the OCR will send a letter discussing the outcome. If it is determined that the covered entity did not comply with HIPAA law, they must:

- voluntarily comply,
- take corrective action, and
- agree to a settlement.

If the covered entity does not comply with the investigative findings and take action to resolve the situation, OCR may impose monetary penalties (HHS, 2018b).

The Health Information Technology for Economic and Clinical Health (HITECH) Act was signed into law in 2009 to promote the adoption of meaningful use of health information technology and to provide awareness of the new enforcement guidelines of strengthening the civil and criminal enforcement of HIPAA guidelines (HHS, 2018b). The HITECH Act addresses the privacy and security concerns associated with electronic transmission of PHI through several provisions. On February 18, 2009, Section 13410(d) of the HITECH Act (HHS, 2017a), which revised section 1176(a) of the Social Security Act, became effective and established:

- four categories of violations that reflect increasing levels of culpability,
- four corresponding tiers of penalty amounts that significantly increase the minimum penalty amount for each violation, and
- a maximum penalty amount of $1.5 million for all violations of an identical provision.

▶ The Evolution of Patient Protection Policies

Like other policies, HIPAA and patient protection policies can change and evolve over time. Policies can go through cycles just to ensure that all areas are covered and everyone is protected. Since the enactment in 1996, many major additions have been added to the HIPAA policy in the last 20 years (HIPAA Journal, 2014). Below are key dates in HIPAA Policy:

- August 1996: HIPAA signed into law
- April 2003: Effective date of HIPAA Privacy Rule
- April 2005: Effective date of HIPAA Security Rule
- March 2006: Effective date of HIPAA Breach Enforcement Rule
- September 2009: Effective date of HITECH and Breach Notification Rule
- March 2013: Effective date of the Final Omnibus Rule (HIPAA Journal, 2014)

The addition of the Enforcement Rule to HIPAA in March 2006 was implemented because of the failure of many covered entities to fully comply with the Privacy and Security Rules that were enacted in 2003 and 2005 (HIPAA Journal, 2014). The HIPAA Enforcement Rule contains provisions relating to compliance and investigations, the imposition of civil money penalties for violations of HIPAA, and procedures for hearings (HHS, 2017b). The most recent act of legislation was the Final Omnibus Rule of 2013. This rule cleared up gray areas of HIPAA and HITECH without adding many new regulations (HIPAA Journal, 2014). Definitions were amended to clear up terms, and the Privacy and Security Rules were amended to allow patients' health information to be held indefinitely—the previous legislation had stipulated that it be held for 50 years (HIPAA Journal, 2014).

▶ Summary

Since HIPAA's inception in 1996, there have been major updates and additions to the law, including changes to the Enforcement Rule, Security Rule, and Privacy Rule. Updating the law to stay current with the healthcare environment is a trend that will continue to evolve over time. The Final Omnibus Rule of 2013 was new but barely enforced new legislation; the purpose of the legislation was to "fill gaps" and "clear up gray areas." The case studies that follow discuss a variety of components regarding the HIPAA law. The key terms are instrumental in the analysis of the case studies and discussion questions.

Key Terms

Covered Entities are defined in the HIPAA rules as (1) health plans, (2) healthcare clearinghouses, and (3) healthcare providers who electronically transmit any health information in connection with transactions for which HHS has adopted standards.

Electronic Health Records (EHR) are digital versions of a patient's paper chart.

Enforcement Rule is a decree from HIPAA that sets out the rules that govern the responsibilities and requirements of covered entities and business associates about how it expects them to cooperate in the enforcement process.

Health Insurance Portability and Accountability Act (HIPAA) is a U.S. law designed to provide privacy standards to protect patients' medical records and other health information provided to health plans, doctors, hospitals, and other healthcare providers.

Office for Civil Rights (OCR) is primarily focused on enforcing civil rights laws that prohibits discrimination on the basis of race, color, national origin, sex, disability, and age.

Patient Bill of Rights is a list of guarantees to those receiving medical care. It may take the form of a law or a nonbinding declaration.

Privacy Officer is a person designated by an organization who routinely handles PHI to develop, implement, and oversee the organization's compliance with the U.S. Health Insurance Portability and Accountability Act (HIPAA) privacy rules.

Privacy Rule establishes national standards to protect individuals' medical records and other personal health information, which applies to health plans, healthcare clearinghouses, and those healthcare providers that conduct certain healthcare transactions electronically.

Protected Health Information (PHI) consists of any information in a medical record that can be used to identify an individual and that was created, used, or disclosed in the course of providing a healthcare service, such as a diagnosis or treatment.

Security Rule requires appropriate administrative, physical, and technical safeguards to ensure the confidentiality, integrity, and security of ePHI.

References

Centers for Medicare and Medicaid Services (CMS). (2018a). Are you a covered entity? https://www.cms.gov/Regulations-and-Guidance/Administrative-Simplification/HIPAA-ACA/AreYouaCoveredEntity.html

Centers for Medicare and Medicaid Services (CMS). (2018b). HIPAA basics for providers: Privacy, Security, and Breach Notification Rules. https://www.cms.gov/Outreach-and-Education/Medicare-Learning-Network-MLN/MLNProducts/Downloads/HIPAAPrivacyandSecurity.pdf

Department of Health and Human Services (HHS). (2017a). HITECH Act Enforcement Interim Final Rule. https://www.hhs.gov/hipaa/for-professionals/special-topics/hitech-act-enforcement-interim-final-rule/index.html

Department of Health and Human Services (HHS). (2017b). The HIPAA Enforcement Rule. https://www.hhs.gov/hipaa/for-professionals/special-topics/enforcement-rule/index.html

Department of Health and Human Services (HHS). (2018a). HIPAA for professionals. https://www.hhs.gov/hipaa/for-professionals/index.html

Department of Health and Human Services (HHS). (2018b). Office for Civil Rights. https://www.hhs.gov/ocr/about-us/index.html

Department of Health and Human Services (HHS). (2018c). Summary of the HIPAA Security Rule. https://www.hhs.gov/hipaa/for-professionals/security/laws-regulations/index.html

HIPAA Journal. (2014). HIPAA history. https://www.hipaajournal.com/hipaa-history/.

⌕ CASE 3-1

What Did I Do?

Wendy M. Whitner, PhD, MPH, Marsha Davenport, MD, MS, MPH, FACPM, & Cassandra Henson, Dr.PA, MBA

HoneyHealth Etc. is a "big box" store that provides pharmacy and healthcare services as well as groceries, clothes, and other basic goods. HoneyHealth Etc. shops are chain stores that are strategically located in lower income areas to provide less costly, convenient health care and pharmacy needs. HoneyHealth Etc. is open 24 hours, 7 days a week, and the clinic side is staffed with one front desk person, a medical assistant, and a nurse practitioner, which is typical of retail clinics (RAND, 2016; Carthon et al., 2017; Martsolf et al., 2017). The pharmacy and the clinic share a reception area, but have different intake (clinic), drop off (pharmacy), and pick-up areas (pharmacy). Sherry J. is a new pharmacist technician and has been with HoneyHealth Etc. for only 90 days.

Hilda B. visits the clinic in HoneyHealth Etc. on a Saturday evening at 10 p.m. because she is not feeling well. After she registers, she is promptly called back for triage and placed in an exam room. She notices the Patient Bill of Rights as well as Health Information Portability & Accountability Act (HIPAA) literature and posters while waiting for the healthcare practitioner. The nurse practitioner enters the exam room and completes her assessment. She asks Hilda B. where she would like to have her prescription filled. Hilda B indicates that she wants it filled at the pharmacy in the store. The nurse practitioner sends the prescription electronically to the pharmacy.

After Hilda B. is discharged from the clinic, she goes directly to the pharmacy side to see if her prescription is ready. As she is waiting in line, she also notices HIPAA and the Patient Bill of Rights posters. When it is her turn, Hilda B. approaches the drop-off station of the pharmacy counter. Hilda B. indicates to Felicia G., a pharmacy technician, that she was seen at the clinic on the other side of the store and that the nurse practitioner electronically sent her prescription to be filled. Felicia G. let Hilda B. know that her medication will be ready in 30 minutes. Meanwhile, Sherry J. is assisting Dr. Lacy, the pharmacist, in the back when she hears a familiar voice. She peeps around the corner to discover, Hilda B., the ex-girlfriend to her current boyfriend, Jaxson Q, who is supposed to have moved to another state the month prior.

Sherry J. looks up Hilda B.'s prescription and notices that the prescription was for a sexually transmitted infection (STI) and that Hilda B.'s address is local. Sherry J. immediately begins texting Jaxson Q., telling him that he better not have given her any "nasty women disease" and accusing him of cheating on her with Hilda. Jaxson Q. texts her back, confused, to say that Hilda B. had moved. Sherry J. texts back: "She is here in the pharmacy getting medication for a STI that you better not have!" Jaxson Q. texts Hilda B. to ask her where she is and what she is doing.

Hilda B. is upset with the text from Jaxson Q. and wonders how he knew where she was and for what. When her medication is ready, she hears over the loudspeaker, "Medicaid patient Hilda B., your STI medication is ready for pick-up," spoken in Hilda B.'s native language, Spanish. She is not happy about the announcement and waits for 10 minutes before going to the counter to pick up her medication. When she arrives at the counter, she recognizes Sherry J. Hilda B. picks up her medication and goes to HoneyHealth Etc. pharmacy and clinic administrator's office to make a complaint about her health condition being announced over the loudspeaker.

Discussion Questions

1. What are the issues in this case?
2. How does HIPAA apply in this case?
3. Who has the authority to act?
4. How could the situations that evolved in the pharmacy been prevented? What are the lessons learned?

References

Carthon, J. M. B., Sammarco, T., Pancir, D., Chittams, J., & Nicely, W. W. (2016). Growth in retail-based clinics after nurse practitioner scope of practice reform. *Nursing Outlook, 65*, 195–201.

Martsolf, G., Fingar, K., Coffey, R., Kandrack, R., Charland, T., Eiber, C., Elixhauser, A., Steiner, C., & Mehrotra, A. (2016). Association between the opening of retail clinics and low-acuity emergency department visits. *Annals of Emergency Medicine, 69*(4): 397–403.

RAND Corporation. (2016). The evolving role of retail clinics. https://www.rand.org/pubs/research_briefs/RB9491-2.html

🔍 *CASE 3-2*

Wait a Minute Mr. Postman: Ensuring HIPAA Compliance during a Release of Information Incident

Kristy Courville, MHA, RHIA

The privacy officer of an acute care hospital was called to meet with the release of information (ROI) supervisor of the Health Information Management department. As the privacy officer arrived for the meeting, the ROI supervisor carried in a box of paper medical records and began to remove portions of paper medical records to display for the privacy officer.

It became immediately apparent to the privacy officer that the medical records were in extremely poor condition. The charts were disassembled, and pages were torn to shreds. The ROI supervisor informed the privacy officer that the box was routed back to the hospital following a standard submission of medical records to the Comprehensive Error Rate Testing (CERT) contractor. CERT contractors are established by the Centers for Medicare & Medicaid Services (CMS) to monitor the accuracy of claim payment in the Medicare Fee-For-Service (FFS) Program (HIPAA Journal, 2017). The CERT program is intended to protect the Medicare Trust Fund by identifying errors and assessing error rates at both the national and regional levels (Rinehart-Thompson, 2018).

The CERT contractor included correspondence within the box of charts that informed the facility that the enclosed charts were delivered to the CERT Documentation Office in the existing deplorable condition. The note further described how the CERT contractor was not able to appropriately conduct the required chart review due to the irreconcilable presentation of the medical records.

The privacy officer and the ROI supervisor began an investigation in an attempt to understand how this situation occurred. Upon further analysis of the contents in the box, it was determined that the medical records belonged to three separate patients treated by the facility. To assist with the investigation, the privacy officer asked that the ROI supervisor provide a listing of all charts released from the facility to the CERT contractor during the timeframe of the incident. Because the investigation could not truly reveal the determining factors of the event, the privacy officer was forced to place a call to the CERT Documentation Office. The CERT case reviewer provided more detail.

The CERT Documentation Office received the medical records in such poor condition that personnel could not determine what documentation belonged to which patient. In addition, a large portion of the documentation was illegible due to the deteriorated condition of the charts. The privacy officer apologized and assured the representative that this was not the condition of the medical records as submitted by the facility. She then conveyed that a second submission of the requested charts would be processed. Before concluding the conversation, the privacy officer confirmed with the CERT representative that all damaged medical records had been returned to the hospital for proper destruction.

The privacy officer's concern over this incident continued to escalate as the investigation continued. The only explanation was that the medical records were destroyed in transit. The standard policy and procedure for submitting medical records to the CERT Office is through United Parcel Service (UPS) via certified mail. Could the incident have occurred under the responsibility of the mail carrier? Meanwhile, the ROI supervisor reported that he could not produce a listing of any charts released to the CERT contractor.

The privacy officer decided to call UPS. The tracking number traced the journey of the box as it traveled through the UPS network. After many phone conversations, the privacy officer finally spoke to a manager who referenced an incident report filed by a UPS Distribution Center in Louisville, Kentucky. As the box of charts made its way through the distribution center, an automated conveyor belt high above the floor of the building navigated the box to the appropriate routing terminal. Apparently, the box became entangled within the equipment causing it to completely fall apart, and medical records poured out all over the floor of the distribution center.

The privacy officer was completely horrified and unable to believe the details of the event. This was definitely the most unique release of information incident during her 20-plus years of healthcare experience. The UPS distribution center manager assured the privacy officer that all employees within the center were required to assist in the collection of the scattered documentation. The manager professed his confidence that all medical information was appropriately recovered, repackaged, and routed for successful delivery to its intended destination.

Discussion Questions

1. Identify if any events in the case study violated the HIPAA Privacy Rule and/or the HIPAA Security Rule.
2. Consider if a breach of PHI, as defined by HITECH, resulted from this incident. Why or why not?
3. Determine if the events of this investigation should be reported to the Department of Health and Human Services' (HHS) Office for Civil Rights (OCR) as outlined by the HIPAA Breach Notification Rule? Why or why not?
4. Evaluate if the ROI supervisor should have been able to produce a list of the charts submitted to the CERT Documentation Office. Explain your answer.
5. Recommend the privacy officer's course of action.

References

HIPAA Journal. (2017, October 12). How should you respond to an accidental HIPAA violation? https://www.hipaajournal.com/accidental-hipaa-violation/

Rinehart-Thompson, L. (2018). *Introduction to health information privacy and security* (2nd ed.). Chicago, IL: AHIMA Press.

🔍 *CASE 3-3*

Patient Protection Policies & Regulations: From Good Intentions to Cruel Intentions on Social Media

Yen Vi Khuu-Eickhoff, MHSA

Southern Health Group is a multi-specialty clinic located in Savannah, Georgia. The practice was established in 1996 by merging two medical groups, Tybee Specialists and Southern Family Practice. Southern Health Group initially started out with seven physicians, including specialists in cardiology and nephrology in addition to primary care.

Today, Southern Health Group has expanded to an additional nine specialties including neurology, allergy and immunology, radiology, ophthalmology, physical therapy, gastroenterology, urology, endocrinology, and pediatrics. The care team has expanded to 85 physicians, 12 nurse practitioners, 9 physician assistants, and about 200 LPNs and MAs. With 15 different campuses along the East Coast, Southern Health Group has quickly become the most popular healthcare organization in the region.

In terms of organizational leadership, there is a board composed of local stakeholders within the community to which the administrator, Michael Carter, reports. Under Michael is the director of operations, human resources director, chief financial officer, and chief information officer. The director of operations oversees 15 practice managers who are responsible for the day-to-day functions of each campus.

While still working on expanding the organization into South Carolina, the director of operations leaves the hiring of another manager for the new location to her lead practice manager, Nicole Wright. Nicole has been with the company for 16 years and is considered an expert in practice management. She often assists in the hiring and training of other managers. Because she has been with the company for so long, she often is very complacent in her work. A friend refers Elizabeth Reid for the position Nicole is seeking to fill. In the midst of many other projects, Nicole decides to hire Elizabeth without a proper interview. Elizabeth attends orientation the next week where she learns about company policies as well as HIPAA policies. The Administrative Simplification Subsection of HIPAA covers healthcare providers, and these regulations govern the job and behavior of those working in the healthcare field (Gartee, 2010).

Elizabeth was previously employed at Coastal Nephrology as a practice manager. She was terminated by the company within a year after discovering that she had been printing "work excuse" notices from the Electronic Medical Record (EMR) for her cousin who is a patient there. Elizabeth was responsible for all charges that come through for her physicians and posting them accordingly. She would often "write off" certain charges on family members that come in. She was caught when a particular physician noticed on his financial statements that he had been charging for fewer visits than the actual number of patients he had seen. Elizabeth was confronted and stated that she "may have made a mistake."

While touring the main campus at Southern Health Group, Elizabeth notices that this organization stays busy, and nurses and physicians often leave their work computers unlocked and accessible to any user. Elizabeth will spend the next 4 months training at this location under Nicole. Nicole barely spends any time training Elizabeth due to her busy schedule in addition to getting ready for a conference.

On the week of the conference, Nicole leaves Elizabeth with a list of things to do. One of the things on the list is to complete random chart audits for physicians. Because Elizabeth is still new, she does not have administrative access in the EMR. Nicole provides Elizabeth with her personal login. While doing chart audits, Elizabeth comes across Shawn Lewis's chart, a friend from high school. She decided to peruse his chart for a while noticing that he has a wife with three children now. In Shawn's chart, the doctor just noted that Shawn has stage 3 prostate cancer. Surprised by this, Elizabeth took a picture of Shawn's chart with her mobile phone. After work, Elizabeth made a post on Facebook stating, "prayers for you, Shawn," along with a picture of his medical record. The post was viewed by many mutual friends between Shawn and Elizabeth. One friend decided to contact Shawn's wife to offer comforting words, but she did not know of Shawn's cancer. The HIPAA Privacy Rule prohibits the use of protected health information (PHI) on social media networks (HIPAA Journal, 2018).

Shawn immediately contacts the office to follow up on the issue, but Nicole is still away at the conference. Shawn speaks with Nicole's assistant, who says she will relay the message to Nicole when she comes back next week. Shawn then calls administration to speak to someone from management. Unfortunately, he is sent to Michael's voicemail and the director of operations is not in the office at the moment.

Discussion Questions

1. List some contributing factors that led to the disclosure of Shawn's medical record on social media.
2. What could the director of operations and Nicole have done differently in each of their roles to prevent such a violation?
3. Does IT have a responsibility in this particular case? Why or why not?
4. Assuming that Shawn's phone call was forwarded to you, the HR director, how would you handle this situation?

References

Gartee, R. (2010). Accreditation, regulation, and HIPAA. *Health information technology and management* (pp.42-73). Upper Saddle River, NJ: Pearson Education.
HIPAA Journal. (2018). HIPAA Social Media rules. https://www.hipaajournal.com/hipaa-social-media/

SECTION 2

Understanding the U.S. Healthcare Delivery System

© exdez/Getty Images

CHAPTER 4

Healthcare Financing and Payment Methods

Rachel Ellison, PhD & Lesley Clack, ScD

▶ Introduction

U.S. healthcare spending reached $3.3 trillion in 2016, an increase of 4.3% from previous years, with an average of $10,348 spent per person (CMS, 2018a). The overall gross domestic product (GDP) related to healthcare spending was 17.9% in 2016, up from 17.7% in 2015 (CMS, 2018a). The growth of healthcare spending has and will continue to increase over the years due to the changing healthcare environment as well as new laws and policies. By 2023, it is expected that healthcare spending in relation to the GDP will reach 19.3%; in other words, one-fifth of the nation's economy will be related to healthcare spending (CMS, 2018a).

▶ Health Spending

Hospital care made up $1.1 trillion of healthcare expenditures in 2016. Hospital care increased by 4.7% over 2015 compared with a 5.7% increase from 2014 to 2015. Hospital care expenditures showed mixed trends across the major payers, with slower growth in Medicaid and private health insurance spending, stable growth in Medicare spending, and faster growth in out-of-pocket spending (CMS, 2018a).

Physician and clinical services spent $664.9 billion in 2016, which outpaced hospital, prescription drugs, dental, and all other professional health services that year (CMS, 2018a). Healthcare is making a positive shift, and physician services are now being used more for preventive care.

Growth in retail prescription drug spending slowed in 2016, increasing just 1.3% to $328.6 billion (CMS, 2018a). Two years previously, the rate was much higher due to increased spending on new medicines and the growth of popular existing brand name drugs. Other professional services, including physical therapy, optometry, podiatry, and chiropractic services, reached $92 billion in 2016. This was an increase of 4.7%. A few years prior, the growth rate was 5.9% (CMS, 2018a).

Spending for dental services accelerated to $124.4 billion in 2016. There was slight growth from 2015 to 2016. In 2015, the growth was 4.4%, and in 2016, the spending increased by 4.6%. Out-of-pocket spending for dental services was the biggest increase and accounted for 40% of spending (CMS, 2018a).

▶ Paying for Health Care

In the United States, healthcare services are paid for by a variety of sources, such as out-of-pocket payments, private health insurance, and public health insurance (Buchbinder & Shanks, 2017). Out-of-pocket payments include payments by individuals who pay for services themselves or payments by individuals who buy insurance policies and pay for part of those services through copayments and deductibles. Private health insurance refers to plans that individuals take out through their employers or on their own, and these payments include health insurance premiums that cover the costs of payments made by the health plan. Public health insurance refers to programs such as Medicare, Medicaid, the Children's Health Insurance Plan (CHIP), and the Military Health System, which are funded by federal, state, and local government programs (Buchbinder & Shanks, 2017). These sources of payment will be discussed in more detail in other chapters throughout this book.

▶ Health Reform Efforts

Although health reform is a hot topic today, health reform efforts in the United States are not new. Health reform has been an issue in U.S. domestic policy since the early 1900s, when Teddy Roosevelt and the Progressive Party attempted one of the first efforts by endorsing social insurance as part of the party platform in 1912 (KFF, 2011). The idea of a national health insurance program has been supported by many presidents, from Roosevelt to Truman to Kennedy, but has never been implemented (KFF, 2011). Historically, health reform has succeeded through the passage of federal legislation governing medical care, which is discussed throughout this book. The most recent health reform effort was the passage of the Patient Protection and Affordable Care Act (PPACA), which was signed into law by President Obama and enacted on March 23, 2010 (CMS, 2018b). The PPACA, also referred to as the ACA or Obamacare, requires that each state establish health insurance exchanges, which are marketplaces where individuals and small businesses can obtain private health insurance coverage (Forsberg, 2018). States have two options for the establishment of exchanges: they can establish a state-based exchange (SBE) on their own, or the Secretary of Health and Human Services (HHS) can establish a federally facilitated exchange (FFE) for them (Forsberg, 2018). Individuals who obtain insurance coverage through the exchange may be eligible for financial assistance from the federal government, which comes in the form of premium tax credits or cost-sharing reductions. The premium tax credit is available to individuals who do not have access to public insurance, such as Medicaid or employer-based coverage. Cost-sharing reductions are available for individuals who meet certain eligibility requirements, and the cost-sharing reductions limit the annual out-of-pocket cap on plans and/or lower the percentage of costs to the individual (Forsberg, 2018).

The PPACA also established additional protections for individuals, including:

- requiring insurance plans to cover people with preexisting health conditions without charging more;
- providing free preventive care;
- giving young adults more coverage options, such as remaining on parent's insurance coverage until age 26 if enrolled in college;
- ending lifetime and yearly dollar limits on coverage of essential health benefits;
- holding insurance companies accountable for rate increases;
- making it illegal for health insurance companies to cancel your health insurance just because you get sick;
- protecting your choice of doctor;
- safeguarding you from employer retaliation; and
- covering mental health and substance abuse services (CMS, 2018c).

Health reform efforts are ongoing in this country and will continue to be a national debate. The many facets of this topic will be explored through different concepts throughout this book.

▶ The Role of Policymakers in Financing Health Care

Policymakers play a large role in the process of passing laws that finance health care. The passing of the PPACA shows the importance of policymakers and the policy-making process in the United States. The distinct role of policymakers will continue to be important as healthcare spending shifts upward. Key stakeholders, including health policy experts, health providers, employers, and payers, are aware of the trend toward increasing healthcare costs. Most stakeholders are conflicted about how to control health spending but know that it must be done. The government has taken strong steps to limit spending, for which they are responsible, by limiting funds to public health insurance programs. Other major players who shoulder the cost (employers, private insurers, and patients) seem reluctant or unable to change behaviors that could significantly lower spending, such as cutting back on unnecessary ordering of supplies, ordering less expensive and fewer elective tests and procedures, and focusing more on preventative health care (Altman & Mechanic, 2018).

Key stakeholders and policymakers work together because everyone has a vested interest in healthcare spending and financing. Individual state governments have taken the initiative to implement programs at the state level to finance health care and to find adequate payment methods. For example, policymakers in Massachusetts implemented the Massachusetts Plan, which sets annual state spending targets, encourages the formation of accountable care organizations, and establishes an independent commission to oversee the performance of the healthcare system (Altman & Mechanic, 2018). Policymakers in the state have addressed health cost containment since 2006, when the landmark health reform bill that provided near-universal health insurance coverage was enacted (Altman & Mechanic, 2018).

▶ Summary

Financing the healthcare system in the United States has been a hot topic for some time. The cost of health care continues to rise annually. Changes in federal healthcare legislation, such as the PPACA, currently do not seem to make a significant difference in overall healthcare expenditure. Major changes are needed from the federal government to show significant improvement in healthcare spending. Some state governments have taken the lead and enacted their own legislation to lessen the burden in their states.

Policymakers have an important role in financing health care. Healthcare spending, financing, reimbursement, and payment methods are all linked to one another. In this text, in-depth discussion regarding reimbursement and payment methods will be discussed in the chapter on Health Insurance and Reimbursement methods. Below are important terms to assist in analyzing this chapter's case studies.

Key Terms

Episode of Care (EOC) is a specific period of relatively continuous care involving one or more healthcare services rendered by a provider in relation to a particular health issue, medical problem, or situation.

Financial Statements are written records of a business's financial situation. There are three reports that depict financial activities: balance sheet, income statement, and statement of cash flows.

Key Performance Indicators (KPI) are a measurable value that demonstrates how effectively a company is achieving key business objectives.

Key Stakeholder is a person, group, or organization that has interest or concern in an organization. Stakeholders can affect or be affected by the organization's actions, objectives, and policies.

Prospective Payment Method is a type of episode-of-care reimbursement in which the third-party payer establishes payment rates for healthcare services in advance for a specific time period.

Retrospective Payment Method is a fee-for-service reimbursement in which providers receive compensation after health services have been rendered.

References

Altman, S., & Mechanic, R. (2018). Health care cost control: Where do we go from here? https://www.healthaffairs.org/do/10.1377/hblog20180705.24704/full/

Buchbinder, S. B., & Shanks, N. H. (2017). *Introduction to health care management* (3rd ed.). Burlington, MA: Jones & Bartlett Learning.

Centers for Medicare and Medicaid Services (CMS). (2018a). National health expenditures highlights 2016. https://www.cms.gov/Research-Statistics-Data-and-Systems/Statistics-Trends-and-Reports/NationalHealthExpendData/downloads/highlights.pdf

Centers for Medicare and Medicaid Services (CMS). (2018b). Patient Protection and Affordable Care Act. https://www.healthcare.gov/glossary/patient-protection-and-affordable-care-act/

Centers for Medicare & Medicaid Services (CMS). (2018c). Rights & Protections. https://www.healthcare.gov/health-care-law-protections/

Forsberg, V. C. (2018). Overview of health insurance exchanges. https://fas.org/sgp/crs/misc/R44065.pdf

Kaiser Family Foundation (KFF). (2011). Timeline: History of health reform in the U.S. https://www.kff.org/health-reform/timeline/history-of-health-reform-efforts-in-the-united-states/

⌕ CASE 4-1

Managing Healthcare Costs: Where to Look When Things Go Wrong

Cassandra R. Henson, Dr.P.A., MBA, Marsha Davenport, MD, MS, MPH, FACPM, & Wendy M. Whitner, PhD, MPH

(*This case assumes a basic understanding of financial concepts and is best used with students who have taken an accounting or finance course.)

Mountain Peak Health System is one of the state's largest healthcare delivery systems, servicing its patients at a number of hospital and neighborhood clinic locations. A full range of services is provided by the highly skilled medical professionals there, using the latest state-of-the-art medical technology. Competing healthcare providers are relatively small with limited services, so competition isn't a real concern to administration. The organization's payer contracts are up to date, and the fee schedule is regularly reviewed. The system is the clear leader in the local market, enjoying years of solid performance and financial viability.

As the senior financial analyst for Mountain Peak Health System, you are responsible for the collection of operating and financial data, as well as the monthly reports to the executive team. The reporting package consists of the following items: (1) a dashboard of key performance indicators (KPIs) for each location, (2) a consolidated dashboard for the entire health system, and (3) an executive summary that provides the highlights of the month's performance. To date, all indicators have been in an acceptable range, with no major red flags in the results.

When preparing this month's reporting package, you notice a few irregularities in the data. The system's bottom line seems to be declining. There have been no significant external events (natural disasters, local crises, etc.) to impact volume, so there must be other causes of this unpredicted change. Has there been a change in healthcare policy (coverage and/or volume)? Maybe a change in clinical/patient care and safety regulations (clinician-to-patient ratio)? As a true financial analyst, you begin to investigate, starting with Mountain Peak's financial statements. The organization's financial statements are provided below, followed by two scenarios (Part A and Part B) for consideration.

Discussion Questions
Part A: Financial Statement Analysis
Analyze and explain the content of financial statements and financial ratios for healthcare organizations. *** Analysis of Mountain Peak's financial statements provided above.

1. Identify at least three financial strengths and three financial weaknesses for Mountain Peak Health System. Support your claims with information presented in the financial or operating data statements.
2. Calculate the following profitability ratio for 2017: a) total margin and b) the return on equity (ROE).
3. Calculate the following debt and asset management ratios for 2017: a) total asset turnover and b) debt-to-equity ratio.
4. Calculate the following operating indicators for 2017: a) revenue per discharge, b) profit per discharge, and c) expense per discharge.

Part B: Labor and Workload Analysis
Perform basic budgeting tasks for healthcare organizations. *** Mountain Peak's new service line ~ PET scans.

TABLE 4-1   Mountain Peak Health System Statement of Operations, Fiscal Years Ending December 31, 2016 and 2017

	2016	2017
Revenues		
Inpatient revenue	$40,125,000	$36,500,250
Outpatient revenue	$29,900,000	$27,048,984
Other operating revenue	$5,575,984	$4,000,000
Total revenues	$75,600,984	$67,549,234
Expenses		
Wages and fringe benefits	$29,203,198	$32,203,198
Agency/contract wages	$3,383,640	$3,183,640
Medical supplies	$699,902	$799,902
Utilities	$362,018	$450,000
Maintenance (equipment)	$3,016,821	$3,216,821
Transportation services	$905,046	$1,253,981
Total expenses	$37,570,625	$41,107,542
Operating income	$38,030,359	$26,441,692
Nonoperating expenses		
Health screenings	$100,000	$100,000
Publications and brochures	$250,000	$250,000
TV and print advertisement	$150,000	$150,000
Total nonoperating expenses	$500,000	$500,000
Net income	$37,530,359	$25,941,692

TABLE 4-2 Mountain Peak Health System Balance Sheet, Fiscal Years Ending December 31, 2016 and 2017

	2016	2017
Assets		
Investments	$4,837,510	$4,729,581
Cash from patients	$100,000	$100,000
Fund raising/charity	$390,000	$390,000
Total assets	$5,327,510	$5,219,581
Liabilities		
Accounts payable	$540,000	$585,490
Salvage receipts	$1,500,000	$1,500,000
Total liabilities	$2,040,000	$2,085,490
Net assets	$3,287,510	$3,134,091

In 2009, the Centers for Medicare & Medicaid Services (CMS) expanded its imaging payment coverage for cancer patients. Mountain Peak is considering the implementation of positron emission tomography (PET) scans for its growing cancer patient population. It already offers magnetic resonance imaging (MRI) and computerized tomography (CT) scans, but this new service will require a separate staff to accommodate the volume of patients. The financial analysis team must estimate the impacts of the new service line and determine its feasibility for the organization. These services will be offered in-house to avoid complications with the Stark Law, which prohibits physician referrals to entities in which they may have financial interest. There are still CMS Medicare physician fee schedule (PFS) capped payment rates to consider, so the labor costs are the first category to be examined. Financial guidance from the U.S. Government Accountability Office (GAO) encourages zero-based budgeting for government programs, so this must be a "ground-up" calculation.

Based upon the annual outpatient ancillary volume shown in the above data, calculate total labor cost using the following full-time employee categories:

1. Medical Doctor/Radiologist @ $175.00 per hour
2. Registered Nurse @ $65.00 per hour
3. Imaging Technicians @ $35.00 per hour
4. 2 hours per patient/imaging procedure
5. Assume fringe benefit percentage of 33%

Costs must be calculated for each labor category separately, monthly, and totaled at the end of the fiscal year.

TABLE 4-3 Mountain Peak Health System Operating Data (Volume), Fiscal Years Ending December 31, 2017

	July-16	August-16	September-16	October-16	November-16	December-16	January-17	February-17	March-17	April-17	May-17	June-17	Total
Medical inpatient days	18,475	17,551	16,674	15,340	17,424	19,166	21,083	19,607	18,235	16,958	19,502	22,427	222,943
Surgical in-patient days	668	793	960	793	818	975	793	758	960	768	783	940	10,009
Outpatient visits	2,690	2,556	2,428	2,306	2,537	2,791	3,070	2,855	2,655	2,469	2,840	3,265	32,461
Total discharges	4,500	4,323	4,525	4,485	4,250	4,100	4,405	4,322	4,120	4,501	3,922	4,495	51,948
Inpatient ancillary	2,170	2,062	1,958	1,861	2,047	2,251	2,476	2,303	2,142	1,992	2,291	2,634	26,186
Outpatient ancillary	3,875	3,681	3,497	3,322	3,655	4,020	4,422	4,112	3,825	3,557	4,090	4,704	46,761
Total patient activity	32,378	30,966	30,042	28,607	30,730	33,303	36,249	33,958	31,936	30,245	33,428	38,466	390,308
Licensed beds	750	750	750	750	750	750	750	750	750	750	750	750	
Occupancy rate	82.34%	78.90%	78.3%	71.54%	81.08%	86.63%	94.09%	96.98%	82.56%	78.78%	87.25%	103.85%	
Average length of stay (days)	4.25	4.24	3.90	3.71	4.29	4.91	4.97	4.71	4.66	3.94	5.17	5.20	

🔍 *CASE 4-2*

Advancing Community Health Improvement through a Hospital-Health Department Collaborative

Erik L. Carlton, DrPH

Since 2013, tax exempt hospitals are under federal requirements to conduct community health needs assessments at least every 3 years (Carlton & Singh, 2018). Additionally, they must develop a community health improvement plan to address identified needs. Similarly, statutory and accreditation guidelines require that local health departments also conduct these assessments and improvement plans (Pennel, McLeroy, Burdine, & Matarrita-Cascante, 2015).

The overlap and duplication of these activities becomes burdensome on local practitioners and citizens alike. It also wastes fiscal and human resources and leads to confusion and disengagement across the community (Rosenbaum & Margulies, 2011).

However, some communities, such as Indigo County, Georgia, are finding significant cost savings and achieving great gains in health improvement through hospital–health department collaboration. With a population of roughly 500,000, the county has five hospitals, each spending nearly $75,000 to complete their assessments. Marie, community improvement manager for one of the hospitals, Indigo County Memorial (ICM), takes a new job at another hospital as director of strategy and planning with ICM's primary market rival, St. Peter's Healthcare. While reviewing the hospital's most recent strategic plan, she finds that St. Peter's community needs assessment and improvement plans largely mirror those that she helped lead at ICM. Knowing what she does of the Indigo County area, Marie expects that the assessments and plans at the county's other hospitals are similar and wonders if there is not a way to share data and experiences. The hospitals have always maintained a strict competitive distance. They do not share data with the regional health information exchange and constantly compete while acquiring new physician practices and service lines. Still, given her personal connections to ICM, Marie begins to wonder if something could be done differently.

Marie begins by reaching out to her former supervisor, Jessica, at ICM who occupies a very similar position to the one she now holds at St. Peter's. Over lunch, Marie initiates a discussion about the similarities she has noticed in their hospitals' respective strategic initiatives. Her colleague at ICM is similarly struck by the significant overlap between the two organizations. Realizing that the community needs assessment and improvement planning activities do not largely inform the broader competitive strategies of their respective hospitals, Marie and Jessica resolve to each approach their hospitals' leaders about the idea of a shared community assessment. Both hospitals are in the early phases of their next assessment, so the timing seems opportune. Much to their surprise, though with some careful cajoling, they each receive approval to work together on a shared assessment.

Though they serve a similar community with largely the same population demographic and socioeconomic profile, Marie and Jessica encounter many difficulties over the next several months. The hospitals' traditional assessments involve many different questions and procedural steps. ICM usually uses an outside consultant to help conduct the assessment using a template the consultant employs nationally, whereas St. Peter's usually involves a broader group of stakeholders and allows those involved from the community to guide the process. After thorough discussion, Marie and Jessica resolve to borrow some key elements of the consultant's model, which they both know from their shared time at ICM, while they also work to engage a group of community stakeholders. They reach out to the new director of the county health department who assigns Zeke, her director of assessment and planning, to participate in the hospitals' joint assessment and planning efforts. He becomes a critical partner, suggesting several ways the two hospitals could share resources and economize their efforts. Over the coming year, their shared work produces a very detailed assessment that captures common community health problems while identifying many overlapping priority areas.

Two years later, Jessica, Marie, and Zeke begin discussing the next round of assessments the hospitals will need to conduct. Zeke indicates that the health department has recently decided to seek accreditation, which requires a high degree of collaboration with local hospitals. Highlighting the many benefits of the collaborative effort, Zeke suggests recruiting the country's other hospitals to a fully integrative and comprehensive community assessment. He proposes a shared resource model whereby each hospital provides a portion of the overall costs, depending on their market share and the comparative size of their annual revenue. The shared financial resources are used to staff two health department positions in community health assessment and improvement planning, which are also jointly funded by the health department. After a prolonged series of meetings and contractual negotiations, each hospital agrees to work together on a shared assessment and improvement plan for Indigo County.

Throughout the ensuing three-year period, the health department staff work closely with Marie, Jessica, and their colleagues at the county's other hospitals. They align the work and investment of these hospitals with the health department. All told, the collaborative effort saves each organization nearly $25,000. More importantly, the deeply integrative work produces a more engaged group of partner organizations, a far superior assessment, and an actionable improvement plan that begins to address pressing public health problems.

Discussion Questions

1. What barriers to greater interorganizational collaboration can you foresee in this case? How would you address these in order to ensure long-term partnership?
2. In addition to healthcare and public health entities, who else could or should be involved to enhance community engagement and shared savings? How would you go about engaging these organizations or individuals?
3. How could policymakers incentivize increased collaboration not only around community health needs assessments and improvement planning but also in terms of actual implementation activities?

References

Carlton, E. L., & Singh, S. M. (2018). Joint community health needs assessments pave the path for local health departments' involvement in non-profit hospitals' implementation planning activities. *American Journal of Public Health, 108*(5), 683–688.

Pennel, C. L., McLeroy, K. R., Burdine, J. N., Matarrita-Cascante, D. (2015). Nonprofit hospitals' approach to community health needs assessment. *American Journal of Public Health,105*(3), e103–e113.

Rosenbaum, S., & Margulies, R. (2011). Tax-exempt hospitals and the Patient Protection and Affordable Care Act: Implications for public health policy and practice. *Public Health Reports, 126*(2), 283–286.

CASE 4-3

Managing the Transition from Volume to Value

Jacqueline Woeppel, ScD, MBA, RHIA, CCS

A seasoned healthcare executive recently joins a mid-size medical practice in a small town. The chief executive officer (CEO) was hired to help the practice adapt to today's new value-based challenges. The multidisciplinary practice includes obstetrics and gynecology, internal medicine, pediatrics, and psychology specialists. The clinicians are committed to effective preventive care and the treatment and management of chronic and acute illnesses. As part of the practice, the organization has developed a holistic approach to patient-centric care but is not fully integrated.

The CEO was initially tasked with evaluating current practice performance to see if the practice is aligned with the state's new value-based initiatives. Episodes of care (EOC), or bundled payments, are part of the new initiatives. The CEO understands the nuances and complexities of EOC programs, which have been defined as related service costs associated with a patient and a particular acute medical problem or surgery procedure (Centers for Medicare & Medicaid Services, 2018). Each EOC has a defined and specific time period across a continuum of care (Division of TennCare, 2018). The CEO focuses on triple aim concepts and looks to drive the practice by controlling cost, improving patient quality, and outcomes. However, the volume of reporting is overwhelming, and there needs to be an evaluation on how many episodes will directly impact the organization.

Episodes are a complex system comprising both incentives and risk sharing as part of the model. The model involves different stakeholder agencies who will set thresholds. The state sets a standard acceptable threshold for each EOC. However, the CEO understands each of the managed care organizations (MCOs) set their own commendable thresholds, which can vary. The CEO makes a mental note that EOC commendable thresholds are associated with gain sharing. In addition, there are several important aspects that have a fundamental impact on the payment model. Integral to the model are the exclusion criteria and risk adjustment methods used to compare EOCs fairly. The state sets exclusion criteria (business and clinical) across all episodes. Conversely, varying risk adjustment methodologies are set by each of the MCOs.

Reports are released quarterly from each of the three MCOs. XYZ, one of the MCOs, has sent preview and interim performance summary reports. Each report comes with an EOC summary as a PDF and an excel spreadsheet with encounter level cost center information (e.g., professional, ancillary, etc.). The XYZ interim performance report contains data on six EOCs, including cholecystectomy, esophagogastroduodenoscopy (EGD), oppositional defiant disorder (ODD), perinatal, respiratory infection (RI), and urinary tract infection (UTI). In addition, XYZ preview reports contain information for attention deficit hyperactivity disorder (ADHD), breast biopsy, human immunodeficiency virus (HIV), otitis media, and skin and soft tissue infection (SSTI) episodes.

The CEO begins to analyze the perinatal episode interim performance summary. Analysis reveals a gap to gain sharing at $490 per episode. Risk adjustment factor (RAF) scores were average. The practice had a slightly higher RAF at 1.02 compared to provider base at 0.99 RAF. The average nonadjusted cost for the practice was $7,082 with a commendable threshold of $6,462. The distribution of the episodes was varied and revealed 40 patients are above the average with approximately 20 patients with costs above $8,144. The CEO observes that over 50 claims were associated with the emergency department (ED) cost category. The ED/observation costs were 5% higher compared to the providers average base. In addition, the CEO notes that the outpatient radiology costs were 19% higher than the provider base. Inpatient facility costs were slightly higher at $3,128 compared to the provider average of $2,792. On a positive note, pharmacy spend was less than the provider average. The CEO concludes the perinatal analysis by evaluating the quality metrics. He notes that not all quality metrics have been met. In particular, HIV quality metrics (which are linked to gain sharing) were at 83% and did not meet the 85% gain sharing standard threshold.

The CEO turns the evaluation process to respiratory infection (RI) episodes. RIs are a low-cost EOC but will have an impact on multiple clinics across the organization. The RI interim performance report from XYZ reveals the practice is neither in the red (risk) or green (gain). There is only a $7 gap to gain sharing. The RI EOC has a total of 262 valid episodes with a nonadjusted cost of $95 and a 1.01 RAF score. The cost distribution was skewed to the left. However, 14% of patients had risk adjusted cost above $141. In addition, the top five drugs prescribed by spend ranged from $316 to $1,177 with an average pharmacy spend of

$40 compared to $34 provider base average. A few other items stood out to the CEO and were worth noting—several patients went to the emergency department (ED) with an average cost of $535 compared to $240 provider base average. Finally, the average lab cost was higher than the provider average—$40 compared to $19.

The CEO is scheduled to meet with the pediatric administrator who is concerned about the future otitis media (OM) EOC and wanted to discuss strategies. The administrator thinks it would be a good idea to review preview reports prior to the performance period. Based on the practice case mix and OM volume (75), they feel OM analysis and strategies might help the clinic. The OM EOC had an average episode cost of $117 and 0.98 RAF for the past year. The commendable threshold was set at $147. If the practice maintained the current path with costs during the performance period, the total upside generated would be $2,057 only if they met the two quality metrics linked to gainsharing. However, non-OM episodes with amoxicillin filled was just shy of meeting QM threshold.

Discussion Questions

1. Based on the new payment reform initiative aimed at value over volume, do episode of care (EOC) reports contain actionable data?
2. Since EOC is a retrospective system, when is the best time to make valuable improvements? What do preview reports offer the practice?
3. Under the value-based initiative, what challenges does this practice face in managing the reports (data and information)?
4. Under the new policy initiative focused in value, does the practice have opportunities to improve the perinatal episode?

References

Centers for Medicare & Medicaid Services (CMS). (2018). State innovation models initiative: General information. https://innovation.cms.gov/initiatives/state-innovations/
Division of TennCare. (2018). Episodes of care. https://www.tn.gov/tenncare/health-care-innovation/episodes-of-care.html

CHAPTER 5

Healthcare Quality and Safety

Rachel Ellison, PhD

▶ Introduction

Patient safety is a public concern in modern healthcare delivery, and providing quality care and minimizing medical errors are top priorities for physicians and healthcare administrators. According to Johns Hopkins Researchers, medical errors are the third leading cause of death in the United States behind heart disease and cancer and range from surgical complications to incorrect medication dosages (Allen & Pierce, 2016). The alarming number of deaths range anywhere from 200,000 to 250,000 per year. To reduce medical errors, healthcare providers must identify the cause, develop solutions, and measure their progress (Grober & Bohen, 2005).

▶ Defining Healthcare Quality

Quality is an attribute of a product or service that involves meeting or exceeding patient expectations (Spath, 2013). Quality is ever-changing and can be improved. The Institute of Medicine (IOM) defines quality as "the degree to which health care services for individuals and populations increase the likelihood of desired health outcomes and are consistent with current professional knowledge" (IOM, 2001).

The IOM Committee on Quality of Health Care in America clarified healthcare quality further in its report, *Crossing the Quality Chasm: A New Health System for the 21st Century*, which was published in 2001. Six dimensions of healthcare quality are identified in the report:

- Safe: avoiding injuries to patients from the care that is intended to help them.
- Effective: providing services based on scientific knowledge to all who could benefit and refraining from providing services to those not likely to benefit

- Patient-centered: providing care that is respectful of and responsive to individual patient preferences, needs, and values and ensuring that patient values guide all clinical decisions
- Timely: reducing waits and sometimes harmful delays for both those who receive and those who give care
- Efficient: avoiding waste, including waste of equipment, supplies, ideas, and energy
- Equitable: providing care that does not vary in quality because of personal characteristics such as gender, ethnicity, geographic location, and socioeconomic status (IOM, 2001)

The IOM definition and dimensions of quality encompass what most consider to be the common attributes of healthcare quality. In 2005, the Institute for Healthcare Improvement (IHI), under the leadership of their president Donald Berwick, described the following expectations for healthcare providers:

- Don't kill me (no needless deaths)
- Help me and don't hurt me (no needless pain)
- Don't make me feel helpless
- Don't keep me waiting
- Don't waste resources (mine or anyone else's) (Spath, 2013)

▶ The Agency for Healthcare Research and Quality

The Agency for Healthcare Research and Quality (AHRQ) is a department within the U.S. Department of Health and Human Services. The department focuses on advancing excellence in health care. The AHRQ has many divisions within the department, in particular the Patient Safety and Quality Improvement Division, which "makes care safer in all settings" (AHRQ, 2018). The AHRQ invests in research and evidence to make healthcare safer and creates training material to educate healthcare systems and healthcare professionals to improve care for their patients. The AHRQ also generates measures and data to track the U.S. healthcare system, in addition to using evidence-based tools and resources to improve quality, safety, effectiveness, and efficiency of health care (AHRQ, 2018). Patient safety and quality are at the forefront of the AHRQ and the Department of Health and Human Services.

▶ Quality Payment Program

To promote quality and safety, the Centers for Medicare and Medicaid Services implemented the Quality Payment Program (QPP). This program was established through the Medicare Access and CHIP Reauthorization Act (MACRA) of 2015, which is discussed further in the chapter on Medicare. The new program is designed to reward providers for their high-level quality care or for participating in the new models of care that promote quality and efficiency (CMS, 2018). The Quality

Payment Program has two different programs that can be chosen depending on the practice size, specialty, location, or patient population.

The Advanced Alternative Payment Model (APM) is an innovative payment approach that gives added incentive payments to provide high-quality and cost-efficient care (CMS, 2018). APMs can apply to a specific clinical condition, a care episode, or a population. For participating in an Advanced APM, a provider might earn an incentive payment through Medicare Part B (CMS, 2018).

The Merit-based Incentive Payment System (MIPS) is a payment program that allows providers to earn a performance-based payment adjustment if certain measures meet standard quality outcomes (CMS, 2018). Under MIPS, providers are included if they are an eligible clinician type and meet the low volume threshold. To determine if the payment adjustment will be awarded, four categories under MIPS are scored (CMS, 2018).

- Quality: This category covers the quality of the care delivered, based on performance measures created by CMS, as well as medical professional and stakeholder groups. Six measures of performance are picked that best fit the practice.
- Promoting Interoperability: This category focuses on patient engagement and the electronic exchange of health information using certified electronic health record technology.
- Improvement Activities: This includes an inventory of activities that assess improvements to the care processes, enhance patient engagement in care, and increase access to care.
- Cost: The cost of the care provided will be calculated by CMS, based on the provider's Medicare claims.

Quality payment programs were designed to link payments to quality and cost-efficient care, drive improvement in care processes and health outcomes, maximize the use of healthcare information, and reduce the cost of care (CMS, 2018). Quality payment programs and their positive outcomes to lower healthcare spending help drive future healthcare polices.

▶ Healthcare Professionals and Patient Safety

The Institute of Medicine (IOM) released *To Err Is Human* in 1999, reporting that over 98,000 people die in hospitals every year from medical mistakes or "preventable medical errors" (Palatnik, 2016). The report discussed how medical errors were not only caused by human error but also as a result of damaged systems and processes that fail to prevent error.

When the report was released, a goal was set to reduce errors by 50% within 5 years. However, in 2013, there were approximately 400,000 deaths by preventable medical errors (Palatnik, 2016). The number of deaths is increasing rather than decreasing.

Healthcare professionals such as nurses and physicians have systems and processes that they implement to provide quality patient care. When a process and/or system is compromised, patient safety is also compromised. The American Nurses Association (ANA) focuses on standards that create a culture of safety. Sixteen years after the report from the IOM was released, the ANA launched a campaign that centered on a culture of safety that displays transparency, mutual trust, accountability, and an environment that promotes learning from errors (Palatnik, 2016). For nurses and other healthcare professionals, a culture of safety empowers individuals to speak up without fear of repercussions when there is a potential safety violation.

All humans make errors. Physician errors are not recklessness but more often are attributable to physician burnout (Sutker, 2008). Like nurses, physicians work in an environment that promotes the culture of patient safety, but the difference lies in the overall culture of medicine that emphasizes individualism and autonomy rather than teamwork. Physicians fear disclosure or admission of medical errors because of concerns about malpractice claims (Sutker, 2008).

▶ Measurement of Healthcare Quality

Total Quality Management (TQM) is a prominent theory in healthcare that was developed by W. Edwards Deming in the early 1950s as an alternative to authoritarian management philosophies (Shaw & Carter, 2015). TQM is firmly based in the statistical analysis of objective data and mobilizes individuals directly involved in a work process to examine and improve the process with the goal of achieving better results (Shaw & Carter, 2015). Avedis Donabedian recognized that TQM could be applied to healthcare services and, in 1966, conceptualized measures into three categories:

- Structure Measures: determines the adequacy of the environment in which patient care is provided
- Process Measures: judges whether patient care and support functions are properly performed
- Outcome Measures: measures the results of patient care and support functions (Spath, 2013)

An example of a structure measure would be the number of beds available in the hospital. An example of a process measure is wait times for emergency rooms. Examples of outcome measures include readmission rates and healthcare-associated infections (HAIs). Gathering data from patient surveys upon discharge is a common way that healthcare organizations evaluate patient safety and quality using these measures. The survey results produce data that can provide important information to the organization and to those who want to make a change or implement a new healthcare policy.

▶ Summary

Keeping patients safe and providing excellent, quality medical care is the top priority for healthcare providers and hospital systems. Hundreds of thousands of people die each year from preventable medical errors, but the federal government has agencies that enforce policies and laws that protect patients. In addition, incentive-based programs are available that entice physicians and healthcare systems to strive for improved quality care. The content in this chapter will guide you throughout your reading of the case studies. The key terms below will lead you through your discussion.

Federal Agencies	
Agency for Healthcare Research and Quality	Focuses on making care safer in all settings
Centers for Medicare & Medicaid Services	Implements healthcare quality improvement mechanisms through hospital discharge programs
Institute of Medicine	Published a document that increased U.S. medical awareness, which increased focus on patient safety and quality
Institute for Healthcare Improvement	Brings awareness of safety and quality to millions, accelerating learning and the systematic improvement of care

Key Terms

Agency for Healthcare Research and Quality (AHRQ)   is a U.S. government agency that functions as a part of the Department of Health & Human Services (HHS) to support research to improve the quality of health care.

Alternative Payment model (APM)   is a payment approach that gives added incentive payments to provide high-quality and cost-efficient care. APMs can apply to a specific clinical condition, a care episode, or a population.

Effective   providing services based on scientific knowledge to all who could benefit and refraining from services to those not likely to benefit

Efficient   avoiding waste, including waste of equipment, supplies, ideas, and energy

Equitable   providing care that does not vary in quality because of personal characteristics such as gender, ethnicity, geographic location, and socioeconomic status

Medical errors   are any preventable adverse effects of medical care, harmful or not.

Merit-Based Incentive Payment System (MIPS)   is one of two tracks under the Quality Payment Program that moves Medicare Part B providers to a performance-based payment system.

Patient-centered   providing care that is respectful of and responsive to individual patient preferences, needs, and values and ensuring that patient values guide all clinical decisions

Quality Care   is the degree to which healthcare services for individuals and populations increase the likelihood of desired health outcomes and are consistent with current professional knowledge.

Quality Payment Program (QPP)   improves Medicare by helping eligible clinicians focus on care quality and making patients healthier.

Safe   avoiding injuries to patients from the care that is intended to help them

Timely   reducing waits and sometimes harmful delays for both those who receive and those who give care

References

Agency for Healthcare Research & Quality (AHRQ). (2018). Agency for Healthcare Research and Quality: A profile. https://www.ahrq.gov/cpi/about/profile/index.html

Allen, M., & Pierce, O. (2016). Medical errors are no. 3 cause of US deaths, researchers say. *National Public Radio (NPR)*. https://www.npr.org/sections/health-shots/2016/05/03/476636183/death-certificates-undercount-toll-of-medical-errors

Centers for Medicare & Medicaid Services (CMS). (2018). Quality Payment Program. https://www
.cms.gov/Medicare/Quality-Payment-Program/Quality-Payment-Program.html

Grober, E. D., & Bohnen, J. M. A. (2005). Defining medical error. *Canadian Journal of Surgery*,
48(1), 39–44.

Institute of Medicine (IOM). (2001). *Crossing the quality chasm: A new health system for the 21st century.*
Washington, DC: National Academies Press.

Palatnik, A, (2016). To err IS human. *Nursing Critical Care, 11*(5), 4. doi: 10.1097/01.CCN.0000490961
.44977.8d.

Shaw, P. L., & Carter, D. (2015). *Quality and performance improvement in healthcare: Theory, practice, and management* (6th ed.). Chicago, IL: AHIMA Press.

Spath, P. (2013). *Introduction to healthcare quality management* (2nd ed.). Chicago, IL: Health
Administration Press.

Sutker W. L. (2008). The physician's role in patient safety: What's in it for me? *Proceedings (Baylor
University. Medical Center), 21*(1), 9–14. doi:10.1080/08998280.2008.11928347.

⌕ CASE 5-1

Rural Healthcare and the Merit-Based Incentive Payment System

Marsha Davenport, MD, MS, MPH, FACPM, Wendy M. Whitner, PhD, MPH, &
Cassandra R. Henson, Dr. P.A., MBA

Wintertime Group Health Care (WGHC) is in Snow County, a rural area about 75 miles from the nearest urban center. WGHC is a privately owned primary care group practice and is known for providing a high quality of care to the community. Snow County comprises primarily low-income families, children, and older adults.

Additional healthcare services provided in Snow County include a 60-bed hospital that is part of a Regional Medical Center linking several other counties, urban areas, and three additional states. The Regional Medical Center provides all levels of care, including emergency, surgical, critical, and various specialties. There are approximately 35,000 people requiring access to health care from the Regional Medical Center. In addition, most of the healthcare clinicians in Snow County work for the Regional Medical Center.

WGHC is fortunate to employ five physicians who do not work for the Regional Medical Center. One of the physicians, Dr. Bird, a geriatrician, is also the owner and the director of WGHC. The four other physicians include two internists, a family practitioner, and a pediatrician. Also, WGHC has two physician assistants (PAs), one nurse midwife, and one nurse practitioner (NP), as well as a registered nurse (RN), two licensed practical nurses (LPNs), and two certified medical assistants (MAs). The final members of the clinical team include two part-time employees: a licensed clinical social worker and a dietician. All members of the clinical team report directly to Dr. Smythe, the family practitioner, who serves as the deputy director for clinical services.

Ms. Brown is the deputy director for administrative services and has two direct reports: the executive officer and the office manager. The executive officer provides support to the director and the two deputy directors. The remaining administrative staff report to Mr. Porter, who is the office manager. Mr. Porter supervises the assistant office manager, a receptionist, a part-time billing clerk, and the two computer systems and health information technology staff.

WGHC is a busy practice, and the clinicians see patients almost continuously throughout the day, except when the office closes from 12–1 p.m. daily for lunch. In addition, WGHC recently expanded its hours to include Tuesday and Thursday evening hours as well as Saturday morning appointments. Although the staff feels that these expanded hours are needed in response to suggestions and feedback from patients, the staff is starting to feel overwhelmed and burned out. Further, Mr. Porter announced at the last staff meeting that he plans to retire at the end of the year to enjoy the holidays and New Year with his grandchildren who live over 200 miles away. He has been with WGHC since it was founded almost 20 years ago.

As the end of the year draws closer, the assistant office manager, Ms. Tree, becomes concerned. All members of the practice, including Ms. Tree, received an email from the Centers for Medicare & Medicaid Services (CMS) that explained the new reporting requirements beginning next year for MIPS. However, no one in the practice is talking about it and the topic has fallen off of the agenda at the last few staff meetings. Ms. Tree plans to ask Mr. Porter to add the topic to the staff meeting next week. She knows that WGHC is usually closed for almost a week during the end of the year so that everyone gets the opportunity to be with their family. Although this is a great benefit of working at WGHC, it means no one will be paying attention to what must be reported for MIPS if new requirements are not discussed soon. Ms. Tree knows that not reporting to CMS on MIPS or reporting poor quality data can have a severe impact on WGHC's financial status, as well as its overall reputation as an excellent healthcare facility. Everyone in the organization will be affected and not in a positive way.

When Ms. Tree approaches Mr. Porter, he is too busy to talk to her. He shouts at her, "There is no need to worry; there is plenty of time to report to MIPS. The deadline is not until next year!" Ms. Tree is stunned and appalled at Mr. Porter's behavior. Rather than try to continue the conversation, Ms. Tree walks away. After a few days, Ms. Tree decides to try to talk to Mr. Porter again. There is now only one staff meeting remaining before the practice closes for the holidays, and everyone is so busy planning the retirement event for Mr. Porter and preparing for the holidays. WGHC will see the last patient for this year next Friday, and the schedule is already filling up for the January. In addition to not talking about MIPS, Ms. Tree is wondering why no potential candidates are being interviewed to replace Mr. Porter.

Ms. Tree decides to ask Dr. Bird what the plans were for hiring a replacement for Mr. Porter and whether they could discuss MIPS at the staff meeting next week. Dr. Bird noted that he had been so busy trying to hire additional physicians, he had not focused on Mr. Porter's position. He thought that it was being addressed by Ms. Brown. When it came to MIPS, Dr. Bird assumed that they were on track because they reported last year, did well, and would probably do the same thing this year. "Why change something that works well?" he said.

Discussion Questions

1. What are the facts in this case?
2. What is the Merit-Based Incentive Payment System (MIPS)?
3. Why is MIPS so important for this group practice?
4. What are some of the ways that the staff reporting to Dr. Smythe can improve the quality of care for patients?
5. What is the role of the healthcare manager in ensuring that the group practice meets its quality metrics?

References

Agency for Healthcare Research and Quality (AHRQ). (2018). TeamStepps. https://www.ahrq.gov/teamstepps/index.html
Centers for Medicare & Medicaid Services (CMS). (2016). Open payments. https://www.cms.gov/OpenPayments/About/Law-and-Policy.html
Centers for Medicare & Medicaid Services (CMS). (2018). Quality Payment Program (QPP). https://www
    .cms.gov/Medicare/Quality-Payment-Program/Quality-Payment-Program.html

🔍 CASE 5-2

Quality of Care: Links to Outcomes and Reimbursement

Lynne Walker MSN, RNC-NIC, CNE & Alice Colwell, MSN, RNC-NIC

Mr. Anderson is an 81-year-old who was admitted to a medical–surgical unit in an inner-city hospital 5 days ago with a diagnosis of congestive heart failure (CHF). Mr. Anderson became confused on the night shift 1 day ago, which was a deviation from his baseline. He has had a Foley catheter for his entire length of stay, which was inserted when he was in the emergency department (ED) before admission. Because of his episode of confusion, the physician ordered a urinalysis and urine culture, and the results indicated Mr. Anderson had a urinary tract infection (UTI). The nurse manager of the unit, Margie, became aware of the situation today during physician rounds.

This is not the news Margie wanted to hear. Yesterday, she was informed by the chief nursing officer that the two units she manages have had increased rates of catheter-associated urinary tract infections (CAUTIs) over the last quarter. She was informed that these increased numbers were unacceptable to the institution and that rates on other inpatient units had remained the same or increased as well. Margie was charged with developing and implementing a plan to decrease the rate of CAUTIs in her units.

Margie is aware that a CAUTI is a hospital-acquired condition (HAC) that is considered preventable by the Centers for Medicare and Medicaid Services (CMS) (CMS, 2015). Healthcare-associated infections (HAIs) are conditions that the patient acquires during the hospital stay and that were not present on admission to the hospital. According to the Centers for Disease Control, in the year 2011, there were an estimated 722,000 HAIs in U.S. hospitals, and approximately 75,000 patients that had acquired HAIs died during their hospitalizations. UTIs are the most frequent HAI reported to the National Healthcare Safety Network, and 75% are related to the use of a urinary catheter. Any patient who has a urinary catheter for an extended amount of time is at risk for developing a UTI (CDC, 2017).

With the implementation of the Affordable Care Act (ACA), Medicare began to reimburse hospitals in such a way as to reward high-quality care and good patient outcomes. Two programs that were implemented by CMS and required by the ACA affect Margie's unit and include the Value-Based Purchasing Program (VBP) and the Hospital Acquired Condition Reduction Program (HACRP). The VBP program gives incentive payments to hospitals based on performance on certain outcomes of care as a measurement of quality. Hospitals can also receive a penalty if they do not meet certain standards of performance. CAUTI is one of the performance outcomes in the VBP program. Second, the HAC program scores hospitals based on their performance on 14 categories of HACs, and the program monitors the rates of central line-associated blood stream infections (CLABSI) and CAUTI. Hospitals that score poorly, indicating unacceptable rates of HACs, will have a 1% reduction in the payment they receive from Medicare (Yakusheva et al., 2015). Therefore, hospitals have made the reduction of CAUTI and CLABSI through the use of evidence-based nursing a high priority.

The prevention of CAUTI also relates to the Hospital National Patient Safety Goals. Accreditation of hospitals is carried out through the Joint Commission. The Joint Commission constructs the Hospital National Patient Safety Goals with the goal of improving patient safety. The 2017 goal "Prevent Infection" states that providers must "use proven guidelines to prevent infections of the urinary tract that are caused by catheters" (The Joint Commission, 2018).

It is understood that there is a relationship between nursing care and patient outcomes. The National Database of Nursing Quality Indicators (NDNQI) has developed 19 measures of quality and performance related to nursing care known as nurse sensitive indicators (NSI) (Heslop & Lu, 2014). These nurse sensitive indicators include things such as CAUTI, CLABSI, falls, ventilator-associated pneumonia (VAP), pressure ulcers, and others that are used to measure what nurses do and the quality of the care that is given. Many HAIs have been linked by the evidence to nursing care, and the costs to Medicare for treating these conditions has been significant (Grace, 2009). If, for example, a hospital is measuring CAUTIs, the rates of CAUTIs occurring in that hospital is an outcome of the nursing care. If care is evidence-based, it should mean that there will be low CAUTI rates and hence good quality of care. It is an expectation that nurses will give high-quality care that will decrease rates of HACs.

Margie believes that the unit nurses should be educated to recognize that the data that is collected and reported on for these specific nurse sensitive quality indicators, such as CAUTIs, need to be analyzed and used to improve nursing care. If deficits exist, they need to be addressed, and a plan for improving the performance on these quality measures must be implemented to achieve quality of care for the patient and improve patient outcomes. These improvement strategies not only have implications for patient outcomes but also on the reimbursement (payment) the hospital will receive for the individual patient's care. Margie recognizes that each individual nurse has the responsibility to contribute to the high-quality care of their patients, but she knows the problem must be addressed on a larger scale.

Although the unit has an evidence-based guideline in place for catheter use, insertion, and maintenance, Margie, with the assistance of the unit nurse educator, begins to investigate ways to improve practice by decreasing the rate of CAUTIs on the unit. She begins by looking at the latest evidence from the CDC to update their existing policy. Margie decides, based on this information that when a CAUTI occurs, all staff who cared for the patient will be called in to a meeting with the manager and educator and made aware of the CAUTI. At that time, an analysis of the patient's situation will take place and a plan to address the problem will be implemented. The plan may include education and involvement of the staff in quality improvement efforts.

Discussion Questions

1. Discuss the links between patient quality of care and reimbursement through Medicare as related to HAIs.
2. What implementation strategies can Margie use to engage the nursing staff in the integration of best practices in regard to CAUTIs on her units?
3. What financial effects are the consequence of preventable HAIs, both individually and on the healthcare system as a whole?
4. What are the advantages to government mandates for quality of care?

References

Centers for Disease Control (CDC). (2017). Catheter-associated urinary tract infections. https://www.cdc .gov/hai/ca_uti/uti.html

Centers for Medicare and Medicaid Services (CMS). (2015). Hospital-acquired conditions. https://www .cms.gov/Medicare/Medicare-Fee-for-Service-Payment/HospitalAcqCond/Hospital-Acquired _Conditions.html

Grace, J. A. (2009). Perspectives on pay for performance in nursing: Key considerations in shaping payment systems to drive better patient care outcomes. Robert Wood Johnson Foundation (RWJF). https://www.rwjf.org/en/library/research/2009/11/cnf-pay-for-performance-in-nursing.html

Heslop, L., & Lu, S. (2014). Nursing-sensitive indicators: A concept analysis. *Journal of Advanced Nursing, 70*(11), 2469–2482.

Joint Commission. (2017). Facts About the National Patient Safety Goals. https://www.jointcommission .org/facts_about_the_national_patient_safety_goals/

Yakusheva, O., Lindrooth, R. C., Weiner, J., Spetz, J., & Pauley, M. V. (2015). How nursing affects Medicare's outcome-based hospital payments. *Interdisciplinary Nursing Quality Research Initiative, (policy brief),* pp. 1–13.

$\mathcal{Q}$ CASE 5-3

There and Not Back Again: A Case Study of Hospital Readmissions

Raymond J. Higbea, PhD, Steven Marzolf, MSA, & Donald Haney, MBA

Continuum Health (CH) is a hospital located in rural Michigan that, as is customary with hospitals around the country, seeks to ensure it is meeting patient safety and quality indicators established by regulatory bodies and payers. In October 2012, CMS began reducing payments for readmission of patients with a limited number of diagnoses

(CMS, 2017a). As the program has matured, CMS has progressively refined the process and added diagnoses. It was in this climate that CH developed a committee to monitor hospital readmissions with the goal of reducing readmissions as much as possible while simultaneously ensuring patients were receiving the highest quality care possible. In October 2014, while reviewing readmissions data, the CH readmissions team noticed that 28% of the readmissions were coming from Crabtree Manor (the local county-owned skilled nursing facility [SNF]). The CH readmissions team recommended that the CH executive leading the team contact his executive peer at Crabtree Manor to begin a discussion about how they could address this concern (Higbea, Marzolf, & Haney, 2017).

When the two leaders met, the Crabtree Manor executive acknowledged a shared concern about the large number of hospital readmissions; she detailed how very disruptive these admissions were to Crabtree Manor residents and that CMS was initiating a SNF 30-day readmission program in late 2017 (CMS, 2017b). As the two leaders discussed these readmissions, they quickly realized this was a problem that they could not solve on their own and agreed to establish a team with representatives from both organizations, including social workers, nurses, providers, and administrators. As the team explored the situation the following facts emerged:

1. The medical director and physician services for Crabtree Manor were provided by an out-of-town contracted medical group that provided routine patient visits with rotating telephone on-call coverage during times they were not physically present. The pattern for the telephone consults was to have the patient transferred to the CH emergency department for workup and likely admission.
2. CH had a hospitalist group that provided inpatient care for patients admitted to the hospital that had additional capacity to care for more patients.
3. The mean readmission charge for Crabtree Manor patients was $19,328.
4. Data analysis of CH and Crabtree Manor patient/resident records revealed readmissions were:
   a. frequently unnecessary and a result of the out-of-town medical group's standard method of evaluation and management of resident care when not on-site,
   b. evenly divided between acute onset illnesses and exacerbation of chronic conditions, and
   c. the causal factor of unnecessary emergency visits and hospital readmissions.
5. Transfers of residents from Crabtree Manor to CH exposed physically and mentally frail residents to unnecessary disruptions and HAI.

The plan for this team was to use the PDCA (Plan-Do-Check-Act) process improvement method to develop and implement a plan using PEPPER data, provided by CMS, to track and validate changes (PEPPER, 2018).

Through use of the PDCA method and the following 6 months of work, the CH/Crabtree Manor team arrived upon a plan that included:

1. replacing the out-of-town medical group with the CH Hospitalist group as medical director and physician services provider;
2. embedding a mid-level practitioner (e.g., PA or NP) at Crabtree Manor Monday through Friday and on-call during off shifts;
3. regular team meetings with representation from both organizations, including shared data tracking;
4. refinement of the plan to address two different regulatory environments;
5. looking for opportunities for increased care coordination and quality of care delivery; and
6. focusing on improving the financial performance of both organizations while reducing patient/resident costs.

Discussion Questions

1. How would you manage this plan across two organizations that are operating in different funding and regulatory environments, and what metrics would you use?
2. How would you measure and demonstrate your results?
3. What quality of care improvements would you anticipate?
4. What were the financial impacts of this plan on both organizations?
5. Could CMS and other payers use this as a model for hospital/SNF collaboration, regardless of community size, throughout the country? What kind of policy design would encourage this type of collaboration?

References

Centers for Medicare and Medicaid Services (CMS). (2017a). Hospital readmission reduction program. https://www.cms.gov/Medicare/Medicare-Fee-for-Service-Payment/AcuteInpatientPPS/Readmissions-Reduction-Program.html

Centers for Medicare and Medicaid Services (CMS). (2017b). Skilled nursing facility value based purchasing program. https://www.cms.gov/Medicare/Quality-Initiatives-Patient-Assessment-Instruments/Value-Based-Programs/Other-VBPs/SNF-VBP.html

Higbea, R.J., Marzolf, S., & Haney, D. (2017). Reducing SNF readmissions through hospital-SNF collaboration. *Healthcare Financial Management, 71*(12), 44–49.

Program for Evaluating Payment Patterns Electronic Report (PEPPER). (2018). Welcome to PEPPER resources. https://www.pepperresources.org/

CHAPTER 6

Health Insurance and Reimbursement Methods

Rachel Ellison, PhD & Lesley Clack, ScD

▶ Introduction

This chapter will discuss the vast complexity of the health insurance and reimbursement system in the United States. Healthcare spending reached $3.3 trillion in 2016 (CMS, 2018). This is the result of a very large and complex system consisting of fragmented pieces (Casto & Forrestal, 2015), including the variety of health services provided as well as those that pay for the services.

▶ Health Insurance

Health insurance in the United States was first documented in 1847 as a "sickness" clause in early health insurance policies (Gabel, 1999). Stand-alone health insurance was not made available until 1929, when Blue Cross offered their first coverage to schoolteachers in Texas. During World War II, the branches of government addressed a labor shortage with policy that, in turn, became the basic structure of health insurance in the United States (Gabel, 1999) and eventually the connection between employment and health insurance that we know today. The first case in this chapter explains the modernization and evolution of health insurance.

In addition to the Patient Protection and Affordable Care Act (PPACA), there are other important laws related to health insurance. The Health Maintenance Organization Act was passed in 1973 to address the rising costs of Medicare by allowing beneficiaries to enroll in HMOs. At the time people were not signing up for HMOs, which caused Medicare spending to increase. Also, the HMO Act of 1973 made federal grants and loans available for planning, starting, and/or expanding HMOs to further decrease Medicare spending (Kongstvedt, 2016). See **TABLE 6-1** to further understand an HMO.

TABLE 6-1 Types of Health Insurance Plans	
Preferred Provider Organizations (PPOs)	PPOs operate off of a list of preferred healthcare providers that patients can choose from for their coverage. Patients save the most money on their healthcare plans by selecting the preferred providers affiliated with a PPO. Providers on the preferred list are considered "in-network," whereas others are "out-of-network" providers. Sometimes an insurance carrier will not cover a person who receives treatment from an out-of-network provider, though PPOs tend to have more coverage options for out-of-network providers than HMOs.
Health Maintenance Organizations (HMOs)	HMOs are groups of physicians, medical facilities, and healthcare services that work to keep patients under the care of providers within their network. Healthcare providers in HMOs coordinate a patient's healthcare decisions and suggest suitable hospitals for care. Because of the close-knit healthcare community in HMOs, members enrolled with these organizations tend to have limited provider options. The upside to HMO membership is that patients tend to pay less in deductibles and receive higher-quality medical care at facilities within the HMO network.
Point-of-Service (POS) Plans	POS plans form a hybrid between PPOs and HMOs. As with HMOs, POS plans allow you to select physicians and services from within a dedicated network of providers. Unlike HMOs, you have the option of coverage for care received from out-of-network providers. However, patients in POS plans must receive a referral from a physician before being covered by out-of-network providers, and this likely falls under their deductible.
High-Deductible Health Plans (HDHPs)	HDHPs are plans with lower insurance premiums and higher deductibles than traditional health insurance plans. Although the monthly premium is lower, individuals typically pay more healthcare costs themselves before the insurance company pays its share of the expenses. A HDHP is typically combined with a health savings account (HSA) to offset some of the medical expenses with untaxed dollars.
Indemnity Plans	Patients with an indemnity policy can receive emergency room care at a hospital of their choice, but they might have to pay a sizable deductible (ranging from a few hundred to several thousand dollars) before insurance carriers will pay for their care. Many indemnity policies allow patients to choose how much they pay for their deductible, and that amount matches the level of coverage they receive from insurance carriers.

Based on Green & Rowell, 2015; Feldstein, 2015

The Employee Retirement Income Security Act of 1974 (ERISA) is a federal law that sets minimum standards for health insurance plans in order to protect individuals (DOL, 2018). For example, ERISA requires that plans provide enrollees with information about plan features and funding, establish a grievance and appeals process for enrollees, and give enrollees the right to sue for benefits (DOL, 2018). One important amendment to ERISA was the Consolidated Omnibus Reconciliation Act (COBRA), passed by Congress and signed by President Reagan in 1985. COBRA mandates that employers allow employees to continue their healthcare coverage after terminating employment (Small Business Majority, 2018). According to federal law, any employer with 20 or more employees is subject to COBRA requirements. Employees have 60 days from when they are notified of their eligibility of COBRA to sign up for coverage, and the length of time employees are eligible to continue coverage depends on eligibility requirements, such as the type of employer (Small Business Majority, 2018).

In the United States, most employers offer health insurance to their employees through their employment benefits package. Employers pay a portion of the health insurance premium, and the employee pays the remainder. Individual coverage insures the employee, and dependent (family) coverage safeguards employees along with spouses, children, or both (Casto & Forrestal, 2013). In most cases, employees pay extra for dependent coverage.

There are also government-based health insurance plans and commercial health insurance plans. Government plans include Medicare, Medicaid, insurance through state health exchanges created by the PPACA, and the Children's Health Insurance Program (CHIP). Commercial health insurance plans are offered by companies such as Blue Cross Blue Shield, Aetna, United Healthcare, and many more.

There are a number of ways in which health insurance can be provided, but they all require coordination between the health provider, insurance carrier, and the person receiving care (Green & Rowell, 2015). In the United States there is no universal health coverage. Currently, 18 countries have universal health care (World Health Organization, 2019). Universal health care coverage means that all people have access to health services without the risk of financial hardship when paying for them (World Health Organization, 2019).

Managed care is one of the most common forms of health insurance coverage. It is administered by organizations that contract with healthcare providers to create an active network of participating providers (Green & Rowell, 2015). There are also indemnity plans that allow people the freedom to choose whatever healthcare provider they want and receive some form of coverage for these services. Patients covered by an indemnity policy can go to any healthcare provider and receive care, even when traveling across state lines (Green & Rowell, 2015). Some of the most common types of health insurance plans are detailed in Table 6-1.

▶ Reimbursement Methods

Reimbursement means being paid for expenses that were already incurred (Casto & Forrestal, 2015). In most situations in which healthcare services are rendered, payment is not expected until after the service is provided and other expenses, such as the cost of supplies, can be requested for reimbursement. There are different characteristics that describe methods of reimbursement, such as:

- the unit of payment,
- the time orientation, and
- the degree of financial risk for the parties

The unit of payment can range from an individual payment for a service like a lab test or a block payment for an entire population for a period of time. The time orientation is retrospective versus prospective. With a retrospective payment method, the payer learns of the costs of the health services after the patient has received the services, and the provider receives payment after services have been provided. With a prospective payment method, payments are set prior to delivery of services (Casto & Forrestal, 2015). Retrospective payment methods place payers, providers, and patients at greater risk because the costs of services are not learned until after the services have already been provided.

There are two distinct reimbursement methods that will be discussed: fee-for-service and episode-of-care. Fee-for-service is when providers receive payment for each service rendered. A specific fee is set for each service. For example, a specific service such as a laboratory test has a set fee associated with that service. The provider charges the fee and the health insurance company pays the fee for each covered service (Casto & Forrestal, 2015). There are advantages and disadvantages of having health insurance plans that reimburse on a fee-for-service basis. They have great flexibility on what health providers those insured can choose, but they tend to have higher deductibles and premiums. In addition, fee-for service models promote volume over value. Because providers are paid a separate amount for each service they provide, providers are incentivized to focus on providing more services.

Episode-of-care reimbursement is when providers receive one lump sum for all the services they provide related to a condition (Casto & Forrestal, 2015). That is, the unit of payment is the episode rather than each individual health service. An episode of care includes any health service that a patient receives during a period of relatively continuous care from a provider (Casto & Forrestal, 2015). Examples of episode-of-care reimbursement are home care services and nonroutine medical supplies provided during a 60-day period. Because this model promotes quality rather than volume, some believe the episode-of-care method helps alleviate problems in reimbursement schemes. Because providers are only reimbursed one lump sum for each episode, providers are not focused on volume of services and thus can focus more on quality services.

▶ Value-Based Purchasing and Pay-for-Performance

The widespread movement in the healthcare system toward improving the quality, efficiency, and value of healthcare has resulted in the value-based purchasing (VBP) and pay-for performance (P4P) systems (Casto & Forrestal, 2015). VBP and P4P systems link quality, performance, and payment. VBP can be defined as a system in which purchasers hold providers of healthcare accountable for both the quality and costs of healthcare (Meyer et al., 1997). In VBP, purchasers are defined as "public and private sector entities that subsidize, arrange, and contract for the cost of healthcare services received by a group" (AHRQ, 2002). Purchasers include employers, federal and state governments, health plans, and other payers (Casto & Forrestal, 2015). In VBP, *value* is defined as "focusing on both quality and cost at the same time in purchasing and delivering health care" (Thomas & Caldis, 2007, p. 1). VBP does the following:

- integrates information on healthcare quality with cost data,
- focuses on managing the use of the healthcare system to reduce inappropriate care, and
- identifies and rewards the best-performing providers (Meyer et al., 1997)

P4P can be defined as any type of payment arrangement for reimbursing providers that includes incentives aligned with performance (Cromwell et al., 2011). P4P systems align payment incentives with specific performance targets. Targets are specific and measurable objectives that are used to judge quality performance (Casto & Forrestal, 2015).

VBP and P4P may at times be used interchangeably, but there are common distinctions:

- Cost
  - VBP results in improved quality for the same cost to the purchaser
  - P4P results in additional payments for higher or increasing quality
- Setting
  - VBP is currently used in the public sector, such as Medicare
  - P4P is common among private health plans
- Duration
  - VBP has been in use since 2005
  - P4P has been in use since 2004 (Casto & Forrestal, 2015)

Models

There are many different VBP and P4P models. The use of these systems are promoted and encouraged by the PPACA. The two primary considerations in the design of VBP and P4P models are awards or penalties and the mechanism of payment (Casto & Forrestal, 2015). The two most common VBP and P4P models are Accountable Care Organizations (ACOs) and Patient-Centered Medical Homes (PCMHs). An ACO is a set of providers who are jointly held accountable for achieving measured improvements in quality and reductions in the rate of spending growth (McClellan et al., 2010). The purpose of an ACO is to improve the quality of care and reduce costs by increasing coordination of healthcare services and reducing fragmentation (Fisher et al., 2007). ACOs are currently being used by Medicare, as well as some commercial payers and state Medicaid programs (Casto & Forrestal, 2015). The three essential characteristics of ACOs are: 1) the ability to manage patients across the continuum of care, including ambulatory, acute, and postacute health services; 2) the capability to prospectively plan budgets and resource needs; and 3) sufficient size to support comprehensive, valid, and reliable measurement of performance (Devers & Berenson, 2009).

PCMHs seek to meet the healthcare needs of patients and to improve patient and staff experiences, safety, outcomes, and system efficiency (Jackson et al.,

TABLE 6-2 Core Functions of Primary Care
Primary Care Functions
Continuous and long-term
Comprehensive, including prevention and wellness, acute care, and chronic care
Coordinated across the continuum of care, including specialty care, hospitals, home health care, and community services and supports
Patient-centered with an orientation toward the whole person, informed engagement of the patient and family, and recognition of each patient's unique needs

Modified from Casto, B. A., & Forrestal, E. (2015). *Principles of Healthcare Reimbursement*, 5th edition. Chicago, IL: AHIMA Press.

2013). PCMH initiatives are organized by payers, health plans, states, providers, or multi-stakeholder groups (Casto & Forrestal, 2015). The PCMH model is currently being used by Medicaid and Medicare. The PCMH model integrates the core functions of primary care (**TABLE 6-2**) with the following:

- multidisciplinary team,
- electronic information systems and online patient portals,
- chronic disease registries,
- population-based management of chronic disease, and
- continuous quality improvement (Casto & Forrestal, 2015)

▶ Summary

Reimbursing healthcare providers is a complex and involved process. In the United States, there is no universal healthcare system, which means that everyone does not have equal access to quality healthcare services. Because healthcare is not a constitutional right, people must buy health insurance on their own, get it through their employer, or be eligible for it through government programs. The vast number of health insurance plans, providers, and people who have insurance make the process of reimbursing providers a daunting process. Accessibility will be the focus of future healthcare policies. This chapter touched on the basics of health insurance and reimbursement payment methods, but the models are more in-depth. Below are important terms to assist in analyzing this chapter's case studies.

Key Terms

Accountable Care Organization (ACO) is a set of providers who are jointly held accountable for achieving measured improvements in quality and reductions in the rate of spending growth.

Episode-of-care (EOC) is a set of services provided to treat a clinical condition or procedure.

Fee-for-service (FFS) is a payment model where services are unbundled and paid for separately.

Health Insurance reimburses the insured for expenses incurred from illness or injury or pays the care provider directly.

Patient-Centered Medical Home (PCMH) seeks to meet the healthcare needs of patients and to improve patient and staff experiences, safety, outcomes, and system efficiency.

Pay-for-performance (P4P) includes any type of payment arrangement for reimbursing providers that includes incentives aligned with performance.

Reimbursement is the action of repaying a person who has spent or lost money.

Retrospective payment is the amount paid that is determined by (or based on) what the provider charged or said it cost to provide the service after tests or services had been rendered to beneficiaries.

Value-based purchasing (VBP) is a system in which purchasers hold providers of healthcare accountable for both the quality and costs of healthcare.

References

Agency for Healthcare Research and Quality (AHRQ). (2002). Evaluating the impact of value-based purchasing: A guide for purchasers. *AHRQ Publication No. 02-0029*. Rockville, MD: AHRQ.

Casto, B. A., & Forrestal, E. (2015). *Principles of healthcare reimbursement* (5th ed.). Chicago, IL: AHIMA Press.

CMS.gov. (2018). National health expenditures highlights 2016. https://www.cms.gov/Research-Statistics-Data-and-Systems/Statistics-Trends-and-Reports/NationalHealthExpendData/downloads/highlights.pdf

Cromwell, J., Trisolini, M. G., Pope, G. C., Mitchell, J. B., & Greenwald, L. M. (2011). *Pay for performance in health care: Methods and approaches*. Raleigh, NC: RTI Press.

Devers, K., & Berenson, R. (2009). Timely analysis of immediate health policy issues: Can Accountable Care Organizations improve the value of health care by solving the cost and quality quandaries? Robert Wood Johnson Foundation. http://www.urban.org/sites/default/files/publication/30736/411979-Can-Accountable-Care-Organizations-Improve-the-Value-of-Health-Care-by-Solving-the-Cost-and-Quality-Quandaries-Summary.PDF

Feldstein, P. J. (2015). *Health policy issues: An economic perspective* (6th ed.). Chicago, IL: Health Administration Press.

Fisher, E. S., Staiger, D. O., Bynum, J. P. W., & Gottlieb, D. J. (2007). Creating Accountable Care Organizations: The extended hospital medical staff. *Health Affairs Web Exclusive, 26*(1), w44–w57.

Gabel, J. R. (1999). Job-based health insurance, 1977–1998: The accidental system under scrutiny. *Health Affairs, 18*(6), 62–74.

Green, M. A., & Rowell, J. C. (2015). *Understanding health insurance* (12th ed.). Stamford, CT: Cengage Learning.

Jackson, G. L., Powers, B. J., Chatterjee, R., Bettger, J. P., Kemper, A. R., Hasselblad, V., Dolor, R. J., Irvine, R. J., Heidenfelder, B. L., Kendrick, A. S., Gray, R., & Williams, J. W. (2013). The patient-centered medical home: A systematic review. *Annals of Internal Medicine, 158*(3), 169–178.

Kongstvedt, P. R. (2016). *Health insurance and managed care: What they are and how they work* (4th ed.). Burlington, MA: Jones & Bartlett Learning.

McClellan, M., McKethan, A. N., Lewis, J. L., Roski, J., and Fisher, E. S. (2010). A national strategy to put Accountable Care into practice. *Health Affairs, 29*(5), 982–990.

Meyer, J., Rybowski, L., Eichler, R., & Fraser, I. (1997). Theory and reality of value-based purchasing: Lessons from the pioneers. *AHCPR Publication No. 98-0004*. Rockville, MD: AHRQ.

Small Business Majority. (2018). Laws related to health insurance. http://healthcoverageguide.org/reference-guide/laws-and-rights/laws-related-to-health-insurance/

Thomas, F. G., & Caldis, T. (2007). Emerging issues of pay-for-performance in health care. *Health Care Financing Review, 29*(1), 1–4.

U.S. Department of Labor (DOL). (2018). Health plans & benefits: ERISA. https://www.dol.gov/general/topic/health-plans/erisa

World Health Organization. (2019). Questions and answers on universal health coverage. https://www.who.int/healthsystems/topics/financing/uhc_qa/en/

🔎 *CASE 6-1*

The Evolution of Modern Health Insurance in the United States

Raymond J. Higbea, PhD & Gregory A. Cline, PhD

Prior to the mid-1800s, the concept of health insurance did not exist in the modern world. The advent of industrial revolution, spurring a population movement from the farm to the city, resulted in an increased need for income security during periods of illness because of changes in family structure and occupations. During the late-1800s, prepaid plans were provided by lumber, railroads, and mining companies for employee coverage. Sickness funds emerged; these did not pay for health services but rather provided a disability payment during illness and convalescence, with individuals personally responsible for payments to physicians and hospitals. Physicians supported sickness funds because the patient was still responsible for payment, and thus sickness fund payments did not influence the physician–patient relationship.

Throughout the first 30 years of the 20th century, Progressives attempted through multiple national commissions, hearings, and legislation to enact a national health insurance plan. All of these attempts failed because of how well sickness funds were working and physician resistance of any intervention, especially from the federal government, into the physician–patient relationship. However, the risk and market relationship between the physician and patient began to shift during this period because of technological advancements such as x-rays, antibiotics, and anesthesia, resulting in increased physician technical (asymmetrical) knowledge and increased cost of care.

Patients found it increasingly difficult to pay their hospital and physician bills. For example, in 1929, Baylor University Hospital was facing bankruptcy because of unpaid hospital bills. In response to this crisis, Baylor hired an executive from the sickness fund industry who established a prepaid plan that restored the hospital to financial viability, became very popular, and ultimately was chartered by the State of Texas: the first Blue Cross plan. Despite physician resistance to insurance, the first Blue Shield plan was chartered ten years later (1939) in California.

On the public policy side, the federal government continued with hearings and legislative attempts to enact a national health insurance plan. Physicians continued to oppose any federal government interventions in healthcare, claiming that it constituted socialism and citing the sacredness of the physician–patient relationship. This physician opposition was so strong that President Roosevelt pulled the national health legislation that was originally part of the Social Security Act for fear that physician opposition would cause the entire act to fail.

During the next 30 years (1935–1965), a number of significant events occurred. First, hospitals became the home of advancements in medical technology, transforming themselves from a less-than-desirable place to die to a place that housed all of the latest life-saving technologies. This transformation came at a price, with the cost of care steadily increasing so high that individuals struggled to afford the out-of-pocket cost, requiring a third party for payment. Second, these technological advancements continued to widen the knowledge gap between physician and patients and stimulated an increase in specialists, both of which added to the cost of care.

From the policy side, two major sets of events occurred. First, the War Labor Board (1943), Supreme Court (1949), and Congress (1951) allowed unions to include health benefits in collective bargaining and provided a tax deduction to employers when providing a health insurance benefit. This established employer-sponsored health insurance as a benefit that, at its peak, covered approximately 70% of the population and provided a means for health insurance coverage to move from the employee only to the employee and family. Second, three events, including passage of the Kerr–Mills bill (1960), Medicare (1965), and Medicaid (1965), set in motion the federal government's involvement as a payer (insurer) for healthcare services. This series of policy events established the federal government as primary payer for the poor and elderly, which has resulted in the federal government becoming the primary payer for healthcare services in the United States. From a physician–patient relationship view, these events led to increased demand for services by both physicians and patients, shifted all financial risk to a third-party payer, and obscured the ability of physicians or patients to be cost-conscious.

Once these policies were established, cost, access, and quality emerged as a third set of policy focus. Cost was initially an access barrier addressed by the passage of Medicare and Medicaid. Once access increased, increasing costs (medical inflation) became the focus of both employers and government; it was partially addressed by bundling payments (prospective payment system—1983), encouraging a shift to capitated payments (HMO Acts of 1973), and a series of initiatives to increase patient cost awareness through copays and deductibles. Around 1990, employers and the federal government began calling out and rewarding positive quality outcomes. Throughout the decades following the passage of Medicare and Medicaid, multiple private and public policy initiatives have attempted to address increasing costs, limited access, and poor-quality outcomes. All of these concerns culminated in the passage of the PPACA in 2010.

TABLE 6-3 provides a summary of how the PPACA addressed several major cost, access, and quality concerns. Two of the major uninsured groups were young adults and low-income single men; this was addressed by allowing children to remain on their parent's insurance up to 26 years of age and the expansion of Medicaid. Health insurance exchanges

TABLE 6-3 PPACA Policy Provisions

Provision	Cost	Access	Quality
Children remain on parent's insurance up to 26 years of age	X	X	
Health insurance exchange	X	X	
Medicaid expansion	X	X	
CMS Innovation Center	X		X
Bundled payments	X		X
Care coordination	X	X	X
Accountable Care Organizations	X		X
Patient-centered medical homes	X		X
Recession	X	X	
Preexisting illness	X	X	
Community rating	X	X	

attempted to increase access by providing a mechanism for purchasing individual health insurance policies. Insurance market reforms included not allowing recession (dropping insurance coverage because of high cost), exclusion from insurance coverage because of a preexisting illness (high insurance cost), and community rating (which disallowed experience rating and limited actuarial variables). The CMS Innovation Center generates changes based on state experiments through a Medicaid waiver process that seeks to reduce cost by linking payment to quality.

Michigan's history with health insurance is unique. It was one of the few states where state law had for many years required guaranteed issue, guaranteed renewal, community rating, and no restrictions for preexisting conditions before the PPACA. Informally, Michigan-based plans kept children covered until age 26. Consequently, the health plans and insurers in Michigan did not need to learn how to price these components. Perhaps just as important, Michigan had in the mid-1990s moved almost all of its Medicaid recipients (nearly 800,000 at that time) into managed care. Thus, Michigan's health plans have had almost 30 years of experience meeting the state's standards for providing coverage to this often-challenging population. So, in the case of Michigan, the transition to the PPACA was smooth. Although several indemnity insurers entered the Michigan market through the federal exchange, these insurers eventually left. However, these insurers left because the existing in-state health plans, experienced in marketing plans under the "new" ACA rules, were consistently better than the out-of-state competitors.

Finally, after several years of private employers complaining about the rising cost of health insurance, several took formal action in 1998. They formed the Leapfrog group, which has been successful in influencing hospital safety and quality outcomes with their ratings and has set the standard for how employers can influence providers. Throughout the ensuing decades, several other private employer groups have formed, with the two most recent entrants being the Health Transformation Alliance, which provides members with buying options, and a yet-to-be-named organization in the formulation stage sponsored by Amazon, Berkshire-Hathaway, and JP Morgan Chase that is focused on addressing cost and quality of care for their employees.

Discussion Questions

1. Based on the above history, would you expect the federal government's involvement in health delivery to increase, remain static, or decrease over the next 20 years? Support your conclusion.
2. Discuss the relationship among cost, access, and quality in the development of health policy.
3. Discuss how the private sector influences the development of health policy.
4. Prior to the 1990s, changes in insurance and reimbursement models were exogenously driven. What happened to change this dynamic?

🔎 CASE 6-2

The Issue with Insurance Networks

Lesley Clack, ScD

The defining feature of health insurance plans lies in their networks. In-network providers are those with whom the health insurance plan has established a contract to reimburse services at a particular rate. Out-of-network providers are those who have not established contractual reimbursement rates with the health insurance plan. This setup encourages health plan enrollees to seek care with providers who are in-network. Blue Cross Blue Shield (BCBS) provides the following example of the benefit of using in-network providers:

A physician may charge a patient $150 for a service, but BCBS may only allow $90 for that service; in-network providers agree to that price, saving the patient $60 (BCBS, 2018). Aetna, another major health insurance provider, estimates that by using in-network providers versus out-of-network providers, a patient could save as much as $78 on an office visit, $920 on an outpatient surgery, and $18,000 on a five-day hospital stay (Aetna, 2012).

Allstate Health is the primary health insurance provider for all state employees in Florida. All hospitals in Florida have historically been in-network with Allstate Health. The contract between Allstate Health and Ocean Hospital, Florida's largest hospital system, is coming up for renewal. Allstate Health and Ocean Hospital have reached a stalemate on negotiations. Ocean Hospital is asking for Allstate Health to reimburse all hospitals in their network at the same rate. Allstate Health continues to assert that reimbursement rates should be set based upon geographic area, meaning that metro area hospitals are reimbursed at a higher rate than smaller regional hospitals. When the contract expires, Allstate Health and Ocean Hospital still have not reached an agreement. All state employees in Florida are informed that they will now have to pay out-of-network charges to see Ocean Hospital physicians or to receive services at Ocean Hospitals.

Alice is a 60-year-old female who has Allstate Health insurance. She has always received care from Ocean Hospital physicians and has used Ocean Hospitals for her care. Two weeks after learning that Ocean Hospital physicians are now out-of-network with her health insurance, Alice finds a lump in her breast while doing a self-exam. She calls her primary physician's office, an Ocean Hospital physician, who schedules a mammogram appointment for her. The physician's office attempts to schedule her with another physician and facility that are in-network with her health insurance but finds that there are long waits. On the advice of her physician's office, Alice goes ahead with the mammogram at Ocean Hospital and finds out that she also needs a biopsy immediately. She has the biopsy done at Ocean Hospital as well and discovers that she has breast cancer. Alice is now faced with surgery, chemotherapy, and radiation therapy. She must determine whether to use her current physicians and facilities at Ocean Hospital, which are out-of-network with her insurance plan, or to start over with new providers and facilities that are in-network.

Discussion Questions

1. What would you do if you were Alice? Explain your rationale.
2. Should policymakers intervene in this situation? Why or why not?
3. Are there policies that could be put in place to prevent this?
4. Should the health insurance industry be more regulated? Why or why not?

References

Aetna. (2012). Save money with Aetna's provider network. http://www.aetna.com/individuals-families
-health-insurance/document-library/2012-aetna-provider-network.pdf
Blue Cross Blue Shield (BCBS). (2018). What's the difference between in network and out of network?
https://www.bcbsm.com/index/health-insurance-help/faqs/topics/how-health-insurance-works
/difference-between-in-network-out-of-network-benefits.html

🔍 CASE 6-3

It Takes a Century: How Payment Evolved

Raymond J. Higbea, PhD & Gregory A. Cline, PhD

This case study examines modern health insurance from a free market lens. Two requirements are necessary for a free market to exist are (1) shared knowledge and (2) understanding of costs. Healthcare services were closest to a free market in the pre-1900 era and has since eroded from increased physician knowledge asymmetry and diminished cost awareness. Although it may be impossible to overcome the knowledge asymmetry, governmental and private insurers have, over the past half century, increasingly sought to restore cost awareness to physicians and patients. This case study will explore how modern health insurance has caused the loss of cost awareness and the efforts put forth by providers to restore it.

Prior to 1900, physicians had little to offer patients other than watchful waiting. Although physicians had greater knowledge of anatomy and physiology than their patients, when it came to treatment, their options were limited and, at times, their knowledge was not much greater than their patients. As the 20th century progressed, medical knowledge and technology increased leading to a change in the difference between physician and patient knowledge so that by the 21st century the knowledge asymmetry was significant.

Pre-1930, the cost for physician services was often what the physician deemed the family able to afford. Hospitals, however, were not as generous and would often require payment prior to the performance of services. Regardless, patients, physicians, or hospitals all had full awareness of costs, and patients had full out-of-pocket cost responsibility. During the late 1800s and early 1900s, sickness funds were effective in blunting the financial impact of illness by providing disability payments to ensure the stability of income. Sickness funds were not intended to provide payment for physician or hospital services. During this period, there was no medical insurance in the United States, although the railroad, mining, and logging industries provided prepaid plans for their employees.

As the 20th century progressed, hospital (1929) and physician (1939) fee-for-service insurance emerged replacing sickness funds and eroding hospital, physician, and patient knowledge of the cost of care. Three federal government events ushered in the proliferation of hospital and physician insurance coverage. First, the War Labor Board (1943) granted employers an exemption to wage and price freezes allowing them to provide noncash wages in the form of a health insurance benefit. Next, the Supreme Court (1949) upheld a National Labor Board ruling allowing unions to include benefits in labor negotiations. Finally, Congress (1951) allowed employers a tax deduction for the provision of a health insurance benefit. These three actions allowed a rapid increase in the growth of health insurance that included the options for family coverage, which peaked at around 70% of the population in the 1970s. The federal government became involved in the payment for health services with the passage and implementation of Medicare (1965) and Medicaid (1965).

Third-party payment for hospital and physician services has been accompanied by an increased demand for services; this can be partially attributed to increased technological advancements and partially to a lack of cost awareness by physicians and patients. With increased physician knowledge asymmetry and absent physician and patient cost awareness, all elements resembling a free market healthcare system were eradicated. In the latter half of the 20th century and into the 21st century, there have been multiple attempts by insurers and policymakers to decrease the cost of care growth by increasing hospital, physician, and patient accountability for the demand for and growth of healthcare services.

Since the inception of hospital and physician insurance, fee-for-service has been the primary means of payment. The fee-for-service concept is embedded in most free market transactions through provision of payment for services rendered. Payment models associated with fee-for-service range from cost-based, itemized billing to bundled payment models and outcome incentivized payments. The free market concept rewards increased productivity with increased income. That is, the more visits, patient-days, or diagnostic procedures a physician or hospital can bill for, the greater the income. Alternatively, the prepaid plans that traditionally have been associated with managed care plans pay a set amount per patient per month (per member per month) and incentivize providing fewer patient services.

TABLE 6-4 Evolution of Payment Services

Years	Technical Advancement	Knowledge Asymmetry	Physician Cost Awareness	Patient Cost Awareness	Patient Out-of-Pocket Cost	Sickness Plans	Fee for Service Insurance	Prepaid Plans Insurance
Pre-1850	Limited	Limited	Full	Full	Full	No	No	No
1850–1899	Limited	Limited	Full	Full	Full	Yes	No	Yes
1900–1919	Yes	Increased	Full	Full	Full	Yes	No	Yes
1920–1939	Yes	Increased	Full	Full	Full	Yes	Yes	Yes
1940–1959	Yes	Increased	Partial	Partial	Partial	No	Yes	Yes
1960–1979	Yes	Increased	None	None	None	No	Yes	Yes
1980–1999	Yes	Increased	Partial	Partial	Partial	No	Yes	Yes
2000–present	Yes	Increased	Partial	Partial	Partial	No	Yes	Yes

Discussion Questions

1. As a policymaker, is it reasonable to think that you could restore health insurance to a free market concept? Why or why not?
2. What kind of legislative approaches could be used to ensure free market concepts?
3. What kind of legislative approaches could be used to ensure (a) provider or (b) patient accountability for health outcomes?
4. What legislative approaches could reduce knowledge asymmetry and increase cost knowledge?

SECTION 3

Government-Funded Programs

CHAPTER 7
Medicare

Rachel Ellison, PhD & Lesley Clack, ScD

▶ Introduction

Medicare is a public insurance program for the elderly and persons with disabilities that is administered by the federal government through the Centers for Medicare & Medicaid Services (CMS), which is part of the U.S. Department of Health and Human Services (DHHS) (Kongstvedt, 2016). Medicare was signed into law by President Lyndon B. Johnson in 1965, and Congress enacted Medicare under Title XVIII of the Social Security Act (CMS, 2018a). Enrollment in Medicare has doubled since its passage, and annual expenditures have increased by about 40-fold, which makes the federal government the nation's single largest healthcare payer (Knickman & Kovner, 2015). In December 2018, there were 38,763,849 people insured by Medicare and 21,655,106 with Medicare Advantage and other supplemental plans (CMS, 2019a). There were 25,656,490 people with prescription drug plans, and 19,007,183 with Medicare Advantage prescription drug coverage (CMS, 2019a).

▶ Medicare Eligibility, Parts, and Coverage

Eligibility

Medicare is a federally funded health insurance program for people age 65 and older, people under age 65 who are disabled, and people of all ages diagnosed with end-stage renal disease (ESRD). To qualify, an individual must be a U.S. resident and have paid the Federal Insurance Contributions Act (FICA) payroll tax for at least 10 years (Knickman & Kovner, 2015). The entitlement was expanded in 1972 to allow people who did not pay FICA for the minimum amount of time to pay a premium for coverage.

Medicare consists of four parts: Part A: Hospital Insurance, Part B: Medical Insurance, Part C: Medicare Advantage, and Part D: Prescription Drug Coverage. Part A is typically paid for through payroll taxes, and Parts B and D are paid for through a monthly premium (CMS, 2018d). When a person enrolls in a Medicare Advantage Plan (Part C), Medicare pays third-party insurers directly to care for the patient each month (CMS, 2018b). The Balanced Budget Act of 1997 established the Medicare+Choice Program, which was designed to build on existing Medicare managed care programs and expand options under Part B (Knickman & Kovner, 2015). Under the George Bush administration pharmaceutical coverage was added through the passage of the Medicare Modernization Act in December 2003. This coverage was expanded for all Medicare enrollees as part of the PPACA in 2010 (Kovner & Knickman, 2015).

Medicare benefits coverage is divided into separate parts—some mandatory and some optional (**TABLE 7-1**). Part A is mandatory for all individuals eligible for Medicare coverage, but Part B is voluntary, and individuals must pay monthly premium payments deducted from their Social Security payments (Kongstvedt, 2016). Parts A and B involve cost sharing, meaning individuals pay a portion of their healthcare costs through premiums, copayments, coinsurance, or deductibles. Parts A and B do not cover the cost of prescription drugs, which is why that benefit was added in 2003 through the Medicare Modernization Act. Prior to that time, seniors did not have prescription drug coverage and could only cover those expenses through a supplemental "MediGap" policy. Medigap policies are sold by private companies, and they are designed to help pay some of the healthcare costs that Original Medicare (Parts A and B) doesn't cover, such as copayments, coinsurance, and deductibles (CMS, 2019c).

Individuals with low income who qualify for Medicare may also qualify for Medicaid. If an individual receives both Medicare and Medicaid, they are considered dual eligible. Typically, Medicare is the primary payer for their medical services, and Medicaid pays the deductibles, coinsurance, and other expenses, in the same fashion as a Medigap policy does (Wagner, 2018). Medicaid is discussed in depth in another chapter in this textbook.

TABLE 7-1 Parts and Coverage	
Part A	▪ Hospital care ▪ Skilled nursing care ▪ Home nursing care ▪ Hospice ▪ Home health services
Part B	▪ Medically necessary services ▪ Preventive services
Part C	▪ Medicare Advantage ▪ Dental ▪ Vision ▪ Hearing
Part D	▪ Prescription drugs (CMS, 2018d)

▶ Applying for Medicare

The Social Security Administration manages eligibility and enrollment for both Social Security and Medicare benefits (Kongstvedt, 2016). Applying for Medicare is situational and differs for many people. Some are automatically enrolled, and some have to sign up for it. Those people who have been diagnosed with ESRD are eligible for Part A and Part B and are automatically enrolled. Like all health insurance plans, there are stipulations and conditions. If a person is under 65 but has a disability as determined by the Social Security Administration (SSA), he or she must receive disability benefits from SSA or the Retirement Railroad Board (RRB) for 24 months before they can apply for Medicare (CMS, 2018d), at which point they become eligible for Part A and Part B. Those individuals who do not receive any Social Security benefits or RRB benefits before turning 65 will have to apply to get Medicare Part A and Part B; they will not automatically be enrolled (CMS, 2018d).

Individuals who are receiving Social Security when they turn 65 will not have to apply. They will automatically be enrolled and coverage will begin the first day of the month they turn 65. If their birthday is on the first day of the month, Part A and Part B will start the first day of the prior month (CMS, 2018d).

Medicare has a Special Enrollment Period for individuals who fall into certain categories based on a spouse's current employment. This period of time allows couples to apply for Medicare Part B during a specific time (SSA, 2018). That specific time can occur any month you remain covered under the group health plan and your, or your spouse's, employment continues or the 8-month period that begins with the month after your group health plan coverage or the employment it is based on ends, whichever comes first (SSA, 2018).

▶ Paying for Medicare Services

Medicare was signed into law on July 30, 1965, by Lyndon B. Johnson. Back then, Part A and Part B were the only provisions of the policy. Today, Part A and B are known as "Original Medicare" (CMS, 2018c). With the new health policy, decisions were made on how to pay physicians and how it would be funded.

Since 1965, many iterations of reimbursing physicians, hospitals, and other healthcare organizations have been made by the CMS. Today, the Medicare Physician Fee Schedule (MPFS) is used. The MPFS is a complete listing of fees that is used by Medicare to pay doctors or other providers on a fee-for-service basis (CMS, 2018e). Medicare pays hospitals for inpatient care on a bundled services payment method referred to as *prospective payment systems* (PPS). All hospitals except children's hospitals, psychiatric hospitals, rehabilitation units, and hospitals with approved waivers are required to participate in PPS (Cleverly & Cleverly, 2018). In other words, PPS provides payment for all hospital nonphysician services provided to hospital inpatients, and MPFS is used to pay physicians who treat patients within the hospital. The bundled service payment method pays the hospital one all-inclusive payment and the hospital has the responsibility to pay the laboratory and other departments included in the PPS (Cleverly & Cleverly, 2018).

The current method used for determining the rate at which Medicare reimburses physicians on a fee-for-service basis is the resource-based relative value scale (RBRVS). RBRVS is calculated using the costs of physician labor, practice overhead, materials, and malpractice insurance, with the resulting amounts adjusted based on geographic location (Wagner, 2018). The three separate relative value units (RVUs) associated with calculating a payment under the Medicare Physicians Fee Schedule are:

- The Work RVU: the relative time and intensity associated with providing a Medicare Physicians Fee Schedule service;
- The Practice Expense RVU: the costs of maintaining a practice (such as office space, supplies and equipment, and staff); and
- The Malpractice RVU: the costs of malpractice insurance (Wagner, 2018)

The Geographic Practice Cost Index (GPCI) is used for each RVU to account for geographic variations in the costs of practicing medicine in different areas of the country, and there is a separate GPCI adjustment for each RVU. After adjusting for GPCI, the conversion factor (CF) is applied to determine the payment for a service. The CF is released by CMS annually, and it is used to translate RVUs into dollars.

The following formula is used to calculate RBRVS:

Payment = CF × [(Work RVU x Work GPCI) + (Practice Expense RVU × Practice Expense GPCI) + (Malpractice RVU × Malpractice GPCI)]

Where CF = conversion factor; RVU = relative value unit; GPCI = Geographic Practice Cost Index

MPFS amounts can be obtained through the CMS MPFS Look-Up Tool (CMS, 2019b).

▶ Medicare Access and CHIP Reauthorization Act (MACRA)

Healthcare has changed over time and will probably continue to do so. Recently, the CMS has taken notice of shift in focus to providing quality healthcare services. Quality initiatives have been identified, such as publicly reporting quality measures for nursing homes, hospitals, and skilled nursing facilities, among other healthcare facilities (CMS, 2018f). The Medicare Access and CHIP Reauthorization Act (MACRA) was enacted in 2015 to create a new provider incentive structure through the Quality Payment Program, previously discussed in the chapter on Healthcare Quality and Safety. MACRA established annual flat-fee adjustments to the MPFS through 2025, and instituted new fee updates beginning in 2019 (Wagner, 2018). MACRA also established the Merit-Based Incentive Payment System (MIPS), which consolidated all of the previous Medicare quality programs into one program. In addition to MIPS, MACRA also established Alternative Payment Models (APMs) for physicians not already in another Medicare alternative payment structure, such as an ACO. APMs are designed to reward providers who outperform others in delivering high-quality, efficient, and coordinated care, whereas MIPS focuses more on performance reporting than actual outcomes (Wagner, 2018). The goals of both programs are the same: to improve quality and reduce costs.

MACRA is a complex law and includes many new requirements. Beginning in 2018, there are five criteria for participation, which all revolve around quality, resource use, technology, and clinical practice improvement activities:

- Protection of patient health information and documentation
- Electronic prescribing
- Coordination of care through patient engagement. The patient should be able to view, download, transmit, correspond via secure messaging, and have access to patient-generated health data and communicate with the physician electronically through a secure messaging application.
- Health information exchange and patient care record exchange, with the ability to request and accept patient care records and to perform clinical information reconciliation
- Public health and clinical data registry reporting, including to immunization registries (Wagner, 2018)

▶ Summary

Since its inception, Medicare has been through many upgrades and has had many milestones. For example, by July 1, 1966, 1 million people were enrolled in Medicare. In 1972, Medicare eligibility was extended to individuals under age 65 with long-term disabilities and to individuals with ESRD (CMS, 2018a). The internet site Medicare.gov was launched to provide updated information about Medicare (CMS, 2018a). Below are key terms that will assist in understanding the case studies and the depth and importance of Medicare in this country.

Key Terms

Alternative Payment Models (APMs) were created under the Quality Payment Program and reward providers who outperform others in delivering high-quality, coordinated, and efficient care.

Center for Medicaid & Medicare Services (CMS) is a federal agency within the U.S. Department of Health and Human Services (HHS) that administers the Medicare program and works in partnership with state governments to administer Medicaid, the Children's Health Insurance Program, and health insurance portability standards.

Medicare Access and CHIP Reauthorization Act (MACRA) created a new provider incentive structure through the Quality Payment Program.

Medicare Part A is managed by Medicare and provides Medicare benefits and coverage for inpatient hospital care.

Medicare Part B covers medical services and supplies that are medically necessary to treat a health condition.

Medicare Part C offers Medicare-covered benefits through private health plans instead of through Original Medicare.

Medicare Part D is a voluntary outpatient prescription drug benefit for people on Medicare.

Medicare Physician Fee Schedule (MPFS) features a complete listing of fees used by Medicare to pay doctors or other providers/suppliers.

Merit-Based Incentive Programs (MIPS) is one of two tracks under the Quality Payment Program, which moves Medicare Part B providers to a performance-based payment system.

Prospective Payment System is used by Medicare to reimburse hospitals a set amount based on the patient's diagnosis-related group (DRG) or ambulatory patient classification (APC).

Resource-based relative value scale (RBRVS) is the physician payment system used by the CMS and most other payers.

References

Centers for Medicare and Medicaid Services (CMS). (2018a). CMS' program history. https://www.cms.gov/About-CMS/Agency-information/History/

Centers for Medicare and Medicaid Services (CMS). (2018b). How Medicare Advantage Plans work. https://www.medicare.gov/sign-up-change-plans/medicare-health-plans/medicare-advantage-plans/how-medicare-advantage-plans-work.html

Centers for Medicare and Medicaid Services (CMS). (2018c). How Original Medicare works. https://www.medicare.gov/sign-up-change-plans/decide-how-to-get-medicare/original-medicare/how-original-medicare-works.html

Centers for Medicare and Medicaid Services (CMS). (2018d). Medicare program—General information. https://www.cms.gov/Medicare/Medicare-General-Information/MedicareGenInfo/index.html

Centers for Medicare and Medicaid Services (CMS). (2018e). Physician fee schedule. https://www.cms.gov/Medicare/Medicare-Fee-for-Service-Payment/PhysicianFeeSched/

Centers for Medicare and Medicaid Services (CMS). (2018f). Quality initiatives—General information. https://www.cms.gov/Medicare/Quality-Initiatives-Patient-Assessment-Instruments/QualityInitiativesGenInfo/index.html

Centers for Medicare and Medicaid Services (CMS). (2019a). Medicare enrollment dashboard. https://www.cms.gov/Research-Statistics-Data-and-Systems/Statistics-Trends-and-Reports/CMSProgramStatistics/Dashboard.html

Centers for Medicare and Medicaid Services (CMS). (2019b). Physician fee schedule look-up tool. https://www.cms.gov/Medicare/Medicare-Fee-for-Service-Payment/PFSLookup/index.html

Centers for Medicare and Medicaid Services (CMS). (2019c). What's Medicare Supplement Insurance (Medigap)? https://www.medicare.gov/supplements-other-insurance/whats-medicare-supplement-insurance-medigap

Cleverly, W., & Cleverly, J. (2018). *Essentials of healthcare finance*. Burlington, MA: Jones & Bartlett Learning.

Knickman, J. R., & Kovner, A. R. (2015). *Jonas & Kovner's health care delivery in the United States* (11th ed.). New York: Springer Publishing Company.

Kongstvedt, P. R. (2016). *Health insurance and managed care: What they are and how they work* (4th ed.). Burlington, MA: Jones & Bartlett Learning.

Social Security Administration (SSA). (2018). Medicare benefits. https://www.ssa.gov/benefits/medicare/

Wagner, S. L. (2018). *Fundamentals of medical practice management*. Chicago, IL: Health Administration Press.

🔍 CASE 7-1

Prescription for Disaster

Kelly L. Colwell EdD, MRC, RRT, NPS, CPFT, AE-C & Alice Colwell MSN, RNC-NIC

Gloria is in her late 70s and has suffered for a number of years with severe back pain as a result of her scoliosis. Although she has had the condition most of her life, it is only in the last 10 years that the pain has become intolerable. At first, Gloria's physician tried her on nonsteroidal anti-inflammatory drugs such as ibuprofen and the popular anti-inflammatory drug Celebrex, an approved, standard treatment for chronic pain. Unfortunately, the benefits and tolerability of these medications were minimal at best because of several side effects including nausea, diarrhea, and vertigo, with no appreciable reduction in her level of pain. Finally, her physician prescribed her the lidocaine patch 5%. The patch is placed in the area of pain and essentially applies a local anesthetic. Gloria was delighted with the results, and better yet, her Medicare Part D Prescription Medication plan covered the cost of the patches. However, recently, Gloria's Part D Medicare plan informed her they would no longer continue to cover the lidocaine patches as they previously had. Gloria is devastated. She has relied on the patches for a couple of years now and benefited greatly, but living on a low fixed income, she cannot afford them herself. She calls the individuals managing her health plan in an attempt to ascertain why the patches she relies on are no longer covered. The customer service representative is polite enough but simply tells her that Medicare Part D plans nationwide are no longer covering "off-label" drugs.

Gloria is confused, so she asks her physician about the change. Dr. Gaff explains, "Off-label means that the reason you are using the drug has not been approved by the FDA and is not mentioned in a Medicare drug compendia, which is basically a medical encyclopedia of approved drug use. So, although off-label drugs are still legal for a doctor to prescribe and can be helpful in treating your medical condition, Medicare does not cover them if they are prescribed for any reason other than what the drug was initially intended for" (Center for Medicare Advocacy, 2010). Gloria looks confused, so Dr. Gaff says, "I prescribed the patches for your diagnosed condition, which is chronic pain as a result of your scoliosis. However, lidocaine patches are only approved by the FDA to treat post-herpetic neuralgia, a complication of shingles, or diabetic neuropathy, and you do not have either." Dr. Gaff looks frustrated. "The patches are the only treatment that has successfully managed your pain, and it is completely legal for me to prescribe it for you. However, Medicare will not pay for the patches because it is not an approved use" (Potter et al., 2018).

Gloria leaves the doctor's office in a state of disbelief. The patches work amazingly well in controlling her pain. There are no side effects, and on top of that, Medicare has covered them for a couple of years. It does not seem to make any sense. And worse than that, Dr. Gaff told her that if she could not afford to continue using the patches, she might have to consider opioids.

In order to be covered under Medicare Part D, drugs must be prescribed for a "medically accepted indication," meaning their use for a particular disease must be approved by the FDA, or supported by one of three Compendia, identified in Section 1927(g)(1)(B)(i) of the Social Security Act (SSA, 2018). The Act was subsequently modified to allow coverage of anti-cancer drugs if their use is supported in peer-reviewed journals. However, under Medicare Part B, all drugs (not just those used in an anti-cancer regimen) may be supported by peer reviewed literature. Off-label drug use is not unusual; in fact, some studies suggest up to 20% of outpatient prescriptions are for off-label uses (Center for Medicare Advocacy, 2010). Studies show that one in five prescriptions written in the United States is for an off-label usage, but as many as 73% of off-label applications have little or no scientific evidence backing up the drug's efficacy in treating the patient's condition (Center for Medicare Advocacy, 2010).

Discussion Questions

1. Gloria has clearly had improved quality of life, and her pain was well managed with the lidocaine patches. If a doctor deems a treatment effective and the results of a treatment are positive, can Medicare still deny coverage? Is a Medicare appeal an option?
2. Medicare Part D plans previously covered the lidocaine patches. The Medicare Part D regulations have not changed recently, so why do you think Part D plans are no longer covering off-label drugs?
3. Lidocaine patches are covered for patients insured under the PPACA, as well as many who have private health insurance. When patients transition to Medicare, the patches are no longer covered. Should Medicare coverage be required to be consistent with the PPACA and private health insurance? Why?
4. ,One of the most pressing public health challenges our country faces today is our epidemic of opioid addiction and overdose. Each day, Americans die of opioid overdoses, while almostmillions of our fellow citizens each year misuse opioids. If Gloria cannot afford to buy the patches herself, her physician says she may have to consider alternative treatments. Is Medicare's position on reimbursement consistent with the current administration's "War on Opioids?" What is the possible societal impact if Medicare denies coverage for other forms of pain control?

References

Center for Medicare Advocacy. (2010). CMA report: Medicare coverage for off-label drug use. http://www.medicareadvocacy.org/cma-report-medicare-coverage-for-off-label-drug-use/

Potter, L. M., Maldonado, A. Q., Lentine, K. L., Schnitzler, M. A., Zhang, Z., Hess, G. P., Garrity, E., Kasiske, B. L., & Axelrod, D. A. (2018). Transplant recipients are vulnerable to coverage denial under Medicare Part D, *American Journal of Transplantation, 18*(6), 1502–1509.

Social Security Administration (SSA). (2018). Payment for covered outpatient drugs. https://www.ssa.gov/OP_Home/ssact/title19/1927.htm

CASE 7-2

The Evolution of How Medicare Pays Doctors

Raymond J. Higbea, PhD & Gregory A. Cline, PhD

This case study chronicles the history of how the federal government has paid physicians for the provision of medical services since 1965 with the passage of Medicare to present day under the MACRA.

History of Medicare

Year	Act
1965	Medicare Part B—Usual & Customary
1989	Physician Fee Schedule—RBRVS
1992	Medical Volume Performance Standards
1997	Sustainable Growth Rate
2015	Medicare Access & CHIP Reauthorization Act

The federal government entered into the realm of physician payment with the passage of Medicare in 1965. Medicare was patterned after 1960s-era Blue Cross and Blue Shield plans, with Part A providing payment for inpatient hospital care and Part B for outpatient care, and 75% of Part B payments going to physician office visits. Reimbursement during this time was usual, customary, and reasonable charges. So, if a physician submitted charges that were average for the geographic area, they were paid without question. Of course, it takes little imagination to comprehend how this type of payment arrangement provided an unlimited source of unquestioned revenue for physicians. In fact, within 20 years (mid-1980s), physician payment had become the largest domestic program funded by general revenues. This rapid growth led Congress to pass PL 101-239 in 1989, which established a physician fee schedule based on the value of a physician's work.

Physician's work was valued through the RBRVS, which rewarded them for the value or complexity of their work, practice expenses, and malpractice risks. The RBRVS also sought to cap payment for physician services by setting the increase in unit service to be inversely proportional to past increases in service quantity. This attempt to cap payment resulted in passage of the Medicare Volume Performance Standards in 1992 that temporarily slowed the physician payment rate of increase. Within a few years of these changes, primary care physicians and surgeons found these standards to be a disadvantage and lobbied Congress for changes and received caps more advantageous to their specialties. An unintended consequence of this bill was that those physicians performing procedures were more richly rewarded than those whose practice was more quality-based, a disequilibrium that was debated but not addressed for 20 years.

Slowed growth in physician payment was very brief, causing Congress to act again in 1997 by passing PL 105-33, the Sustainable Growth Rate (SGR). The SGR calculation included the estimated: (1) percentage change in fee for physician services, (2) percentage change in the average number of Medicare fee-for-service beneficiaries, (3) 10-year average annual percentage change in real gross domestic product per capita, and (4) percentage change in expenditures due to changes in regulations (Clemons, 2014). The SGR worked extremely well in controlling physician expenses to the point that it resulted in negative payment increases ranging from 4.8% to 20% for the years 2002 to 2014. However, Congress did not let any of these negative increases take effect and instead passed modest increases of no more than 2% each year. Finally, in 2015, both chambers of Congress tired of this and passed PL 114-10 (MACRA) as the "permanent doc fix" to address these annual payment concerns.

MACRA is a bipartisan bill that consolidated physician payment into the Merit Incentive Payment System (MIPS) and Alternative Payment Models (APM). MIPS consolidates the Physician Quality Reporting System (PQRS); Meaningful Use; Value Based Model; and Improvement Activities. PQRS is an incentive-based program that encourages physicians to report on quality measures relevant to their area of practice. Meaningful Use incentivized physicians to acquire and use an electronic health record in a meaningful way. The Value Based Model is applied to the physician fee schedule and rewards physicians for providing high-quality care at a low cost. Finally, Improvement Activities rewards physicians for providing care focused on care coordination, patient engagement, and patient safety. Alternative Payment Models (APM) are programs such as ACOs that provide physicians with a 5% additional incentive for assuming some risk in the provision of high-quality care for patients with specific clinical conditions, episodes of care, or populations.

An examination of how physicians are paid is incomplete without a brief discussion about how much physicians are paid. The U.S. Bureau of Labor Statistics (2016) data lists the mean physician and surgeon wage as $210,270. Compare this with the mean wage for lawyers ($139,880) and management occupations ($118,220). Physicians and surgeons are firmly in the top quintile of U.S. income earners (2015 quintile mean, $202,366), and specialists are in the top 5% (2015 quintile mean, $350,870). Although physicians are certainly well paid, the lingering question is whether they are overpaid. When U.S. physician wages are compared to the wages of their Organization for Economic and Cooperative Development

(OECD) peers, their wages are comparable. Further, physician density per 100,000 population is similar to that of their OECD peers.

Since 1965 when the federal government entered the realm of physician payment, they have consistently sought to pay physicians appropriately for the services they have provided. What has changed over the years has been the desire to control the growth and predictability of payments. Since 2006, additional measures associated with payment have included quality of care, patient safety, and use of an electronic medical record in a meaningful way. Stated otherwise, we have moved from paying for cost to paying for value (quality/cost).

Discussion Questions

1. Based on the above history, how would you anticipate Medicare payment policy has driven the organization of physician practice?
2. How can Medicare payment policy direct the delivery of patient care?
3. How can Medicare payment policy affect attempts to reduce the cost of medical care?
4. Should Medicare physician payment policies gradually erode overall physician pay? Why or why not?

References

Clemons, M. K. (2014). Estimated sustainable growth rate and conversion factor, for Medicare payments to physicians in 2015. https://www.cms.gov/Medicare/Medicare-Fee-for-Service -Payment/SustainableGRatesConFact/index.html

U.S. Bureau of Labor Statistics. (2016). Wages. https://www.bls.gov/oes/current/oes_nat.htm#29-0000

🔍 *CASE 7-3*

Who Saves? The Medicare Quality and Cost Conundrum

Gregory A. Cline, PhD & Raymond J. Higbea, PhD

TRIUNE health system was formed in 2000 from two separate faith-based health systems to achieve three overarching goals. The primary goal of the merger was to create a new entity with the capital to become a recognized lead innovator in both service delivery and management. The secondary goal was to design, test, and implement across all 50 subordinate health systems a "first in the nation" (FIN) integrated information system across all clinical, financial, and enterprise resource planning (ERP) systems. The third goal was to become a leader in "smart" community benefit operations.

Just 5 years later, TRIUNE had made substantial progress on all three goals. It led one of the 15 partnerships in the Agency for Healthcare Research and Quality's (AHRQ) Accelerating Change and Transformation in Organizations and Networks (ACTION) initiatives— "a model of field-based research designed to promote innovation in health care delivery by accelerating the diffusion of research into practice" (AHRQ, 2018). It had successfully tested its FIN, starting implementation across all subordinate health systems. A senior community benefit analyst from TRIUNE chaired the Religious Health Association (RHA) community benefit committee.

Near the same time that TRIUNE began implementation of FIN, the Centers for Medicare and Medicaid Services (CMS) began a series of waiver demonstrations seeking to increase quality while reducing costs, with some savings being returned to any partner health systems meeting the goals of each demonstration. While TRIUNE did not bid on these CMS waiver demonstrations, the senior leadership tracked the goals and methods of each as a way to anticipate future CMS policy changes related to cost and quality driven by the outcomes of each. By 2009, TRIUNE leadership determined that the outcomes from the CMS waiver demonstrations would eventually result in new legislation tying Medicare reimbursement to quality and that while these changes would begin with carrots, one day they would become sticks. The leadership team decided that developing solutions for avoiding future penalties should begin well in advance of the penalties coming into force.

TRIUNE leadership (including board members) determined that community benefit activities could play a role in developing solutions. This was termed "smart" community benefit and would consist of innovations to further all three goals. An internal competitive funding initiative was created to foster competition among subordinate health systems for community benefit innovations. The focus of "smart" community benefit was entitled *Programs to Policy*. The long-term goal of *Programs* was to build an inventory of successful community benefit projects that could be replicated across interested subordinate systems. To receive *Programs to Policy*, funding proposed projects needed to address access, quality improvement, return on investment, and relevance for future health policy advocacy.

By 2016, the *Programs to Policy*–funded innovations began producing second-generation innovations, capitalizing on learning from prior innovations by combining components from earlier successful projects. One important second-generation innovation focused on reducing readmissions among vulnerable Medicare patients, an area where in 2012 "carrots" had already changed to "sticks" (see **FIGURE 7-1**).

One of the most recent *Programs to Policy* innovations demonstrated the success of iterative innovations, which build on prior successes, that targeted vulnerable Medicare patients. After an 18-month trial period, the effort yielded demonstrated savings of $7,000.00 to $20,000.00 for each Medicare patient through avoided readmissions. Most surprising, almost all of the "unnecessary variation" in services and negative health outcomes had

FIGURE 7-1 Progression of CMS Quality & Value-Based Purchasing Initiatives

disappeared among the treatment group (Laffel & Blumenthal, 1989). The government affairs team of TRIUNE health began using the findings from this study to advocate for receiving some share of the savings to CMS, arguing that CMS savings were also lost revenue for health systems that deliver high-quality, low-cost services.

Discussion Questions

1. Is CMS at risk of not providing an equitable return to innovators like TRIUNE that produce savings well above those from avoided readmissions?
2. Should CMS replicate this system of increasing accountability for quality outcomes to state Medicaid programs?
3. What might cause CMS to ask Congress for additional legislation supporting the broadening of this successful quality–cost initiative that has produced unexpected improvements in other health outcomes?
4. What policy changes might be suggested by the findings to encourage community-based social support agencies to link?

References

Agency for Healthcare Research and Quality (AHRQ). (2018). Accelerating change and transformation in organizations and networks. https://www.ahrq.gov/research/findings/factsheets/translating/action/index.html.

Laffel G., & Blumenthal, D. (1989). The case for using industrial quality management science in health care organizations. *JAMA, 262*(20), 2869–2873.

CHAPTER 8
Medicaid

Rachel Ellison, PhD & Lesley Clack, ScD

▶ Introduction

The second largest provider of health insurance in the United States is Medicaid. It is a means-tested program, meaning that it is a needs-based social welfare program in which eligibility is based on income (Buchbinder & Shanks, 2017). In 1965, under the administration of President Lyndon B. Johnson, Medicaid was created by adding Title XIX to the Social Security Act (SSA, 2018). Medicaid is jointly funded by the states and the federal government but is administered by the states according to federal requirements. The primary goal of Medicaid is to provide health coverage for low-income adults, children, pregnant women, elderly adults, and people with disabilities.

▶ Medicaid Eligibility

Eligibility requirements are set by each state, but by law the federal government requires that certain groups of people are eligible for Medicaid (CMS, 2018a):

- low-income families,
- qualified pregnant women and children, and
- individuals receiving Supplemental Security Income.

The states also decide what type of benefits individuals of their state receive, except for the mandatory benefits that the federal government requires each state to provide (CMS, 2018a). The federal government allows each state to offer optional benefits if they choose to do so (**TABLE 8-1**).

▶ Medicaid Funding

Funding Medicaid is a joint effort. The federal government pays states a percentage of program expenditures (CMS, 2018a), which vary by state and are calculated by

TABLE 8-1 Medicaid Benefits (CMS, 2018b)

Mandatory Benefits	Optional Benefits
Inpatient hospital services	Prescription drugs
Outpatient hospital services	Clinic services
EPSDT: Early and periodic screening, diagnostic, and treatment services	Physical therapy
Nursing facility services	Occupational therapy
Home health services	Speech, hearing, and language disorder services
Physician services	Respiratory care services
Rural health clinic services	Other diagnostic, screening, preventive, and rehabilitative services
Federally qualified health center (FQHC) services	Podiatry services
Laboratory and X-ray services	Optometry services
Family planning services	Dental services
Nurse midwife services	Prosthetics
Certified pediatric and family nurse practitioner services	Eyeglasses
Freestanding birth center services (when licensed or otherwise recognized by the state)	Chiropractic services
Transportation to medical care	Other practitioner services
Tobacco cessation counseling for pregnant women	Nursing services and case management

Data from Centers for Medicare & Medicaid Services (CMS). (2018). Medicaid Benefits. Link: https://www.medicaid.gov
/medicaid/benefits/index.html

the Department of Health & Human Services (HHS). States must be sure they have enough money to fund the remaining costs. Depending on the state, some physicians are reimbursed well from treating patients with Medicaid; others are not.

Billions of dollars every year are lost by states from Medicaid fraud, abuse, and waste. Medicaid fraud and abuse has been defined as the following: "Medicaid fraud involves knowingly misrepresenting the truth to obtain unauthorized benefit, abuse includes any practice that is inconsistent with acceptable fiscal, business, or medical practices that unnecessarily increase costs, and overutilization or resources and inaccurate payments for services" (NCSL, 2018). States must balance innovative ways to control costs while also fighting fraud and abuse. There are several important fraud and abuse laws to offer protection. The False Claims Act protects the government from fraud and abuse and makes it illegal to submit claims for payment to Medicare or Medicaid knowing that they are fraudulent (HHS, 2018). A false claim may result in a fine of $11,000 per claim filed, plus fines of up to three times the programs' loss (HHS, 2018). Another law enacted to combat fraud and abuse is the Anti-Kickback Statute (AKS), which was passed by Congress in 1972 and amended in 1987 (American Bar Association, 2018). The AKS prohibits knowing and willful payment in return for referring an individual to another person or entity or recommending or arranging for the ordering of any services reimbursed by a federal healthcare program. AKS makes it illegal to solicit or accept payments for referrals or for generating Medicare or Medicaid business (American Bar Association, 2018). The Stark Law, which is discussed in the chapter on Federal Legislation Governing Medical Care, also protects the Medicare and Medicaid programs from fraud and abuse.

▶ Medicaid Expansion

One of the key provisions of the Patient Protection and Affordable Care Act (PPACA) for reducing the number of uninsured individuals in the United States was to expand Medicaid by establishing a minimum income eligibility across the country rather than leaving it up to each state (Shi & Singh, 2015). As the law was written, states would be mandated to cover all legal U.S. residents under the age of 65 with incomes up to 138% of the federal poverty level (FPL) starting January 2014 (Shi & Singh, 2015). The U.S. Supreme Court declared the mandate unconstitutional and left it up to each state to choose whether they wanted to expand their Medicaid program. As of February 2019, 37 states have expanded their Medicaid programs, and 14 states have not (**TABLE 8-2**).

TABLE 8-2 Status of State Action on the Medicaid Expansion Decision	
State	**Current Status of Medicaid Expansion (February 2019)**
Alabama	Not expanded
Arkansas	Expanded
Arizona	Expanded
Arkansas	Expanded
California	Expanded

(continues)

TABLE 8-2 Status of State Action on the Medicaid
Expansion Decision   *(continued)*

State	Current Status of Medicaid Expansion (February 2019)
Colorado	Expanded
Connecticut	Expanded
Delaware	Expanded
District of Columbia (DC)	Expanded
Florida	Not expanded
Georgia	Not expanded
Hawaii	Expanded
Idaho	Expanded
Illinois	Expanded
Indiana	Expanded
Iowa	Expanded
Kansas	Not expanded
Kentucky	Expanded
Louisiana	Expanded
Maine	Expanded
Maryland	Expanded
Massachusetts	Expanded
Michigan	Expanded
Minnesota	Expanded
Mississippi	Not expanded
Missouri	Not expanded
Montana	Expanded
Nebraska	Expanded

State	Current Status of Medicaid Expansion (February 2019)
Nevada	Expanded
New Hampshire	Expanded
New Jersey	Expanded
New Mexico	Expanded
New York	Expanded
North Carolina	Not expanded
North Dakota	Expanded
Ohio	Expanded
Oklahoma	Not expanded
Oregon	Expanded
Pennsylvania	Expanded
Rhode Island	Expanded
South Carolina	Not expanded
South Dakota	Not expanded
Tennessee	Not expanded
Texas	Not expanded
Utah	Expanded
Vermont	Expanded
Virginia	Expanded
Washington	Expanded
West Virginia	Expanded
Wisconsin	Not expanded
Wyoming	Not expanded

KFF's State Health Facts. Status of State Action on the Medicaid Expansion Decision, Kaiser Family Foundation (KFF), April 9, 2019. URL: https://www.kff.org/health-reform/state-indicator/state-activity-around-expanding-medicaid-under-the-affordable-care -act/?activeTab=map&currentTimeframe=0&selectedDistributions=current-status-of-medicaid-expansion-decision&sortModel =%7B%22colId%22:%22Location%22,%22sort%22:%22asc%22%7D#notes

▶ Summary

As you have read, Medicaid is a large health insurance program that provides coverage to certain groups of people. The policy is funded jointly by federal and state governments. Eligibility differs across the board by state. Each state sets requirements but must follow certain criteria set forth by the federal government. Because Medicaid is essentially different in every state, benefits are different for everyone. This tends to cause a stir for the controversial policy. The case studies that follow illustrate the vast differences in Medicaid among states. Below are important terms to assist in analyzing this chapter's case studies.

▶ Key Terms

Abuse occurs if an activity misuses the healthcare system, such as charging outrageous fees or using billing codes that are related to, but pay higher than, the code for the service that was actually provided.

Fraud happens when someone misrepresents or falsifies a fact related to healthcare services to receive payment from a health plan or the government.

Medicaid is a healthcare program that assists low-income families or individuals in paying for doctor visits, hospital stays, long-term medical costs, custodial care costs, and more.

Medicaid Expansion is a provision in the PPACA that called for expanding Medicaid eligibility in order to cover more low-income people.

Waste includes unnecessary costs and use of resources, such as spending on services that lack evidence of producing better outcomes than less expensive alternatives.

References

American Bar Association. (2018). *What is the Anti-Kickback Statute?* https://www.americanbar .org/groups/young_lawyers/publications/tyl/topics/health-law/what-is-anti-kickback-statute .html

Buchbinder, S. B., & Shanks, N. H. (2017). *Introduction to health care management* (3rd ed.). Burlington, MA: Jones & Bartlett Learning.

Burns, S. (2018). Supporting Medicaid in Virginia. *Exigence, 2*(1), 1–26. https://commons.vccs.edu /exigence/vol2/iss1/2

Centers for Medicare & Medicaid Services (CMS). (2018a). *CMS' program history.* https://www.cms .gov/About-CMS/Agency-information/History/

Centers for Medicare & Medicaid Services (CMS). (2018b). *Medicaid benefits.* https://www.medicaid .gov/medicaid/benefits/index.html

Department of Health and Human Services (HHS). (2018*). A roadmap for new physicians: Fraud & abuse laws.* https://oig.hhs.gov/compliance/physician-education/01laws.asp

Kaiser Family Foundation (KFF). (2019). *Status of state action on the Medicaid expansion decision.* https://www.kff.org/health-reform/state-indicator/state-activity-around-expanding-medicaid -under-the-affordable-care-act/?activeTab=map&currentTimeframe=0&selectedDistributions =current-status-of-medicaid-expansion-decision&sortModel=%7B%22colId%22:%22Location %22,%22sort%22:%22asc%22%7D

National Conference of State Legislatures (NCSL). (2018). *Medicaid fraud and abuse.* http://www .ncsl.org/research/health/medicaid-fraud-and-abuse.aspx

Shi, L., & Singh, D. A. (2015). *Delivering health care in America: A systems approach.* Burlington, MA: Jones & Bartlett Learning.

Social Security Administration (SSA). (2018). *Social Security history.* https://www.ssa.gov/history/ssa /lbjmedicare1.html

🔍 CASE 8-1

A State Approach to Medicaid

Christina Juris Bennett, JD

Medicaid is a state–federal program that provides no- or low-cost health care for particular populations. To qualify for Medicaid, a person must fit into a category while also satisfying financial requirements. Categories include, but are not limited to, aged, blind, disabled, children under age 18, and breast and cervical cancer patients. Financial qualifications usually require that the enrollee or enrollee's family live at or below some percentage of the federal poverty line. If a person meets both the categorical and financial requirements, then they may be enrolled in Medicaid. By enrolling, the program subsidizes that person's healthcare costs so long as they are within the scope of the program. For instance, the program will pay for nursing home care but not nonmedically necessary nose jobs.

Medicaid is funded through a partnership between the state and federal government. Each state agrees that it will provide Medicaid services that the federal government requires, and in exchange, the federal government agrees to pay a particular percentage of the costs accrued. States may also enroll additional populations or provide additional benefits beyond those required by the federal government. As one might guess, the more people enrolled or the higher the costs of care provided, the higher the total bill and the individual state or federal components. Since Medicaid's inception in 1965, healthcare costs in the United States have skyrocketed. This has led to states trying different approaches to contain their costs.

In contrast, other states used the managed care model, which adds a middleman, known as a managed care organization (MCO), between the providers and the enrollees. The MCO bears administrative duties related to building and sustaining pools of enrollees and providers and bears financial risk. The state agency pays the MCO a capitation rate—a specific amount of money per enrollee per month—for its expenses. If the enrollees use more care than the total capitated payment for a month, then the MCO loses money. If the enrollees use less care than the total capitated payment for a month, then the MCO yields a profit. Obviously, for MCOs, the strategy is to have a large enrollment of healthy, noncare-seeking people. This case study describes the whirlwind development of Tennessee's managed care Medicaid program and the policymaking process on both the state and federal levels.

In the 1980s, Tennessee, like other states, worked hard to provide healthcare coverage to its poorest and neediest citizens. When the options for expanding Medicaid coverage arose, state leaders seized the opportunities. Consequently, by the early 1990s, the state was carrying its heaviest load of enrollees, and the program proved to be quite costly. The choices were to cut benefits, cut enrollees, or change the program. Cutting benefits and enrollees was not popular, so policymakers began looking for ways to change the program. Managed care entered as a way to control costs, and one of its key proponents was Arkansas governor and future president Bill Clinton. Tennessee, led by Governor Ned McWherter, a longtime friend of Clinton, began considering managed care to change its Medicaid program.

In 1993, Governor McWherter approached the state legislature and asked for a bill granting him authority to revise the Medicaid program from a fee-for-service model to the managed care model. Wanting to begin its recess and trusting the governor immensely because of his previous experience as a legislator, the legislature passed such a bill on May 17, 1993. The law passed was one page long, one of McWherter's requirements, and it stated that the legislature authorized Medicaid to operate pursuant to a federal waiver as of January 1, 1994, and revise[d] provisions necessary for obtaining waiver. There was no other guiding language. By June 16, the governor submitted a full proposal to the HHS to modify the program. The proposal contained detailed information about how the program would operate, what companies would be used as managed care organizations (MCOs), and who supported this policy change. The proposal included one additional critical piece: it expanded enrollee eligibility categories and expanded benefits so people would operate through an insurance program and rely less on charity care.

Time passed, and the governor heard nothing. After a few months, Secretary Donna Shalala of the HHS expressed her concern about the appropriate funding of the MCOs and the proposed expansion of benefits and enrollees. In particular, the vast majority of the MCOs were newly incorporated, and she feared the capitation rates insufficiently funded the start-up costs. Governor McWherter was in a bind. HHS refused to fund portions of the existing Tennessee Medicaid program because it was hemorrhaging money. Cutting benefits and enrollees was political suicide, and it required a lengthy notice and comment period for due process concerns—time that the state did not have. The state had put all its hopes in this new plan, but the federal government still was not supporting it. Without federal funding, the program would cease to exist and leave roughly 20% of Tennesseans without health care, and most of those would be vulnerable populations.

Needing to get approval quickly for this new program, Governor McWherter reached above Secretary Shalala to his friend, President Bill Clinton. In November, McWherter spent a weekend at the White House, and after that visit, Secretary Shalala approved the TennCare proposal. Tennessee's government had approximately one month to convert its Medicaid program of 775,000 people from fee-for-service into managed care. Likewise, the MCOs had one month to build their operational infrastructure and strategize about enrollment. On January 1, 1994, the program went live, and within six months, it had about 1.2 million enrollees.

Discussion Questions

1. If Governor McWherter did not change the TennCare program, he would not have received any federal funding. Knowing that the federal government paid $2 for every $1 the state spent, speculate on the possible consequences if the program had lost federal funding.
2. Would you have tried to cut benefits or enrollees instead of changing the program's structure? Explain your answer.
3. Medicaid is often described as a partnership between the federal and state governments. Discuss whether Tennessee and the federal government, as represented by Secretary Shalala, were equal partners.

🔎 CASE 8-2

The Issue with Access to Care for Patients with Medicaid

Lesley Clack, ScD

Access to care has become a cause for concern for patients with Medicaid. Physicians are not required to accept Medicaid, and thus many doctors choose not to see patients with Medicaid because of increased billing requirements (Agarwal, 2017). According to Health and Human Services (HHS) Secretary Tom Price, "One out of every three physicians in this nation aren't seeing Medicaid patients" (Robertson, 2017).

Mary is a 56-year-old African American female with limited income, and Medicaid is her only source of health insurance. Mary has recently moved to rural Georgia, and there is only one physician within a 50-mile radius of her home who accepts patients with Medicaid. Mary needs to establish a relationship with a primary care physician in order to continue her blood pressure and cholesterol medication. She calls the physician's office to make an appointment and is told that there is a 1-month wait for an appointment with the doctor. Mary does not have the financial resources to pay to see a doctor who does not accept Medicaid, and she does not have the ability to travel 50 miles to see the next available doctor who accepts it. She has no options other than to wait. During the month that she is waiting for her appointment, Mary runs out of her blood pressure and cholesterol medication. She calls the physician's office to see if she can get an earlier appointment, but she is told that there is nothing available and she will have to wait until her scheduled appointment. Within the week, Mary's blood pressure spikes, and she has to go to the local emergency room (ER) for treatment.

Discussion Questions
1. Should physicians be allowed to refuse to see Medicaid patients? Why or why not?
2. What could be done from a policy standpoint to address this issue? Explain.
3. How do the issues present in this case affect the healthcare system as a whole?

References

Agarwal, S. (2017). *Physicians who refuse to accept Medicaid patients breach their contract with society.* STATNews. https://www.statnews.com/2017/12/28/medicaid-physicians-social-contract/
Robertson, L. (2017). *Medicaid's doctor participation rates.* The Wire. https://www.factcheck.org/2017/03/medicaids-doctor-participation-rates/

🔍 *CASE 8-3*

Closing the Gap on Medicaid through Expansion

Yen Vi Khuu-Eickhoff, MHSA

Medicaid is a federally funded program to assist residents with healthcare coverage. In 2012, the PPACA initiated the expansion of Medicaid in all states; however, a ruling from the Supreme Court allowed for each state to make the decision to expand independently. The expansion means that residents may qualify for Medicaid on income alone rather than based on a combination of income, household size, and family status.

Georgia, a state that did not expand Medicaid, is estimated to have about 10.1 million residents (KFF, 2017). About 37% of that population is low income (at 200% or below the FPL). Kurt and Barbara Johnson are one the many low-income families relying on Medicaid for healthcare coverage.

The couple and their 6-year-old son, Nathan Johnson, reside in Brunswick, a small town in southeast Georgia. Kurt is employed locally as a handyman. His annual salary is $35,000. Barbara works at a local grocery store as a cashier, making about $25,000 annually. Due to financial struggles, they cannot afford insurance for themselves. They were able to obtain insurance for Nathan through PeachCare, a state program through which parents can purchase insurance for children at a low cost.

Recently, Kurt has been feeling unwell. He is experiencing symptoms of fatigue, shortness of breath, and lightheadedness. Barbara suspects something is wrong with Kurt, so she advises him to go to the ER despite their financial constraints. There, Kurt is diagnosed with hypertension and is told he is at risk for cardiovascular disease. He is given 3 days of medications and told to see his primary care physician within 72 hours to obtain more.

Because Kurt and Barbara are not insured, they do not have a primary care provider. A coworker suggests that Kurt apply for Medicaid to seek treatment because he is at risk for other diseases if his hypertension is left untreated. Kurt's research reveals that he is ineligible for Medicaid because of his family's annual income. To be eligible for Medicaid in Georgia, one has to meet one of the following basic criteria (Georgia Department of Community Health, 2018):

- Currently pregnant
- A child or teenager
- 65 years of age or older
- Legally blind
- Have a disability
- Need nursing home care

Kurt and Barbara have discussed getting insurance through the state exchange; however, they cannot pay the deductible nor the monthly premiums. Kurt decides to ignore his medical condition and continue working, although this does mean he visits the ER frequently because that is the only place that he can get treatment in emergency situations.

Discussion Questions

1. If Georgia had expanded Medicaid, how would the situation differ for Kurt and Barbara?
2. What do you think would be a reasonable way for Kurt to seek treatment in this case?
3. As noted at the end of the case, Kurt frequents the ER because he does not have other means to receive treatment. What do you think the long-term impact of Kurt going to the ER is?
4. Would you recommend Kurt get insurance through the state exchange? Why or why not?

References

Georgia Department of Community Health. (2018). *Applying for Medicaid*. https://dch.georgia.gov /applying-medicaid

Kaiser Family Foundation (KFF). (2017). *Medicaid in Georgia*. http://files.kff.org/attachment/ fact-sheet-medicaid-state-GA

CHAPTER 9
Children's Health Insurance Program

Rachel Ellison, PhD & Lesley Clack, ScD

▶ Introduction

The Children's Health Insurance Program (CHIP), coded as Title 21 of the Social Security Act, was enacted in 1997 under the Balanced Budget Act (BBA) to expand coverage to uninsured children who are not eligible for Medicaid but can't afford private health insurance (Shi & Singh, 2017). In 2017, it was reported that 9.4 million children were enrolled (HHS, 2018a). CHIP was renewed and strengthened through the Children's Health Insurance Program Reauthorization Act (CHIPRA) of 2009, which provides states with significant new funding, programmatic options, and a range of incentives for covering children through Medicaid and CHIP (Casto & Forrestal, 2015). In 2012, CHIP helped reduce the rate of uninsured children to a record low of 7% (HHS, 2018a).

The program is jointly funded by individual states and the federal government. CHIP is state administered, and each state has its own guidelines regarding eligibility and services, in accordance with federal guidelines. In 2010, the Patient Protection and Affordable Care Act (PPACA) contained provisions to strengthen the program. Since the inception of the PPACA in 2010, CHIP is funded by state and federal funds. The PPACA extended CHIP funding until September 30, 2015, and required states to prolong eligibility guidelines through 2019 (CMS, 2018b). On January 22, 2018, Congress passed a 6-year extension of CHIP funding. Federal funding for CHIP had expired as of September 30, 2017, but services were not cut, and emergency funds were used to continue treating children in the program. The CHIP funding extension that was passed in September 2017:

- provided federal funding for CHIP for 6 years, from FY 2018 through FY 2023;
- continued the 23% federal match rate for CHIP that was established by the PPACA but reduced the federal match rate to the regular CHIP rate over time; and

- extended the requirement for states to maintain coverage for children from 2019 through 2023; after October 1, 2019, the requirement is limited to children in families with incomes at or below 300% of the federal poverty level (FPL) (Kaiser Family Foundation, 2018)

▶ Eligibility & Benefits

CHIP serves uninsured children up to the age of 19 in families with incomes that are too high to qualify them for Medicaid. States have the discretion in setting their income eligibility standards, and eligibility varies across states (CMS, 2018b). In order to be eligible for CHIP, families must also meet income eligibility requirements.

Income Eligibility

- Forty-six states and the District of Columbia cover children up to or above 200% of the FPL.
- Twenty-four of these states offer coverage to children in families with income at 250% of the FPL or higher.
- States may get the CHIP-enhanced match for coverage up to 300% of the FPL.
- States that expand coverage above 300% of the FPL get the Medicaid matching rate. (CMS, 2018b)

Like Medicaid, CHIP provides comprehensive benefits (**TABLE 9-1**). Each state has the choice to offer optional benefits. The optional benefits vary by state and are mainly determined by funding (CMS, 2018b). Because the program is jointly funded by the federal government, there are mandatory benefits that are required by each state (CMS, 2018b).

TABLE 9-1 CHIP Benefits (CMS, 2018b)	
Mandatory Benefits	**Optional Benefits**
Well-baby and well-child care including age-appropriate immunizations	Inpatient mental health services
Emergency services	Outpatient mental health services
Dental services	Durable medical equipment
Inpatient hospital services	Nursing care services
Outpatient hospital services	Hospice care
Physician surgical and medical services	Medical transportation
Laboratory and X-ray services	

▶ Quality Health Care for Children

The Children's Health Insurance Program not only wants to provide children healthcare coverage but also strives to provide good quality care. To ensure the healthcare services are up to the quality standard of the federal government, the Centers for Medicare and Medicaid Services (CMS) has implemented quality improvement initiatives that specifically focus on the care of children (CMS, 2018a). These initiatives include screening, oral health, maternal and infant health, and vaccines. For example, the Early and Periodic Screening, Diagnostic, and Treatment (EPSDT) quality improvement initiative is a service provided to all children enrolled in Medicaid and CHIP. EPSDT is key to ensuring that children and adolescents receive appropriate preventive, dental, mental health, developmental, and specialty services (CMS, 2018c).

Early and Periodic Screening, Diagnostic, and Treatment Initiative

- **Early:** Assessing and identifying problems early
- **Periodic:** Checking children's health at periodic, age-appropriate intervals
- **Screening:** Providing physical, mental, developmental, dental, hearing, vision, and other screening tests to detect potential problems
- **Diagnostic:** Performing diagnostic tests to follow up when a risk is identified
- **Treatment:** Control, correct, or reduce health problems found (CMS, 2018c)

With this specific initiative each state must report findings annually to CMS. The purpose of quality improvement initiatives is to collect data, analyze it, and then decide what improvements need to be made to ensure the children are receiving quality healthcare services and are thriving (CMS, 2018d).

▶ Cost Sharing for CHIP

States may elect to impose limited enrollment fees, premiums, deductibles, coinsurance, and copayments for children enrolled in CHIP. Cost sharing is generally limited to 5% of a family's income and is prohibited for services such as well-baby and well-child visits (CMS, 2019). As of January 2017, there were 26 states charging monthly or quarterly premiums and 4 states charging annual enrollment fees for CHIP. Premium amounts vary by state and most states use an income-based sliding-fee scale (Brooks et al., 2017).

▶ Summary

The Children's Health Insurance Program provides healthcare coverage to those children who are not eligible for Medicaid. Each state sets its own eligibility guidelines and benefits. The program is funded jointly by the federal government and individual states. Since 1997 when the policy was implemented, the rate of uninsured children has decreased drastically (HHS, 2018b). The case studies in this chapter depict unique situations involving CHIP. Below are important terms to assist in analyzing this chapter's case studies.

Key Terms

Patient Protection and Affordable Care Act (ACA) is a healthcare law passed by Congress in 2010 during the administration of President Barack Obama.

Children's Health Insurance Program (CHIP) provides medical coverage for individuals under age 19 whose parents earn too much income to qualify for Medicaid but not enough to pay for private coverage.

Children's Health Insurance Program Reauthorization Act (CHIPRA) provides states with significant new funding, new programmatic options, and a range of new incentives for covering children through Medicaid and CHIP beginning in 2009.

Cost Sharing is the portion of healthcare expenses covered by insurance that individuals pay out of their own pocket.

Federal Poverty Level (FPL) is a measure of income used by the U.S. government to determine who is eligible for subsidies, programs, and benefits.

References

Brooks, T., Wagnerman, K., Artiga, S., Cornachione, E., & Ubri, P. (2017). *Medicaid and CHIP eligibility, enrollment, renewal, and cost sharing policies as of January 2017: Findings from a 50-state survey.* Kaiser Family Foundation. https://www.kff.org/report-section/medicaid-and-chip-eligibility-enrollment-renewal-and-cost-sharing-policies-as-of-january-2017-premiums-and-cost-sharing/

Casto, A. B., & Forrestal, E. (2015). *Principles of healthcare reimbursement* (5th ed.). Chicago, IL: AHIMA Press.

Centers for Medicare & Medicaid Services (CMS). (2018a). *Children's health care quality measures.* https://www.medicaid.gov/medicaid/quality-of-care/performance-measurement/child-core-set/index.html

Centers for Medicare & Medicaid Services (CMS). (2018b). *Children's Health Insurance Program.* https://www.medicaid.gov/CHIP/index.html

Centers for Medicare & Medicaid Services (CMS). (2018c). *Early and periodic screening, diagnostic, and treatment.* https://www.medicaid.gov/medicaid/benefits/epsdt/index.html

Centers for Medicare and Medicaid Services (CMS). (2018d). *Reports & evaluation.* https://www.medicaid.gov/chip/reports-and-evaluations/index.html

Centers for Medicare & Medicaid Services (CMS). (2019). *Cost sharing.* https://www.medicaid.gov/chip/cost-sharing/index.html

Department of Health and Human Services (HHS). (2018a). *The Children's Health Insurance Program.* https://www.healthcare.gov/medicaid-chip/childrens-health-insurance-program/

Department of Health and Human Services (HHS). (2018b). *2016 Child and adult health care quality measures.* https://data.medicaid.gov/Quality/2016-Child-and-Adult-Health-Care-Quality-Measures/vncf-b8xx

Kaiser Family Foundation. (2018). *Summary of the 2018 CHIP funding extension.* http://files.kff.org/attachment/Fact-Sheet-Summary-of-the-2018-CHIP-Funding-Extension

Shi, L., & Singh, D. A. (2017). *Essentials of the U.S. health care system* (4th ed.). Burlington, MA: Jones & Bartlett Learning.

🔍 CASE 9-1

Understanding the Children's Health Insurance Program (CHIP) in Today's Changing Marketplace

Kim Johnson, PMHNP-BC, FNP-C, RN

Children and pregnant women need well-care visits, vaccinations, and regular check-ups with primary care and specialist providers. With the changing insurance marketplace, parents have fewer options for providing their families with healthcare plans. Any family whose income is below the FPL is provided Medicaid to meet their children's healthcare needs; however, families who make more than the FPL may not qualify for Medicaid. Despite this, employees may not have access to company-subsidized family health insurance because businesses are having a hard time furnishing expensive healthcare plans for their employees.

The Children's Health Insurance Program (CHIP) provides a safety net for families who don't qualify for Medicaid. CHIP has been instrumental in the provision of resources for childcare since its inception in 1997. The value of CHIP is intensified for families with children who have chronic health conditions that require long-term treatment (Rosenbaum et al., 2017). Congress determines whether to federally fund CHIP; the funding extension debate occurs in Congress every few years and is a public concern for American families who need health care.

Medicaid, with state-assisted CHIP coverage, contributes to long-term positive outcomes in health, school performance, educational attainment, and economic success (Brooks et al., 2017). CHIP operates much like Medicaid by providing federal matching payments for program expenses for children's health care. Federal funds are provided to states at a higher rate than is paid for by traditional Medicaid plans to cover increasing healthcare expenses. The PPACA enhanced CHIP by offering special protections for out-of-pocket spending and to fill the gap of PPACA's "Family Glitch." The "Family Glitch" denies health insurance marketplace assistance for family coverage for parents who can afford employer coverage for themselves (Rosenbaum et al., 2017).

States can use their CHIP funds to expand Medicaid, operate their own CHIP programs, or combine the two approaches. By 2015 estimates, CHIP covered 8.4 million children and provided maternity coverage for approximately 370,000 women. As the population increases, so will the number of children and pregnant women who will require CHIP funds for their healthcare needs (Rosenbaum et al., 2017).

The Family Health Clinic is a place where children from birth to the age of 18 may obtain preventive healthcare services, well-care visits, vaccinations, and sick visits by licensed providers including MDs, nurse practitioners, nurses, lab technicians, and case workers. To fund the clinic, practice managers depend on Medicaid, which in this state is partially supported by CHIP. The Family Health Clinic is open 12 hours daily, 7 days a week and provides accessible, affordable, and coordinated care for families with children. The Family Health Clinic sees over 100 children per day. The clinic has operated for over 15 years in this capacity and has been able to support itself using a combination of Medicaid with CHIP assistance, private insurance reimbursement, and sliding-fee scales.

A family familiar with the clinic has 2 children ages 5 and 7. The mother and children of the family experienced emotional trauma when the father became addicted to cocaine. According to the mother, the father broke into the house one night, woke the kids, and held the mother at gunpoint, demanding money. After the father was arrested, it became apparent that the children were experiencing residual effects from the trauma, including nightmares with awakening, inability to go to the bathroom by themselves, and various somatic complaints. The mother was concerned about their ability to concentrate at school. She herself was struggling with the aftereffects of being held at gunpoint by a man she trusted. Compounding her problems were the financial losses from her husband's stealing and his insufficient contribution to the family's income. The mother made a minimal salary at her day job, which was classified as "part-time." Even though she picked up as many hours as she could, the company limited her to 24 hours per week to avoid having to provide her and her children with group health insurance. She had few options for after-school daycare because her family lived more than 3 hours away, impeding her ability to obtain work on a full-time basis. Because she made 100% of the FPL, the children weren't eligible for Medicaid. Once it became apparent the father would continue using drugs, and the effects of the trauma would be long-lasting, she went to the clinic to ask for help.

Nearly 9 of 10 children live in families with incomes at or below the FPL (KFF, 2018). As employer-sponsored coverage for children has declined over many years, Medicaid and CHIP have filled the gap for low- to moderate-income children (Whitener et al., 2016). Unfortunately, the Family Health Clinic does not provide child and adolescent psychiatry services. Indeed, there were only two psychiatric providers in the surrounding rural area available—a psychiatric nurse practitioner and a licensed counselor. The nurse practitioner could provide medication management if needed and could refer them to individual and family therapy; however, both providers only took private insurance and Medicaid. The clinic wanted to help them by providing free help; however, psychiatric treatment was out of the current physician's scope of practice. Further, the clinic could not take them free of charge.

Discussion Questions

1. How does the CHIP assist Medicaid in providing for child healthcare visits?
2. How does the PPACA influence CHIP Plan and Medicaid eligibility and coverage standards? Explain the PPACA's "Family Glitch."
3. What medical services does CHIP provide? Describe vulnerable populations where CHIP makes the most impact.
4. When employed in healthcare delivery organizations, how might you influence health policy and decision-making in your state for the provision of CHIP? How can you help influence policy decisions regarding CHIP as a citizen?

References

Artiga, S. & Ubri, P. (2017). *Key issues in Children's Health Coverage. Kaiser Family Foundation.* https://www.kff .org/medicaid/issue-brief/key-issues-in-childrens-health-coverage/

Brooks, T., Miskell, S., Artiga, S., Cornachione, E., & Gates, A. (2017). *Medicaid and CHIP eligibility, enrollment, renewal, and cost-sharing policies as of January 2016: Findings from a 50-state survey.* Kaiser Family Foundation. https://www.kff.org/medicaid/report/medicaid-and-chip-eligibility-enrollment -renewal-and-cost-sharing-policies-as-of-january-2016-findings-from-a-50-state-survey/ http://www.urban.org/sites/default/files/publication/90301/2017.4.26_lessons_from_partnerships _finalized_1.pdf

Kaiser Family Foundation (KFF). (2018). *Enhanced Federal Medical Assistance Percentage (FMAP) for CHIP.* https://www.kff.org/other/state-indicator/enhanced-federal-matching-rate-chip/?currentTimeframe =0&sortModel=%7B%22colId%22:%22Location%22,%22sort%22:%22asc%22%7D

Rosenbaum, S., Gunsalus, R., Rothenberg, S., & Schmucker, S. (2017). *Extending the Children's Health Insurance Program: High Stakes for Families and States.* The Commonwealth Fund. https://www .commonwealthfund.org/publications/issue-briefs/2017/sep/extending-childrens-health -insurance-program-high-stakes?redirect_source=/publications/issue-briefs/2017/sep /extending-chip-high-stakes-families-states

Whitener, K., Volk, J., Miskell, S., & Alker, J. (2016). *Children in the marketplace.* Georgetown University Health Policy Institute Center for Children & Families. https://ccf.georgetown.edu/wp-content/ uploads/2016/06/Kids-in-Marketplace-final-6-02.pdf

⌕ *CASE 9-2*

Innovative State Approaches to Children's Health

Lesley Clack, ScD

According to the CMS, 9.4 million children were enrolled in CHIP in 2017 (CMS, 2018). Many states use innovative approaches to improve the quality of pediatric care and preventive services (King et al., 2018). States are allowed to implement performance measurement incentives and improvement projects to promote children's access to preventive services. As such, 24 states have a performance measure or incentive plan in place for their Medicaid program (NASHP, 2016). Some of those specifically related to children or CHIP are detailed in **TABLE 9-2**.

Seventy percent of existing Medicaid pay-for-performance programs operate in managed care or primary care case management, with a focus on children, adolescent, women's health, and preventive services. The majority of state Medicaid directors said their pay-for-performance priority is on improving quality of care rather than reducing cost (NASHP, 2016).

Discussion Questions

1. Because all states have CHIP, how would a state benefit from choosing to implement a performance measure or improvement project?
2. How do children benefit from these mandates?
3. Why do you think only half of all states have implemented such projects? Should policymakers intervene and federally mandate states to have performance measures or improvement projects? Why or why not?

TABLE 9-2 Innovative State Approaches to Insuring Children

State	Program Description
Idaho	Idaho's Preventive Health Assistance (PHA) Program uses incentives that target Medicaid and CHIP beneficiaries to promote healthy behaviors and encourage parents to help children and adolescents adopt healthy lifestyle changes.
Tennessee	Tennessee adopted a pay-for-performance program that rewards improvement on Healthcare Effectiveness Data and Information Set (HEDIS) quality measures for pediatric preventive services.
Minnesota	Minnesota has statewide measures based on the state health reform law for both depression and mental health screening.
Oregon	Oregon requires mental, physical, and dental health assessments within 60 days for children in Department of Human Services (DHS) custody.
Maine	Maine offers primary care physician incentive payments for pediatric preventive health screenings.

References

Centers for Medicare and Medicaid Services. (CMS). (2018). *Children's Health Insurance Program (CHIP)*.
    https://www.medicaid.gov/chip/index.html
National Academy for State Health Policy (NASHP). (2016). *State strategies for promoting children's preventive
    services*. https://nashp.org/state-strategies-for-promoting-childrens-preventive-services/
King, A., Housberger, K., Hanlon, C., & NASHP Staff. (2018). *Case studies: Innovative state programs that
    promote children's health*. National Academy for State Health Policy (NASHP). https://nashp.org
    /case-studies-innovative-state-programs-that-promote-childrens-health/

🔍 CASE 9-3

The Jeffersons and CHIP: Are They Eligible?

Rachel Ellison, PhD

The Jefferson family made the move from Arizona to Colorado for a fresh beginning and
a new job opportunity for Mr. Jefferson. Mr. Jefferson's new job is a great opportunity, but
it does not come with health insurance. Mr. and Mrs. Jefferson have the daunting task of
finding the best healthcare coverage for their family. Because this is a new state they have
never lived in, they do not know about the government health programs that are offered in
Colorado.

They do know that Medicaid is available in Colorado and the federal government
funds it, but each state sets the funding amount, programs, and so on. They had Medicaid in
Arizona and had great coverage for all of their children, but they were not eligible for CHIP
because Mr. Jefferson's income was too high. They are interested to see if their children will
be eligible for CHIP in the state of Colorado.

To check their eligibility, they decide to go online and apply. They gather all of the
necessary information and begin the process. They know the application process takes
time, and the questions are very in-depth, so they are prepared to spend the afternoon
completing the application. When they begin the CHIP application, the first screen that pops
up contains the following general information:

All About CHIP

- The Children's Health Insurance Program (CHIP) was signed into law in 1997.
- It provides federal matching funds to states to provide health coverage to children
  in families with incomes too high to qualify for Medicaid but who can't afford private
  coverage (CMS, 2018).
- In some states, CHIP covers pregnant women.
- All providers do not accept patients covered by CHIP. Patients must obtain services from
  providers that are eligible for reimbursement through CHIP. Most CHIP programs have
  websites that tell you which providers are available.
- You can enroll in CHIP at any time. There is no open enrollment period.
- Teens are eligible for coverage until their 19th birthday.

What Services Does CHIP Cover?

All states cover comprehensive coverage, including:

- routine check-ups,
- immunizations,
- doctor visits,
- prescriptions,
- dental and vision care,

- inpatient and outpatient hospital care,
- laboratory and X-ray services, and
- emergency services.

States may cover other CHIP benefits. It's best to check with your individual state for covered benefits (HHS, 2018).

What Does CHIP Cost?
- Routine "well child" visits are free.
- Routine dental visits are free.
- There may be a copayment based on the type of service provided.

The costs are different from state to state, but you won't have to pay more than 5% of your family's income for the year (HHS, 2018).

The Jeffersons found this information to be very helpful. They felt more informed and educated about CHIP, what it offers, who is eligible, and the overall cost. They realize that each state is very different when it comes to the benefits of CHIP, just like Medicaid. Just because the children were not eligible for CHIP or any publicly funded government program in Arizona doesn't mean it will be the same situation for them in Colorado.

After submitting the application, the Jeffersons decided to research other health insurance plans as a backup in case the family was not eligible for CHIP. After about a month, the Jeffersons received an email confirming that the four children were eligible for CHIP. Mr. and Mrs. Jefferson were not eligible for Colorado Medicaid because their combined household income was too high, but they were eligible for coverage through the state's health insurance marketplace. The Jeffersons are very happy that the kids will be receiving great healthcare coverage. They are pleased that the move to Colorado has started out so well, because they knew obtaining quality health insurance coverage was a priority.

Discussion Questions
1. Who funds the Children's Health Insurance Program?
2. Why does each state have different benefits?
3. If the Jefferson's were not eligible for CHIP what other avenue could they take for health insurance coverage?

References
Department of Health and Human Services (HHS). (2018). *The Children's Health Insurance Program.*
    https://www.healthcare.gov/medicaid-chip/childrens-health-insurance-program/
Centers for Medicare & Medicaid Services (CMS). (2018). *Program history.* https://www.medicaid.gov
    /about-us/program-history/index.html

SECTION 4
Access to Care

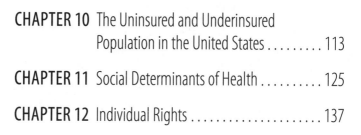

CHAPTER 10

The Uninsured and Underinsured Population in the United States

Lesley Clack, ScD

▶ Introduction

The uninsured and underinsured population in the United States is vast. However, the federal government has provisions in place to ensure that these underserved populations have access to health services. The Patient Protection and Affordable Care Act (PPACA) and other legislations have helped to reduce this population, with nearly 20 million Americans gaining coverage as a result of the PPACA. These vulnerable populations have many obstacles to overcome.

▶ The Uninsured

The term *uninsured* refers to those individuals who do not have public or private health insurance coverage (Shi & Singh, 2015). The majority of the uninsured are low-income individuals. In 2016, 45% of uninsured adults cited the cost of coverage as their main reason for not having insurance (KFF, 2017).

Historically, a lack of access to affordable private insurance and gaps in the public insurance system left millions without insurance. The government sought to reduce the number of uninsured through the passage of the PPACA, which led to expanded coverage for millions of previously uninsured Americans through the establishment of Health Insurance Exchanges and expansion of Medicaid in some states. According to the Kaiser Family Foundation, since passage of the PPACA, the number of uninsured nonelderly Americans decreased from 44 million in 2013 to less than 28 million at the end of 2016 (KFF, 2017).

▶ The Underinsured

According to a Commonwealth Fund report, 28% of working age adults in the United States who had health insurance in 2016 were underinsured, an increase from 23% in 2014. Underinsured refers to those individuals who have high deductibles and high out-of-pocket expenses relative to their income (The Commonwealth Fund, 2017). For individuals with low income, this includes those who spend 5% of their income or more on health care. For individuals with higher income, this includes those who spend 10% of their income or more on health care. Being underinsured is a significant issue; in 2016, 52% of the underinsured had medical debt problems, and 45% went without needed health care because of cost (The Commonwealth Fund, 2017).

▶ Issues Faced by the Uninsured and Underinsured

The consequences of being uninsured and underinsured are well known. The uninsured and underinsured face inequities in access to care, avoidable mortality, poor quality care, and financial burdens (Davis, 2007). In addition, the Institute of Medicine (IOM) estimates that 18,000 lives are lost each year due to gaps in health insurance coverage (IOM, 2003). While the uninsured and underinsured are less likely to seek care, when they do require assistance, they are more likely to receive poorer quality and less coordinated care due to the lack of a primary care provider. Uninsured individuals are twice as likely to use the emergency room to manage chronic conditions than individuals who are insured (Collins et al., 2006).

▶ Provisions for Underserved Populations

The Health Resources and Services Administration (HRSA) has developed criteria for designated shortage areas by determining whether a geographic area, population group, or facility is considered to be a Health Professional Shortage Area (HPSA) or a Medically Underserved Area or Population (MUA or MUP). HPSAs have a shortage of either primary medical care, dental care, or mental health providers and may be urban or rural areas. MUAs may consist of an entire county or group of counties where residents have a shortage of health services. MUPs are groups of individuals who face economic or cultural barriers to accessing healthcare (HHS, 2018).

Community Health Centers (CHCs) provide essential access to comprehensive primary care in underserved communities and are a key component of our healthcare system. In 2016, CHCs served 25.9 million patients at more than 10,400 urban and rural locations; 23% of those were uninsured patients (Rosenbaum et al., 2018). CHCs, also known as federally qualified health centers (FQHCs), were established through Section 330 of the Public Health Service Act (KFF, 2012). According to U.S. Code Title 42, Section 254b, in order to qualify as a FQHC facilities must meet the following four requirements:

1. location in or service to MUAs/MUPs,
2. provision of comprehensive primary health care in accordance with federal guidelines,
3. prospective adjustment of changes in accordance with patients' ability to pay, and
4. governance by a board of directors, a majority of whose members must be patients of the health center (GPO, 2018).

FQHCs that meet these requirements are eligible for federal Section 330 grants to support care for the uninsured. In 2010, there were 1,124 FQHCs operating in every state, in more than 8,100 locations (KFF, 2012).

Another type of facility created to meet the needs of MUAs are critical access hospitals (CAHs). CAHs, which are hospitals of 25 beds or fewer, were created by Congress under the Balanced Budget Act of 1997. There are currently 1,343 CAHs (out of 5,000 hospitals in the United States) (Gaston & Walker, 2018).

▶ Summary

The inequities of the uninsured and underinsured are astounding. Many lives are lost each year due to these injustices (i.e., specifically access to adequate healthcare services), which are causes for concern in the United States. Health policies, such as the PPACA and other programs including CHCs and FQHCs, have helped to address these issues over the years. Stakeholders, including hospitals, policymakers, and key players, must come together to combat the issue of providing quality care to the uninsured and underinsured. Access to quality healthcare services is slowly improving for the uninsured and underinsured population, but more policies and regulations are needed. The only way this will happen successfully is for more action to take place.

Key Terms

Federally Qualified Health Center (FQHC) provides essential access to comprehensive primary care in underserved communities (MUAs) and are a key component of our healthcare system.

Health Professional Shortage Area (HPSA) has a shortage of either primary medical care, dental care, or mental health providers, and may be in urban or rural areas.

Medically Underserved Area (MUA) constitutes an entire county or group of counties where residents have a shortage of health services.

Underinsured Population are made up of citizens who have inadequate healthcare coverage.

Uninsured Population are citizens who lack health insurance coverage.

Vulnerable Population are the economically disadvantaged, racial and ethnic minorities, the uninsured, low-income children, the elderly, the homeless, those with human immunodeficiency virus (HIV), and those with other chronic health conditions, including severe mental illness.

References

Collins, S. R., Davis, K., Doty, M. M., Kriss, J. L., & Holmgren, A. L. (2006). *Gaps in health insurance coverage: An all-American problem.* New York: Commonwealth Fund.

Davis, K. (2007). Uninsured in America: Problems & possible solutions. *BMJ, 334*(758), 346–348.

Gaston, S. M., & Walker, B. W. (2018). Critical access hospitals: Meeting underserved community needs. *Nursing2018, 48*(5), 51–54.

Institute of Medicine (IOM). (2003). *Committee on the consequences of uninsurance. Hidden costs, value lost: Uninsurance in America.* Washington, DC: National Academies Press.

Kaiser Family Foundation (KFF). (2012). *Medicaid and CHCs: The relationship between coverage for adults and primary care capacity in medically underserved communities.* https://www.kff.org /health-reform/issue-brief/medicaid-and-community-health-centers-the-relationship/

Kaiser Family Foundation (KFF). (2017). *Key facts about the uninsured population.* https://www.kff .org/uninsured/fact-sheet/key-facts-about-the-uninsured-population/

Rosenbaum, S., Tolbert, J., Sharac, J., Shin, P., Gunsalus, R., & Zur, J. (2018). *Community health centers: Growing importance in a changing health care system.* Henry J Kaiser Family Foundation (KFF). https://www.kff.org/medicaid/issue-brief/community-health-centers-growing -importance-in-a-changing-health-care-system/

Shi, L., & Singh, D. A., (2015). *Delivering health care in America: A systems approach.* Burlington, MA: Jones & Bartlett Learning.

The Commonwealth Fund. (2017). *Underinsured rate increased sharply in 2016: More than two of five marketplace enrollees and a quarter of people with employer health insurance plans are now underinsured.* https://www.commonwealthfund.org/press-release/2017/underinsured-rate -increased-sharply-2016-more-two-five-marketplace-enrollees-and

US Department of Health and Human Services (HHS). (2018). *HRSA data warehouse.* https:// datawarehouse.hrsa.gov/topics/shortageareas.aspx

U.S. Government Publishing Office (GPO). (2018). 42 U.S.C. 254B-health centers. https:// www.gpo.gov/fdsys/granule/USCODE-2010-title42/USCODE-2010-title42-chap6A -subchapII-partD-subparti-sec254b

🔎 CASE 10-1

Ever-Changing Guidelines for Breast Cancer Screening: Utilizing Mobile Mammography Outreach in Underinsured Women

Cathy Coleman, DNP, MSN, PHN, CNL, CPHQ, OCN & Mary Mcginty, RT(R) (M) (ARRT)

In 2018, 268,670 people will be diagnosed with invasive breast cancer in the United States; a majority will be women, and the estimated deaths include 41,000 women and 480 men (American Cancer Society, 2018). Black women are more likely to die from the disease, followed by white, American Indian, Alaska Native, and Hispanic or Pacific Islander women (American Cancer Society, 2018; Coleman, 2017). Breast cancer is second only to lung cancer as a major cause of cancer deaths in women, and a majority of the risk for breast cancer occurs with increasing age (American Cancer Society, 2018). However, most findings in the breast are not breast cancer, which can be reassuring to individuals who commonly associate the word "cancer" with any new lump or symptom that is detected through breast self-examination or in a routine clinical breast exam by a licensed healthcare provider. The purpose of screening is to identify abnormalities before signs or symptoms become visible (i.e., changes in the nipple or skin of the breast) or palpable (i.e., a thickening or lump can be felt by touch in the breast tissue or axillae).

Because the hallmark of curable breast cancer is finding a tumor that is small (preferably less than 15 millimeters), mammography, or x-rays of the breast, are used to identify preclinical or nonpalpable findings in healthy women without symptoms (Coleman, 2017). This is key because a breast cancer tumor can grow at various rates (often up to 6 years before it can be felt) depending upon the type of tumor and its level of aggressiveness. Therefore, in the mid-1970s and 1980s, esteemed radiologists and researchers around the world perfected the art of screening with periodic, comparative mammography to monitor breast tissue over time and find tiny tumors that were most likely limited to the breast. These tumors, if diagnosed as malignant, are less likely to spread or "metastasize" to distant sites such as the lung, bone, or brain, which can lead to death (Coleman, 2017). Vigorous global studies in large populations of women proved that routine screening with mammography could reduce mortality (Arleo et al., 2017). Screening and early detection exams, known as secondary prevention methods, have been used because there remains no means of primary prevention.

The controversies surrounding breast cancer screening with mammography were based not on the proven value of finding curable breast cancer 85 to 90% of the time, but at what age to begin and stop screening in asymptomatic women, as well as the frequency of exams (Coleman, 2017). The recommendations are different for women at average risk of getting the disease (most women over 40 years of age) and women at higher than average risk of developing it based on their personal history (the 5 to 10% affected by familial genetic predisposition) (Arleo et al., 2017; Monticciolo et al., 2018). The interval between regular mammography exams is particularly crucial because tumors grow at different rates. The goal is to screen frequently enough to obtain an acceptable rate of cancer detection without allowing a cancer that might be present to go undetected. The most hotly contested issue is beginning screening at 40 years of age. A variety of researchers have interpreted the data differently, which has influenced government and insurance carrier decisions to fund or not fund screening in some subgroups based on individual risk factors or age (Arleo et al., 2017).

In the United States, over the past 3 decades, several organizations (see **TABLE 10-1**) including nonprofit cancer control agencies (American Cancer Society), the federal

TABLE 10-1 Resource Organizations—Breast Cancer Screening

Organization	Website
Agency for Healthcare Research and Quality	https://www.ahrq.gov/research/findings/nhqrdr/nhqdr16/index.html
American Cancer Society	https://www.cancer.org/cancer/breast-cancer.html
American College of Radiology	https://www.acraccreditation.org/accredited-facility-search https://www.acraccreditation.org/Breast-Imaging-Center-of-Excellence
Centers for Disease Control and Prevention National Breast and Cervical Cancer Early Detection Program	https://www.cdc.gov/cancer/nbccedp https://www.cdc.gov/cancer/nbccedp/pdf/breastcanceractionguide.pdf
Centers for Medicare & Medicaid Services	https://ecqi.healthit.gov/ecqm/measures/cms125v6
International Cancer Control Partnership	http://www.iccp-portal.org http://www.iccp-portal.org/resources-search?f%5B0%5D=search_api_aggregation_5%3A503
Mammography Quality Standards Act	http://www.fda.gov/Radiation-EmittingProducts/MammographyQualityStandardsActandProgram
National Cancer Institute	https://www.cancer.gov/types/breast https://www.cancer.gov/publications/dictionaries/cancer-terms
National Committee for Quality Assurance	http://www.ncqa.org/report-cards/health-plans/state-of-health-care-quality/2017-table-of-contents/breast-cancer
National Comprehensive Cancer Network	https://www.nccn.org https://www.nccn.org/professionals/physician_gls/default.aspx#detection
National Quality Forum	http://www.qualityforum.org/Patient_Passport.aspx http://www.qualityforum.org/Guidance_to_Improve_Shared_Decision_Making.aspx

Organization	Website
National Quality Strategy	https://www.ahrq.gov/workingforquality/about/index.html
Think Cultural Health	https://www.thinkculturalhealth.hhs.gov/
Union for International Cancer Control	http://www.uicc.org/sites/main/files/atoms/files/WCLS2016_Report_FA.pdf
U.S. Department of Health & Human Services	https://www.healthypeople.gov/2020/topics-objectives/topic/Access-to-Health-Services

government (Centers for Disease Control and Prevention), insurance payers (Centers for Medicare & Medicaid Services), and professional societies (American College of Radiology) have debated the costs, risks, and benefits of screening in both individuals and populations. Three major sets of guidelines and policies were recommended to the American public, policy makers, insurance companies, and physician groups, which led to mixed messages and confusion regarding who to believe about the benefits versus risks, who should pay for screening and follow up tests, and which set of guidelines to follow. However, a recent analysis revealed that starting annual screening at age 40 prevents most deaths (Arleo et al., 2017). Campaigns to educate women about the benefits and risks associated with breast cancer screening have become commonplace.

Common Barriers Lead to a MammoVan

In addition to confusion about recommended screening guidelines, many subgroups of women at average or high risk also face other barriers to screening (Monticciolo et al., 2018). Some of the most detrimental barriers include a lack of insurance at diagnosis and socioeconomic factors, such as living in low-income, inner-city areas and in neighborhoods without breast cancer screening centers (Hsu et al., 2017). Based on this recurring trend, a safety-net hospital in one urban city was able to receive funding in 2005 for a mobile mammography van with outreach to approximately 11 underserved neighborhoods and community health clinics. Many of the women served had difficulty obtaining transportation to and from the central breast center, lacked a personal healthcare provider they could trust, or had affiliations with organizations that lacked cultural and linguistic sensitivity in treating clients. Other factors included fear of cancer, pain or discomfort with the procedure, competing priorities that outweighed the desire for preventive services, or a general lack of awareness about the importance of screening. Despite controversies and questions regarding the value and frequency of screening, the breast center MammoVan team was able to create trusting and reliable relationships with local neighborhood community health clinics, promote shared decision-making between clinicians and clients, and recruit and maintain regular screening schedules year after year. The efforts paid off. Screenings for asymptomatic women increased from 233 patients in 2010 to 1,600 in 2017. This resulted in 10 screen-detected (i.e., small), curable cancers being identified in 2017 in this underserved, relatively poor, and underinsured population (McGinty, personal communication, May 9, 2018). Multilingual, layperson patient navigators also supported success.

In a recent integrative review, Truglio-Londrigan and Slyer (2018) found that barriers to shared decision-making are reduced when providers and patients work together within a specific healthcare context. They suggest that organizational models (such as the mobile mammography van) can facilitate access to care and promote teamwork and collaboration while reducing fragmentation. With ongoing advocacy and consciously chosen policies that promote equality in insurance coverage and access to quality screening services, positive trends in survival are likely to prevail (Milstead & Short, 2019).

Discussion Questions

1. Lack of insurance at the time of breast cancer diagnosis is a critical barrier that affects access to care and survival. List two other factors that may impact uninsured or underinsured women related to breast cancer screening.
2. Explain how advocacy and health policy can impact breast cancer screening in low-income women.
3. Locate the Mammography Quality Standards Act (MQSA) resource in Table 10-1 and follow the link to learn about it. Please describe the impact of the MQSA on consumers.
4. Find an accredited mammography facility near you by looking in Table 10-1 and searching one of the American College of Radiology sites.

References

American Cancer Society. (2018). *Cancer facts & figures 2018*. https://www.cancer.org/content/dam/cancer-org/research/cancer-facts-and-statistics/annual-cancer-facts-and-figures/2018/cancer-facts-and-figures-2018.pdf

American Society of Clinical Oncology. (2017). The state of cancer care in America 2017: A report by the American Society of Clinical Oncology. *Journal of Oncology Practice, 13*(4), 256–260.

Arleo, E. K., Hendrick, R. E., Helvie, M. A., & Sickles, E. A. (2017). Comparison of recommendations for screening mammography using CISNET models. *Cancer, 123*(19), 3673–3680.

Coleman, C. (2017). Early detection and screening for breast cancer. *Seminars in Oncology Nursing, 33*(2), 141–155.

Hewitt, M. E., & Simone, J. V. (eds.). (1999). *Ensuring quality cancer care*. Institute of Medicine. https://www.nap.edu/download/6467#

Hsu, C. D., Wang, X., Habif, D. V., Ma, C. X., & Johnson, K. J. (2017). Breast cancer stage variation and survival in association with insurance status and sociodemographic factors in U.S. women 18–64 years old. *Cancer, 123*(16), 3125–3131.

Milstead, J. A., & Short, N. M. (2019). *Health policy and politics—A nurse's guide* (6th ed.). Burlington, MA: Jones & Bartlett Learning.

Monticciolo, D. L., Newell, M. S., Moy, L., Niell, B., Monsees, B., & Sickles, E. A. (2018). Breast cancer screening in women at higher-than-average risk: Recommendations from the ACR. *Journal of the American College of Radiology, 15*, 408–415.

Truglio-Londrigan, M., & Slyer, J. T. (2018). Shared decision-making for nursing practice: An integrative review. *The Open Nursing Journal, 12*, 1–14.

$\mathcal{P}$ CASE 10-2

Collaboration for Access: How States Maximize Federal Resources

Gregory A. Cline, PhD & Raymond J. Higbea, PhD

Background

The story of how government policy has responded to issues of access is a textbook example of incrementalist theories of policy change, meaning that the government has typically addressed the access problem through small policy changes over time. Two approaches were taken with near simultaneity: one approach was to develop infrastructure, such as clinics for the uninsured/underserved. The other approach was to entice providers to practice in underserved areas (either at the clinics or as independent practitioners— see **FIGURE 10-1**).

Alongside these two policy approaches was a separate, but closely linked, process to develop a common definition of underserved populations as defined by geographic location (see **FIGURE 10-2**).

In the initial stages of the government focusing on policies related to access, the policy activity was confined almost wholly within the Health Resources and Services Administration (HRSA) located within the Department of Health and Human Services (DHHS). Government efforts to address these two frames for defining the access problem (barriers defined by geography and ethnicity) began in 1965 with the first federal funding for Community Health Centers (CHCs). The policy decision authorizing the funding of CHCs was taken in the executive branch through the interpretation of administrative rules governing the Office of Economic Opportunity (OEO).

This decision led to the first attempts to define Health Professional Shortage Areas (HPSAs) and then define the operationalization of CHCs. The success of these federally funded health centers in increasing access to underserved, uninsured adults led to steady increases in funding, the founding of more centers, and attempts to better define areas with constrained access. In the 1980s, an expansion of federal policy addressing access problems by geography occurred by the creation of the Office of Rural Health Policy (ORHP) within HRSA. This group focused on rural hospitals—formally defined as critical access hospitals (CAHs)—and the networks of rural healthcare providers necessary for the long-term sustainability of healthcare delivery in rural communities.

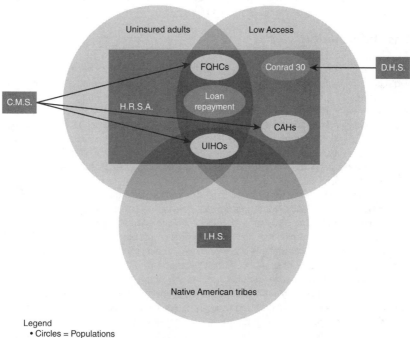

Legend
  • Circles = Populations
  • Rectangles = Federal government agencies
  • Light gray ovals = Nonprofit healthcare organizations
  • Dark gray ovals = Federal programs

FIGURE 10-1 Federal Programming for Increasing Access: Populations, Agencies, Organizations

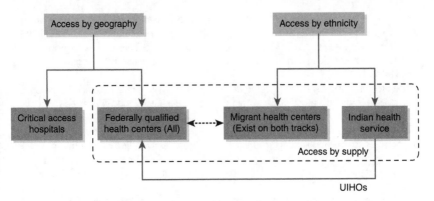

FIGURE 10-2 Federal Programming for Increasing Access: Geography, Ethnicity & Supply

The story of healthcare workforce policy addressing access involving four separate areas of the federal government—the Health Resources and Services Administration, Centers for Medicare and Medicaid Services, the Department of Homeland Security, and the Indian Health Service—appears disjointed and awkward when viewed from the federal level. Although at the state level, the appearance is largely opposite. The healthcare workforce programs supported by these areas in the federal government are normally housed within one state agency responsible for health, often within one subunit of the agency. This approach for coordination at the state level produces coordinated and "seamless" policy implementation across communities receiving supports.

Case Information

The Department of Health and Human Services in the state has placed the coordination of federal programs and funding streams for healthcare in the Bureau of Health Policy and Legislation. In addition to federal funds, two decades prior, the Superior state legislature decided to provide supplemental funding for federal loan repayment entitled the State Loan Repayment Program (SLRP). Around the same time as the creation of the SLRP, the state legislature decided to fund 10 additional safety net clinics—eight qualified as CHCs and the two others attended to underserved populations. Lastly, the state legislature also funds the State Office of Rural Health (SORH) to augment federal supports to better coordinate rural health resources statewide including support for rural Critical Access Hospitals and Certified Rural Health Clinics.

Elizabeth Paisley is the administrator tasked with coordinating the use and pass-through of these funds. Not surprisingly, Ms. Paisley found that ensuring that communities produce smooth, seamless delivery of healthcare services from the apparent chaos of federal programming required her to master not just program management but also coordinate efforts with multiple agency partners, frequently assess the potential effects of future changes, and maintain a close working relationship with the healthcare committees in both chambers of the state legislature.

Ms. Paisley discovered that federal agencies regularly implement small changes to ongoing programs and occasionally legislation is passed by Congress that introduces both large and small programmatic changes. She knows that staying on top of both sources of policy change, while always remaining flexible in how to best respond, is an ongoing process. Only through such ongoing attention and flexibility can she maximize the effectiveness of coordinated federal programming delivered to her state's communities. This attention begins with her partners in coordination—the Superior Primary Care Association (SPCA), the statewide association for all HRSA-funded clinics, and the Superior Center for Rural Health (SCRH), the statewide representative for all rural hospitals. Formal coordination with partners occurs quarterly, at a minimum, in regularly scheduled workforce meetings. Informal coordination occurs much more frequently, using e-mail and phone.

Ms. Paisley has, over the past several years, coordinated and overseen multiple state-level policy changes to maximize the positive impact of all resources in a changing policy environment. These policy changes included altering the mix of funding sources for SLRP, removal of state fees for physicians that are in the United States on a visa, and moving qualifying primary care provider applicants on a visa to a separate visa waiver program enacted under the federal Department of Health and Human Services (HHS). She also led the effort to promote efficiency through the removal of bureaucratic barriers. These included the elimination of her department as the pass-through of ORHP funds to SCRH, moving to a three-share funding model for SLRP—now each provider contract is funded by a mix of federal, state, and facility money. Lastly, with the efficiencies gained within her office, she brought the HPSA designation process back to her staff, saving the expense of the external contractor that had performed this function.

Discussion Questions

1. Within what political context might we anticipate federal policy change to alter the level of match funding that states are required to provide for uninsured and underinsured programs?
2. Why do you think Lara Paisley lobbied to remove the state fees for physicians on a visa to address uninsured and underinsured concerns?
3. Which of the uninsured and underinsured policy changes by the Superior legislature or Lara Paisley's office required a preexisting context of close collaboration, both with multiple agencies and across political parties?

⌕ CASE 10-3

The Uninsured Homeless Population

Rachel Ellison, PhD

For a variety of reasons, such as the warmer climate, the state of Florida has a large homeless population. Sunset Hospital is located in Palms, Florida, one of those warmer climate cities. Sunset is a nonprofit hospital that serves a large percentage of the indigent and homeless population in the area. Because they are a nonprofit hospital, they are required by the government to provide charity care, and they also provide many services to the community and surrounding areas.

Across the street from Sunset Hospital is a homeless shelter known as "Tent City." The tents are set up on plywood boards that are raised up off of the ground to ensure the tents will not be infested with bugs or get flooded by rain. The residents of Tent City are well taken care of and enjoy the amenities of the shelter, such as help with job placements, food, warm showers, and assistance with applying for disability and Medicaid. The shelter is funded by a nonprofit organization and is operated mostly by volunteers. One other major benefit of Tent City is having Sunset Hospital and physician offices right next door. Some would think this would be a perk to the people living at Tent City, but many of the residents do not utilize the healthcare services.

Homeless and indigent people do not utilize healthcare services and forgo treatment because of the lack of empathy and the discrimination they feel they receive (Wen et al., 2007). According to the U.S. Department of Housing and Urban Development's 2018 Annual Homeless Assessment Report (AHAR) to Congress, 553,000 people were homeless in the United States in 2018. Most homeless people do not have access to healthcare services.

Some states and communities have programs where the homeless population do have access and can utilize healthcare services, but they often refuse until they are too ill and don't have a choice. Homeless people's attitudes toward healthcare services and healthcare workers are sometimes shaped based on previous interactions (Wen et al., 2007). This is another reason the homeless population may stay away from obtaining care after receiving it the first time. When this is the case, it drives up the cost of healthcare, because tertiary care is much more expensive than primary care. When patients wait to get care until they are very ill, the cost to treat them is financially very high.

Recently, a specific case rocked Sunset Hospital. A 55-year-old female resident of Tent City was brought into the hospital via ambulance because she lost consciousness at the shelter. She had been ill for quite some time but had taken a turn for the worse. The homeless and indigent population of Palms, Florida, are eligible for the community health program. Many go to the Health Department for medical, dental, and behavioral treatment. Because of the high demand for care in the area, the resident could not get an appointment for 2 months. She refused to go to the hospital across the street from the shelter because 1) she didn't have health insurance, and 2) she didn't want to be discriminated against because she was homeless.

Once the resident was stabilized and all tests had been performed, the results showed that she had stage IV lung cancer that had metastasized to her liver and kidneys. She was told by the oncologist that there was nothing that could be done. There were no treatment options for her, and she was told she had a few months to live. Because the patient was so ill, her application for Social Security Disability was quickly submitted, which would get her approved for Medicaid. This would allow her to be moved to a healthcare facility where she would spend the rest of her life.

The resident could have gone to the hospital to get care before her disease became terminal. Even though there was a hospital right across the street, she could not seek treatment. She did what she was supposed to do by setting up an appointment at the health department, but it was too late. The cancer had spread and became terminal.

The homeless population run into many barriers when accessing healthcare services. Most do not have health insurance; therefore, their benefits are limited. If they have insurance or are enrolled in a community health program, they tend to forgo treatment because of the discrimination and unwelcoming behavior that is often displayed by health providers (Rosenbaum & Zuvekas, 2006).

Discussion Questions

1. Read the article by Wen, Hudak, and Hwang (see references below). Put yourself in the homeless person's shoes. Would you seek out healthcare treatment? Explain your answer with facts from the article.
2. Why do you think health providers discriminate against homeless, uninsured, and underinsured people? Explain.
3. Research health programs and health policies in your state that protect the uninsured and underinsured populations. How easy or difficult do you think it would be to apply for insurance without a permanent address?

References

Rosenbaum, S., & Zuvekas, A. (2006). Healthcare use by homeless persons: Implications for public policy. *Health Services Research, 34*(6): 1303–1305.

Wen, C., Hudak, P., & Hwang, S. (2007). Homeless people's perceptions of welcomeness and unwelcomeness in healthcare encounters. *Journal of General Internal Medicine, 22*(7), 1011–1017.

CHAPTER 11
Social Determinants of Health

Lesley Clack, ScD

▶ Introduction

Addressing the social determinants of health (SDOH) is a goal identified by Healthy People 2020 to "create social and physical environments that promote good health for all" (HHS, 2010). The World Health Organization (WHO) further defines SDOH as "the conditions in which people are born, grow, work, live and age, and the wider set of forces and systems shaping the conditions of daily life" (WHO, 2018). This refers to forces and systems, such as economic policies and systems, social norms, social policies, and political systems (WHO, 2018). The term *SDOH* refers to the conditions that affect an individual's health and health outcomes and the availability of resources that can enhance his or her health state (HHS, 2010). Determinants of health can be classified as either social or physical, as illustrated in the examples listed in **BOXES 11-1** and **11-2**.

A framework for addressing SDOH was developed by Healthy People 2020. This framework identifies five key areas of determinants: Economic Stability, Education, Social and Community Context, Health and Health Care, and Neighborhood and Built Environment (HHS, 2010). The key issues of each of the five determinant areas are listed in **TABLE 11-1**.

Economic Stability

Economic stability/instability is a key component of the SDOH framework. Unemployment, food insecurity, housing insecurity, and poverty are all indicators of economic instability. Employment is directly correlated with a person's health. When the rate of unemployment increases, illness and premature death also increase (Kushel et al., 2006). Unemployed adults are more likely to delay or not receive

---

BOX 11-1   Examples of Social Determinants

Availability of resources to meet daily needs
Access to educational, economic, and job opportunities
Access to healthcare services
Quality of education and job training
Availability of community-based resources in support of community living
Transportation options
Public safety
Social support
Social norms and attitudes
Exposure to crime, violence, and social disorder
Socioeconomic conditions
Residential segregation
Language/literacy
Access to mass media and emerging technologies
Culture

Source: Overview, Access to Health Services, Healthy People 2020. Washington, DC: U.S. Department of Health and Human Services, Office of Disease Prevention and Health Promotion. Available from https://www.healthypeople.gov/2020/topics -objectives/topic/Access-to-Health-Services

---

BOX 11-2   Examples of Physical Determinants

Natural environment, such as green space or weather
Built environment, such as buildings, sidewalks, bike lanes, and roads
Worksites, schools, and recreational settings
Housing and community design
Exposure to toxic substances and other physical hazards
Physical barriers, especially for people with disabilities
Aesthetic elements, such as good lighting, trees, and benches

Source: Overview, Access to Health Services, Healthy People 2020. Washington, DC: U.S. Department of Health and Human Services, Office of Disease Prevention and Health Promotion. Available from https://www.healthypeople.gov/2020/topics -objectives/topic/Access-to-Health-Services

---

needed medical care when compared with employed adults (WHO, 2018). The association between poor health and unemployment has been well recognized (Marmot & Wilkinson, 2006; Paul et al., 2005. Research has shown that chronic disease, mental health, and premature mortality are higher in unemployed individuals (Paul et al., 2005). In addition, research has shown that unemployment is associated with unhealthy behaviors, such as increased alcohol and tobacco use and decreased physical activity (Dooley et al., 1992; Lee et al., 1991).

Where a person lives and works can also affect health outcomes. Housing insecurity, which is linked to economic instability, is associated with poorer health outcomes (Kushel et al., 2006). Approximately 11.4 million of all U.S. households paid more than half of their income for housing in 2014 (JCHS, 2016). This significant

TABLE 11-1 Key Issues within the Five Determinant Areas

Economic stability	Employment Food insecurity Housing instability Poverty
Education	Early childhood education and development Enrollment in higher education High school graduation Language and literacy
Social and community context	Civic participation Discrimination Incarceration Social cohesion
Health and health care	Access to health care Access to primary care Healthy literacy
Neighborhood and built environment	Access to foods that support healthy eating patterns Crime and violence Environmental conditions Quality of housing

Source: Overview, Social Determinants of Health, Healthy People 2020. Washington, DC: U.S. Department of Health and Human Services, Office of Disease Prevention and Health Promotion. Available from https://www.healthypeople.gov/2020/topics-objectives/topic/Access-to-Health-Services

financial burden can result in serious health consequences and can lead to increased risk of illness and early mortality (RWJF, 2009). Housing insecurity has been linked with poor mental health, problems sleeping, increased risk for high blood pressure, respiratory issues, and exposure to infectious disease (Cardoso et al., 2004).

Another indicator of health is food insecurity, which is an important indicator of economic instability. Most adults who experience food insecurity report going hungry due to not having enough money for food and not eating at all over the course of an entire day (Coleman-Jensen et al., 2017). A healthy diet can result in positive health outcomes, and inability to access healthy foods can lead to health problems. Food insecurity has been shown to increase consumption of foods high in fat that can lead to weight gain, poor physical health, chronic disease, and healthy risk behaviors (Jyoti et al., 2005; Vozoris & Tarasuk, 2003).

Household income, in terms of poverty, is another key issue of economic instability. Low income and the poverty level are strongly correlated with poor health. Individuals with lower incomes are commonly less healthy than individuals with greater means (WHO, 2018). In addition, individuals with social, economic, and environmental disadvantages often report poorer health statuses and disease risk factors (Meyer et al., 2013). Research has shown that people with lower incomes are more likely to engage in risky health behaviors, such as drinking, smoking, eating unhealthy foods, and lower levels of physical activity (NCIOM, 2009). Adults in poverty are more likely to have chronic disease, such as diabetes, heart disease, or other chronic illnesses that limit physical activity (NCIOM, 2009).

Education

Another key determinant in the SDOH framework is education. As defined by Healthy People 2020, the education domain encompasses individual factors such as high school graduation, enrollment in higher education, language and literacy, and early childhood education and development (HHS, 2010). Education is a strong predictor of quality of life, because education produces benefits that later predispose individuals to better health outcomes (Zimmerman et al., 2015). Individuals with low education levels are at greater risk for poor health, higher levels of stress, and lower self-confidence (WHO, 2018). In addition, researchers have found dramatic differences in morbidity and mortality related to education levels (WHO, 2008). Educational attainment affects an individual's ability to achieve positive health outcomes due to a variety of factors such as soft skills, hard skills, and health literacy. Health literacy refers to the ability of patients to understand their health needs, read and follow instructions, advocate for themselves and family members, and communicate effectively with healthcare providers (Zimmerman et al., 2015).

Research has shown that individuals with lower health literacy have poorer health-related knowledge and comprehension, a lower ability to demonstrate taking medications properly, and a lower ability to interpret medication labels and health messages. In addition, individuals with lower health literacy also have increased hospitalizations and utilization of the emergency room for care and decreased use of preventive care (Berkman et al., 2011). Adults with higher education levels are less likely to engage in risky health behaviors, such as smoking and drinking, and more likely to have healthy behaviors regarding diet and exercise. Education provides individuals with the opportunity to learn more about health and health risks, while increasing their health literacy, which can lead to positive health outcomes (Zimmerman et al., 2015).

Social and Community Context

Social and community context is another key determinant in the SDOH framework; it refers to social cohesion, civic participation, discrimination, and incarceration (HHS, 2010). Social cohesion refers to the strength of relationships among members of a community, and an indicator of social cohesion is the amount of shared group resources available in a community (Kawachi & Berkman, 2000). Individuals have access to these resources through their social relationships. Relationships are important for health and well-being (Umberson & Montez, 2010). High levels of social support can positively impact health outcomes through behavioral and psychological influences (Uchino, 2006). Individuals who have strong social support systems may eat healthier, be more physically active, and have less emotional stress (Thoits, 2011). Being active in the community after incarceration and being included and not discriminated against is a positive indicator for social cohesion (Umberson & Montez, 2010).

Health and Health Care

The health and healthcare domain within the SDOH framework includes access to health care, primary care, and health literacy (HHS, 2010). One of the largest barriers to healthcare access in the United States is being uninsured or underinsured (Call et al., 2014). Individuals who are unemployed, have lower income levels, or lower education levels are more likely to be uninsured or underinsured. A lack of health insurance can have a negative impact on health, because uninsured individuals are less likely to receive preventive care (IOM, 2009). Individuals who have health insurance have better access to care, although health insurance alone does not provide access to care. Other barriers are a lack of transportation, reduced availability of providers due to longer wait times, and physician shortages in rural areas (Bodenheimer & Pham, 2010). A key issue in the health and healthcare domain is the lack of access to primary care providers. Primary care providers offer preventive care, early detection and treatment of disease, and chronic disease management. Individuals with a primary care provider are more likely to receive recommended preventive services such as immunizations and screenings (Friedberg et al., 2010). Access to primary care is critical for reducing health disparities and improving health outcomes.

Neighborhood and Built Environment

The last key determinant in the SDOH framework, neighborhood and built environment, includes access to foods that support healthy eating patterns, quality of housing, crime and violence, and environmental conditions (HHS, 2010). Crime and violence in a community is a public health issue. Violence can be experienced in many forms, such as being a victim of violence, witnessing violence, or crimes occurring in the community (Hartinger-Saunders et al., 2012). Violence impacts health outcomes because it can lead to premature mortality or can cause injuries (Krug et al., 2002). Low-income neighborhoods are more likely to be affected by crime and violence (Kang, 2016). Repeated exposure to violence can be linked to negative health outcomes (Margolin et al., 2010). Exposure to crime and violence in the community can cause short-term and long-term health effects. Thus, addressing exposure to crime and violence can help prevent or reduce harm and lead to improved health outcomes.

Environmental conditions, such as polluted air, contaminated water, and extreme heat, can negatively impact health outcomes (HHS, 2010). Individuals who are economically disadvantaged are at a greater risk of being affected by environmental conditions (Evans & Kantrowitz, 2002). Neighborhoods higher in poverty report poorer quality housing (Fauth et al., 2004). Quality of housing refers to the physical condition of an individual's home and the environment in which the home is located. Housing quality includes aspects such as air quality, home safety, space per individual, and presence of environmental hazards and toxins (Bonnefoy, 2007). Poorer quality housing is associated with negative health outcomes, such as chronic disease, injury, and poor mental health (Krieger & Higgins, 2002). Individuals with lower incomes may be more likely to experience poor quality housing and lack of access to food that promotes healthy eating (Office of the Surgeon General, 2009). Reducing harmful environmental exposures and having access to better quality housing and access to foods that support healthy eating patterns can contribute to positive health outcomes.

▶ Health Behaviors

Health behavior is a term used to refer to behaviors that are beneficial to health; however, the term is most commonly used to denote the lack of those behaviors or behaviors that are harmful to health (Goldsteen & Goldsteen, 2013). The SDOH approach seeks to understand how the environment shapes an individual's health through health behaviors (Short & Mollborn, 2015). There are five categories of behavior that have been consistently correlated with increased morbidity and mortality (Spring et al., 2012):

1. Consuming a diet high in calories, fat, and sodium, and low in nutrients
2. Low levels of physical activity and high levels of sedentary activity
3. Smoking cigarettes
4. Abusing substances including alcohol, prescription drugs, and illicit drugs
5. Engaging in risky sexual behaviors

Health protective behaviors are those that reduce susceptibility to disease or facilitate restoration of health. Three health protective behaviors that have been linked with better health and recovery from illness are being physically active, eating fruits and vegetables, and being adherent with prescribed medication (Spring et al., 2012). Unhealthy behaviors are prevalent in the United States, with two-thirds of the population currently exceeding a healthy weight (Spring et al., 2012). Thus, policy interventions are needed to address health behaviors in order to improve the overall health of the population.

▶ Summary

The circumstances surrounding each SDOH play a very large role in healthcare policy and policy creation. Local, state, and federal governments take into account the framework of the five social determinants: Economic Stability; Education; Social and Community; Health and Health Care; and Neighborhood and Built Environment. The WHO and the U.S. Department of Health and Human Services make it a priority to address SDOH and reevaluate related goals regularly to ensure provisions are in place to keep people healthy. They do this by evaluating evidence of the social determinants through research and data. Policies are created to change, update, and alter goals to ensure that everyone is safe and healthy.

Key Terms

Civic Participation promotes the quality of life in a community, through both political and nonpolitical processes.

Discrimination is the unjust or prejudicial treatment of different categories of people or things, especially on the grounds of race, age, or sex.

Health Literacy is the degree to which individuals have the capacity to obtain, process, and understand basic health information and services needed to make appropriate health decisions.

Social Cohesion describes the willingness of members of a society to cooperate with each other in order to survive and prosper.

Social Determinants of Health (SDOH) are conditions in which people are born, grow, live, work, and age. These circumstances are shaped by the distribution of money, power, and resources at global, national, and local levels.

World Health Organization (WHO) has the primary role of directing and coordinating international health within the United Nations system. Its main areas of work are health systems, health through the life-course, noncommunicable and communicable diseases, preparedness, surveillance and response, and corporate services.

References

Berkman, N. D., Sheridan, S. L., Donahue, K. E., Halpern, D. J., & Crotty, K. (2011). Low health literacy and health outcomes: An updated systematic review. *Annals of Internal Medicine, 155*(2), 97–107.

Bodenheimer, T., & Pham, H. H. (2010). Primary care: Current problems and proposed solutions. *Health Affairs, 29*(5), 799–805.

Bonnefoy, X. (2007). Inadequate housing and health: An overview. *International Journal of Environment and Pollution, 30*(3), 411–429.

Call, K., McAlpine, D., Garcia, C., Shippee, N., Beebe, T., Adeniyi, T., & Shippee, T. (2014). Barriers to care in an ethnically diverse publicly insured population: Is health care reform enough? *Medical Care, 52*, 720–727.

Cardoso, M. R., de Goes Siqueira, L. F., Alves, F. M., & D'Angelo, L. A. (2004). Crowding: Risk factor or protective factor for lower respiratory disease in young children? *BMC Public Health, 4*, 19.

Coleman-Jensen, A., Rabbitt, M. P., Gregory, C. A., & Singh, A. (2017). *Household food security in the United States in 2016.* United States Department of Agriculture Economic Research Service. https://www.ers.usda.gov/publications/pub-details/?pubid=84972

Dooley, D., Catalano, R., & Hough, R. (1992). Unemployment and alcohol disorder in 1910 and 1990: Drift versus social causation. *Journal of Occupational and Organizational Psychology, 65*, 277–290.

Evans, G. W., & Kantrowitz, E. (2002). Socioeconomic status and health: The potential role of environmental risk exposure. *Annual Review of Public Health, 23*(1), 303–331.

Fauth, R. C., Leventhal, T., & Brooks-Gunn, J. (2004). Short-term effects of moving from public housing in poor to middle-class neighborhoods on low-income, minority adults' outcomes. *Social Science Medicine, 59*(11), 2271–2284.

Friedberg, M. W., Hussey, P. S., & Schneider, E. C. (2010). Primary care: A critical review of the evidence on quality and costs of health care. *Health Affairs, 29*(5), 766–772.

Goldsteen, R. L., & Goldsteen, K. (2013). *Jonas' introduction to the U.S. health care system* (7th ed.). New York: Springer Publishing Company.

Hartinger-Saunders, R. M., Rine, C. M., Nochajski, T., & Wieczorek, W. (2012). Neighborhood crime and perception of safety as predictors of victimization and offending among youth: A call for macro-level prevention and intervention models. *Child Youth Services Review, 34*(9), 1966–1973.

Department of Health and Human Services (HHS). (2010). *Social determinants of health.* Healthy People 2020. https://www.healthypeople.gov/2020/topics-objectives/topic/social-determinants-of-health

Institute of Medicine (IOM). (2009). *Committee on health insurance. America's uninsured crisis: Consequences for health and health care.* Washington, DC: National Academies Press.

Joint Center for Housing Studies (JCHS) of Harvard University. (2016). *The state of the nation's housing.* http://www.jchs.harvard.edu/sites/default/files/jchs_2016_state_of_the_nations_housing_lowres.pdf

Jyoti, D. F., Frongillo, E. A., & Jones, S. J. (2005). Food insecurity affects school children's academic performance, weight gain, and social skills. *Journal of Nutrition, 135*(12), 2831–2839.

Kang, S. (2016). Inequality and crime revisited: Effects of local inequality and economic segregation on crime. *Journal of Population Economics, 29*(2), 593–626.

Kawachi, I., & Berkman, L. (2000). Social cohesion, social capital, and health. In L. F. Berkman & I. Kawachi (Eds.), *Social epidemiology,* pp. 174–190. New York: Oxford University Press.

Krieger, J., & Higgins, D. L. (2002). Housing and health: Time again for public health action. *American Journal of Public Health, 92*(5), 758–768.

Krug, E. G., Mercy, J. A., Dahlberg, L. L., & Zwi, A. B. (2002). The world report on violence and health. *Lancet, 360*(9339), 1083–1088.

Kushel, M. B., Gupta, R., Gee, L., & Haas, J. S. (2006). Housing instability and food insecurity as barriers to health care among low-income Americans. *Journal of General Internal Medicine, 21*(1), 71–77.

Lee, A. J., Crombie, I. K., Smith, W. C. S., & Tunstall-Pedoe, H. D. (1991). Cigarette smoking and employment status. *Social Science and Medicine, 33*(11), 1309–1312.

Margolin, G., Vickerman, K. A., Oliver, P. H., & Gordis, E. B. (2010). Violence exposure in multiple interpersonal domains: Cumulative and differential effects. *Journal of Adolescent Health, 47*(2), 198–205.

Marmot, M., & Wilkinson, R. (2006). *Social determinants of health* (2nd ed.). London: Oxford University Press.

Meyer, P., Yoon, P., & Kaufmann, R. (2013). CDC Health Disparities & Inequalities Report—United States. *Morbidity & Mortality Weekly Report (MMWR) Supplement, 62*(3), 1–187.

North Carolina Institute of Medicine (NCIOM). (2009). *Socioeconomic determinants of health.* Prevention for the Health of North Carolina: Prevention Action Plan. http://nciom.org/wp-content/uploads/2017/07/Prevention-Chpt11.pdf

Office of the Surgeon General. (2009). *The Surgeon General's Call to Action to Promote Healthy Homes.* Rockville, MD: Office of the Surgeon General.

Paul, K. I., Geithner, E., Moser, K., Song, Z., Wanberg, C. R., & Kinicki, A. J. (2005). Psychological and physical well-being during unemployment: A meta-analytic study. *Journal of Applied Psychology, 90*(1), 53–76.

Robert Wood Johnson Foundation (RWJF). (2009). *Improving the health of all Americans through safe and healthy housing.* https://www.rwjf.org/en/library/research/2009/07/improving-the-health-of-all-americans-through-safe-and-healthy-h.html

Short, S. E., & Mollborn, S. (2015). Social determinants and health behaviors: Conceptual frames and empirical advances. *Current Opinions in Psychology, 5*, 78–84.

Spring, B., Moller, A. C., & Coons, M. J. (2012). Multiple health behaviors: Overview and implications. *Journal of Public Health, 34* (Suppl 1), i3–i10.

Thoits, P. A. (2011). Mechanisms linking social ties and support to physical and mental health. *Journal of Health & Social Behavior, 52*(2), 145–161.

Uchino, B. (2006). Social support and health: A review of physiological processes potentially underlying links to disease outcomes. *Journal of Behavioral Medicine, 29*, 377–387.

Umberson, D., & Montez, J. K. (2010). Social relationships and health a flashpoint for health policy. *Journal of Health & Social Behavior, 51*(1 Suppl), S54–66.

World Health Organization (WHO). (2008). *Closing the gap in a generation: Health equity through action on the social determinants of health.* Geneva, Switzerland: World Health Organization, Commission on Social Determinants of Health. http://www.who.int/social_determinants/thecommission/finalreport/en/

World Health Organization (WHO). (2018). *Social determinants of health.* http://www.who.int/social_determinants/en/

Vozoris, N. T., & Tarasuk, V. S. (2003). Household food insufficiency is associated with poorer health. *Journal of Nutrition, 133*, 120–126.

Zimmerman, E. B., Woolf, S. H., & Haley, A. (2015). *Understanding the relationship between education and health: A review of the evidence and an examination of community perspectives.* https://www.ahrq.gov/professionals/education/curriculum-tools/population-health/zimmerman.html

🔍 CASE 11-1

The Opioid Epidemic: An SDOH Approach

Kathy J. Keister, PHD, RN, CNE

John Thomas's parents divorced when he was 6 years old. His mother relocated John and his siblings to another state to be closer to her family and remarried when John was 8 years old. His alcoholic stepfather was physically and emotionally abusive to John and his stepbrother, so much so that John attempted suicide when he was 9. John loved his mother, but did not like her, because she allowed the abuse to continue. John had several uncles he adored, all of whom had served in the military. John could not wait until he was old enough to join the army and serve his country as his uncles had. A secondary benefit was to escape his stepfather.

John's mother signed the paperwork necessary for John to enlist in the army at the age of 17 at the end of his junior year of high school. John thrived in the military environment. While in the military, he finished his high school education, graduating from his hometown high school. As part of his training, he took college credit courses at a university where he was stationed. John quickly rose to the rank of a noncommissioned officer and served both as a medic and an engineer throughout his tenure.

Today, John is a divorced 39-year-old male army veteran who served in Iran, Iraq, and Afghanistan. In fact, his unit was among the first to be deployed to Afghanistan following 9/11 (Operation Enduring Freedom). In 2003, John was deployed to Iraq for Operation Iraqi Freedom. During his deployment to Iraq, he was injured when a rocket-propelled grenade buried him under a brick wall, ending his 22-year military career. John suffered a traumatic brain injury (TBI), and multiple areas of his body were peppered with shrapnel. He spent two weeks in the critical care unit of a Veterans Administration (VA) Medical Center before stabilizing and being discharged to live with his mother.

John has a monthly pension of $3,000 and uses the VA system for his healthcare needs. He is being treated for depression, due to the involuntary end of his military service and the fact that his wife cheated on him during his deployment, leading to his divorce. Since discharge, transcutaneous electrical nerve stimulation and a variety of nonopioids (nonsteroidal anti-inflammatory drugs, selective serotonin reuptake inhibitors, and tricyclic antidepressants) and opioids (hydrocodone, oxycodone, and morphine) have been prescribed to treat his chronic pain. However, John reports none of these options have adequately managed his pain.

Until recently, John's healthcare provider willingly renewed his opioid prescription on a monthly basis. However, since the release of new prescribing guidelines recommended by the Centers for Disease Control and Prevention (2018), John has received only a 7-day supply of his pain medication. In response, John has turned to alcohol and illegally purchased oxycodone to cope with his chronic pain as well as his mental illness.

Discussion Questions

1. What evidence exists regarding opioid abuse, especially in the veteran population?
2. Which SDOH impact John's misuse of opioids?
3. Go to https://www.congress.gov/ and search for federal legislation that has been proposed to address the opioid epidemic. What federal legislation has been proposed to address the opioid epidemic? Select two and provide an overview of the legislation.
4. What gaps exist in current efforts to address the opioid crisis in terms of SDOH for veterans?
5. What recommendations do you have for addressing specific SDOH to interrupt the opioid misuse cycle to promote veteran health?

Reference

Centers for Disease Control & Prevention (CDC). (2018). *Prescription opioid data*. https://www.cdc.gov /drugoverdose/data/prescribing.html

🔎 CASE 11-2

No Home? No Money? No Rights?

Barbara Cohen, PhD, JD, RN

Sam F. is a healthy, 48-year-old male who has lived on the streets of New York City for most of his life. Although Sam has a long history of substance abuse and schizophrenia, he is otherwise in good health with no chronic illness. He is accustomed to panhandling and working odd jobs for money and has nearly always managed to care for his most basic needs—food, clothing, and shelter. He is familiar with the shelter system, the location of various soup kitchens, and safer street-based places to sleep. He has occasionally been arrested for minor crimes primarily during the times when he has needed money for drugs. He has never had any incident that endangered anyone other than himself.

During his last arrest, he was referred to a Mental Health Court, and, in accordance with the resolution of his criminal case, he chose to enter into a supportive living environment rather than serve jail time. In Sam's words: "Do I have a choice? Why can't you just let me live in the streets? I can do it!" He has had no further arrests since he qualified for an apartment in Happy Trails 2 You, a supportive living environment for formerly homeless chronically mentally ill individuals.

He has been medically cleared by the facility's retained internist and is being monitored by the facility's psychiatrist who visits the facility once a week. Sam's current medications are: Suboxone, 8 mg/2 mg, sublingual twice daily; and intramuscular risperidone, 37.5 mg every two weeks. As a condition of being accepted into permanent housing, Sam agreed to have his medications provided by the on-site team twice a day, to see the nurse every two weeks for his risperidone injections, and to allow his case manager to handle his funds until further assessment of his money management skills can be completed.

Although Sam's clothes are clean and weather appropriate and he is showering regularly, his apartment is littered in garbage and attracting pests. Further, Sam has consistently missed medication times set for the residents. He generally arrives late for both morning and afternoon medication administration, demanding both doses of medication simultaneously, and berating staff "for neglect" when these demands are not met. When taking his sublingual medications, Sam refuses to remain present with the staff until the tablet is dissolved. He insists on walking away, placing a tissue to his mouth, leaving the staff with the belief that he is hoarding his medications to either increase his later doses or to sell. He threatens the staff, demanding missed doses of suboxone "for later" and ridiculing staff for incompetence when his demands are declined. Sam accepted his first risperidone injection but is now refusing any more. He states he will only accept this medication if he is granted immediate unlimited access to his monthly funds. When the staff impose limits per the interdisciplinary team's plan, thus refusing access to missed doses and monetary funds, Sam becomes enraged, threatening to "go on the street and use," calling his psychiatrist "an idiot," screaming at the nurse, demanding his medication immediately, and stating angrily, "I gotta get outta here."

Sam has been a resident at Happy Trails 2 U for all of two weeks. The exhausted interdisciplinary team seeks your advice as a fellow member of the interdisciplinary healthcare team.

Discussion Questions

1. Make a list of the political, legal, societal, and healthcare issues that have arisen with respect to Sam's current life situation beginning with his arrest and appearance in mental health court. Next to each issue, list the various stakeholders involved and describe their respective rights and interests.
2. Make a list of the SDOH that may be impacting Sam's life events. What national and local efforts have been made to date to diminish the disparate impact of these social determinants on Sam's well-being?
3. What plan would you suggest to resolve Sam's current healthcare and related behavioral issues so as to maximize his adjustment to his new home and new behavioral restrictions?
4. What outside resources would be most beneficial for Sam so as to continue his access to his apartment?
5. What steps can the interdisciplinary team take to support themselves while facing Sam's threatening conduct?

🔍 CASE 11-3

We Can Do It: Employing SDOH to Improve Patient Outcomes

Raymond J. Higbea, PhD, Lara J. Jaskiewicz, PhD, & Ramona Wallace, DO

Sofia Madison, DO, was medical director of Majestic River Family Care (MRFC), a federally qualified health center in Majestic River, Michigan. Like most providers, she struggles with addressing her patients' SDOH, including a lack of resources and support from integrative care providers. The support system in place at MRFC is not reimbursable by current payor systems and is supported by funding that is not sustainable. Although the providers have always recognized the influence of SDOH on the low-income population of patients treated by MRFC, it recently has become a priority to develop a sustainable model of care linkages. For example, in early 2017, the State of Michigan shared a SDOH screening tool with Medicaid providers with the expectation that providers would begin using this screening tool and address the findings.

Rather than recoil from a new requirement, Dr. Madison views this as an opportunity to begin addressing some of her long-held concerns about her patient's social needs. Even with the State mandate to screen patients for SDOH needs, she found herself in an operational and procedural dilemma over how to begin screening patients, what to do with the information, and how to make SDOH treatments part of each patient's plan of care. Several challenges become readily apparent: implementing a system, cost of support to address the patients' needs, and provider "buy in" to ask another list of questions. The practice administrator develops a standard workflow around the checklist with a design to track data. The implementing and operationalizing of the plan to address patient SDOH needs is completed in 2 weeks. Within 5 months, MRFC is able to screen over 5,000 members. These data, on an aggregate as well as an individual level, provide the basis for further development of community care linkages to address chronic health conditions.

Dr. Madison and the practice administrator successfully pull together a team from case management, finance, and coding to explore how to implement and operationalize the screening tool. The team very quickly finds a way to include the SDOH screening tool as part of the assessment process, develop referral protocols, and identify payment codes. Soon after this, Dr. Madison implements this process with her patients before rolling it out to the other practice providers. Six months postimplementation, MRFC improves quality measures, decreases the behavioral health no-show rate, improves patient satisfaction, and sees a marked reduction in pain control prescriptions.

Discussion Questions

1. As an administrator, what incentives would you have to offer to implement such a program, and how would you engage your medical and support staff in the new initiative?
2. How would you organize the development of referral networks and other managerial processes to support this new initiative? Explain.
3. How should payers address SDOH payment when developing payment policies? Explain.
4. Should payment for SDOH be written into statute or handled by the regulatory process? Explain.

CHAPTER 12
Individual Rights

Lesley Clack, ScD

▶ Introduction

All individuals have a right to health care that meets the highest standard, and "understanding health as a human right creates a legal obligation on states to ensure access to timely, acceptable, and affordable health care of appropriate quality" (WHO, 2017). In addition, rights to health care include "providing for the underlying determinants of health, such as safe and potable water, sanitation, food, housing, health-related information and education, and gender equality" (WHO, 2017). The concept of individual rights in patient care refers to the application of human rights principles in the context of health care (Cohen & Ezer, 2013). Unfortunately, human rights violations can and do occur in healthcare. Both patients and providers have rights, as well as responsibilities, as providers and consumers of health care.

▶ The Right to Health

According to the World Health Organization (WHO), the right to health is one of the internationally agreed upon human rights, and achieving the right to health is central to the realization of other human rights, such as food, housing, work, education, information, and participation (WHO, 2017). The WHO Constitution proclaims "the highest attainable standard of health" as a "fundamental right of every human being" (WHO, 2006). This right set forth by WHO creates a legal obligation on states to ensure appropriate health, including access to timely, acceptable, and affordable health care, for all people, without discrimination (WHO, 2017). Core components of the right to health are availability, accessibility, acceptability, and quality, as defined in **TABLE 12-1**. The human right to health also involves the procedural principles (**TABLE 12-2**) that apply to all human rights (NESRI, 2018). The right to health must be provided without discrimination on the grounds of race,

TABLE 12-1 Core Components of the Right to Health

Core Components of the Right to Health	Definition
Availability	The need for a sufficient quantity of functioning public health and healthcare facilities and equitable services.
Accessibility	The requirement that health facilities and services must be accessible to everyone. Accessibility has four overlapping dimensions: nondiscrimination, physical accessibility, economical accessibility, and information accessibility.
Acceptability	This relates to respect for medical ethics and culturally appropriate services. Acceptability requires that health facilities and services are patient-centered and designed for the specific needs of diverse population groups and in accordance with standards of medical ethics for confidentiality and informed consent.
Quality	Facilities, goods, and services must be scientifically and medically approved. Quality health services should be safe, effective, patient-centered, timely, equitable, and efficient.

Data from Human rights and health, WHO, 29 December 2017. URL: https://www.who.int/news-room/fact-sheets/detail/human-rights-and-health

TABLE 12-2 Procedural Principles of the Right to Health (NESRI, 2018)

Nondiscrimination	Health care must be accessible and provided without discrimination (in intent or effect) based on health status, race, ethnicity, age, sex, sexuality, disability, language, religion, national origin, income, or social status.
Transparency	Health information must be easily accessible for everyone, enabling people to protect their health and claim quality health services. Institutions that organize, finance, or deliver health care must operate in a transparent way.
Participation	Individuals and communities must be able to take an active role in decisions that affect their health, including in the organization and implementation of healthcare services.
Accountability	Private companies and public agencies must be held accountable for protecting the right to health care through enforceable standards, regulations, and independent compliance monitoring.

Source: NESRI, 2018; *What is the Human Right to Health and Health Care?* https://www.nesri.org/programs/what-is-the-human-right-to-health-and-health-care

age, ethnicity, or any other status. Equality requires states to take steps to redress any discriminatory law, practice, or policy. Another feature of rights-based approaches is meaningful participation. Participation means ensuring that national stakeholders, including nongovernmental organizations, are meaningfully involved in all phases of programming, including assessment, analysis, planning, implementation, monitoring, and evaluation (WHO, 2017).

▶ Patient Rights and Responsibilities

Patients have rights, whether established by federal law, state law, or the healthcare facility. Some of these rights include the right to information confidentiality, the right to informed consent, the right to refuse treatment, and the right to emergency treatment without the ability to pay. The right to information confidentiality was set forth by the Health Insurance Portability and Accountability Act (HIPAA) of 1996 (HHS, 2013). Prior to passage of the HIPAA, there were no specific standards or requirements for privacy and security of health information.

Another important patient right is informed consent. Informed consent refers to the requirement that healthcare providers must provide patients with all of the information that they need to make an educated decision about their care. Patients and providers both benefit when a patient is fully informed by clear communication between the patient and provider and full patient understanding of treatment occurs prior to providing consent.

The right to refuse treatment is recognized as a fundamental principle of liberty or freedom as set forth by the U.S. Constitution. Patients have the right to decide whether or not to undergo treatment, and it is unethical for providers to force patients to undergo treatment against their will. There are a few exceptions in which patients do not have the ability to refuse treatment, such as patients with altered mental status, children, patients who are a threat to themselves or others, and in life-threatening emergency situations. Patients also have the right to emergency treatment without the ability to pay. This right was set forth by the Emergency Medical Treatment & Labor Act (EMTALA) in 1986 (CMS, 2012).

Patients also have responsibilities as consumers of medical services, such as asking questions of providers, providing accurate information to providers, and following the care plan agreed upon with their provider. In order to ensure the best possible health outcomes, patients must be active and responsible participants in their health care.

▶ Provider Rights and Responsibilities

Although providers have an obligation to provide the best patient care while respecting patient rights, providers also have rights. Providers have the right to be treated with fairness and dignity by employers, to be protected from harassment, and to excuse themselves from patient care with which they disagree. Providers also have responsibilities, which include practicing in accordance with state and federal laws, practicing in accordance with licensure and malpractice laws, and following professional standards and codes of ethics.

▶ Violation of Human Health Rights

Serious health consequences may result from violations of human rights in health care. Violations, such as overt discrimination in the delivery of healthcare services, can act as a barrier to patients receiving healthcare services and contributes to poor quality care (WHO, 2017). Vulnerable populations, such as individuals with mental illness, individuals with disabilities, indigenous populations, LGBTQ, and people who use drugs, are at greater risk for dealing with abuse of human health rights (WHO, 2017). Legal issues often arise regarding a patient's right to refuse treatment, particularly surrounding vulnerable populations (Shi & Singh, 2015). The Patient Self-Determination Act of 1990 applies to all healthcare facilities participating in Medicare or Medicaid, and it requires that hospitals and other facilities must provide all patients, upon admission, with information on patients' rights (Shi & Singh, 2015). Most healthcare facilities have a patient's bill of rights, which reflects legal issues such as confidentiality and consent.

▶ Summary

Individuals have rights as patients. They have the right to obtain the highest standard of care, regardless of their ability to pay. Over the years, access and other rights have evolved. Individuals have the right to decide if they want treatments; they have the right to decide which option they want regarding surgery or end-of-life decisions. They also have the right to keep their information private and confidential. The evolution of individual rights has come far and will continue to do so as new healthcare policy standards change.

Key Terms

Individual Rights guarantee certain freedoms without interference from the government or other individuals.

Informed Consent requires that healthcare providers afford their patients with all of the information that they need to make an educated decision about their care.

Patient Rights are the rights to make decisions regarding medical care, to accept or refuse treatment, and to formulate advance directives.

Provider Rights are the rights to be treated with fairness and dignity by employers, to be protected from harassment, and to excuse themselves from patient care with which they disagree.

Right to Health is a legal obligation on states to ensure appropriate health, including access to timely, acceptable, and affordable health care, for all people, without discrimination.

References

Centers for Medicare & Medicaid Services (CMS). (2012). *Emergency Medical Treatment & Labor Act (EMTALA)*. https://www.cms.gov/Regulations-and-Guidance/Legislation/EMTALA/

Cohen, J., & Ezer, T. (2013). Human rights in patient care: A theoretical and practical framework. *Health & Human Rights, 15*(2), 368–386.

National Economic and Social Rights Initiative (NESRI). (2018). *What is the human right to health and health care?* https://www.nesri.org/programs/what-is-the-human-right-to-health -and-health-care

Shi, L., & Singh, D. A. (2015). *Delivering health care in America: A systems approach* (6th ed.). Burlington, MA: Jones & Bartlett Learning.

U.S. Department of Health and Human Services (HHS). (2013). *Summary of the HIPAA Security Rule.* https://www.hhs.gov/hipaa/for-professionals/privacy/laws-regulations/index.html

World Health Organization (WHO). (2006). *Constitution of the World Health Organization.* http://www.who.int/governance/eb/who_constitution_en.pdf

World Health Organization (WHO). (2017). *Human rights and health.* http://www.who.int/news-room/fact-sheets/detail/human-rights-and-health

🔍 CASE 12-1

Living on the Wild Side: Policy in the Adult Film Industry

Christina Juris Bennett, JD

This case study focuses on the policy battles between public health initiatives to prevent the spread of sexually transmitted diseases (in particular, HIV) and a person's individual right to pursue an economic endeavor. The adult film industry (AFI) is a thriving business in California, San Fernando Valley, where a majority of American sex films are shot. San Fernando Valley is about 25 miles north of Los Angeles and has pet names like Porn Valley and San Pornando (Robinson, 2016). According to The Statistic Brain Research Institute (2016), roughly 11,000 adult films are released worldwide each year, and they yield $13.3 billion in revenue. California, in particular, realizes $36 million in taxes from this industry. In the United States in the mid-2000s, there were about 200 production companies and 1,200–1,500 performers. The performers were generally paid $400–1,000 per shoot, and higher risk shots (meaning that performers were more likely to contract a disease) commanded higher prices (Grudzen & Kerndt, 2007). Particularly high-risk acts, such as double penetration and repeated facial ejaculations, are called "money shots," and they have been on the rise since 2007.

Hand-in-hand with sex-based films go concerns about sexually transmitted infections (STIs). In 2017, the Centers for Disease Control (CDC) reported that the previous year had the highest number of cases of chlamydia, gonorrhea, and syphilis ever (CDC, 2017b). All three diseases may be cured through antibiotics; however, they may also cause long-term, irreversible harm. Other common sexually transmitted diseases include the incurable human papillomavirus (HPV) and HIV (CDC, 2018). HIV can take weeks or months to be detected in a person's blood, and it becomes fatal by developing into AIDS (HHS, 2017). The CDC has estimated that the lifetime treatment costs of an HIV infection are $379,668 in 2010 dollars (CDC, 2017a).

Beginning in the 1990s, both the federal (29 CFR § 1910.1030) and California's Occupational Safety And Health Administration (OSHA and Cal/OSHA) (Cal. CFR § 5193) began requiring that employers provide a place of employment free from hazards that cause or are likely to cause death or serious harm (Wilken et al., 2016). Cal/OSHA took the requirement even further and required that employers provide personal protective equipment, along with implementing other procedures, to prevent contact with blood, semen, vaginal secretions, and other potentially infectious materials. This requirement applied to any work site, including the AFI, where the performers are at high risk for exposure.

Despite those provisions, the AFI remained relatively unregulated. In 1997, the Adult Industry Medical Health Foundation (AIM) was established to protect adult film performers from HIV and STIs and support them through treatment (Jordan, 2005). With AIM, the industry began regulating itself, and performers were tested monthly for HIV and other STIs. Performers must pay for tests themselves and consent to disclosures in order to film in California. This testing is critical because only about 17% of adult performers in heterosexual films wear condoms (Grudzen & Kerndt, 2007). Only HIV+ females are automatically banned from future filming.

Propelled by the rise in STIs and the desire to protect AFI performers and the public, AIDS activists joined with public health policymakers in 2012 to propose Measure B, also known as the County of Los Angeles Safer Sex in the Adult Film Industry Act (Verrier, 2014). Measure B, which passed, added safety requirements to adult film productions within the Los Angeles city limits (11 Los Angeles County Health and Safety Code Ch. 11.39). Production companies were required to obtain a filming permit from the Department of Public Health, complete bloodborne pathogen training, and submit an exposure control plan. They also agreed to surprise inspections, and the performers were required to wear condoms during vaginal and anal sex. Penalties included injunctions (stopping the filming process) and fines. Within a year's time, the number of permits for adult film productions fell by 90%, and the production of films was claimed to have moved to less-regulated areas like Nevada, Brazil, and Europe (Verrier, 2014). FilmLA, the group that handles the permits, stated that the decrease in film production negatively impacted the entire production staff, from the performer to the caterers to the cameramen.

Measure B was subsequently challenged in the lawsuit *Vivid Entertainment v. Fielding*, 774 F.3d 556 (9th Cir. 2014). On appellate review, the 9th circuit court ruled in favor of the city's permits, inspection, and injunctions on the ground of protecting the public's health. The court opined in December 2014 that condom and barrier requirements did not infringe free speech and that there were alternative methods of expressing oneself.

Despite the victory in Los Angeles, public health officials remained worried about HIV infections in the AFI. Lending credence to their concerns, in 2014, one male AFI performer was diagnosed with HIV and rectal gonorrhea, and public health authorities discovered he infected several of his work- and nonwork-related sexual contacts (Wilken et al., 2016). Thus, policymakers chose to push for a statewide condom requirement for adult film production.

In 2014, Los Angeles representative Isadore Hall III introduced a bill to the California legislature that would require condom use statewide in film production and mandatory testing of adult film performers at the employer's expense (AIDS Health, 2014). This bill, California AB 1576, survived initial committee votes, but it eventually died in the Senate Appropriations Committee without discussion. In contrast with the Los Angeles Measure B, this bill attached criminal prosecution as a penalty for noncompliance. Proponents, including the bill's sponsor, the AIDS Healthcare Foundation, argued the bill would protect the health of performers and their partners. Industry members rejected the bill and claimed they would film elsewhere (Verrier, 2014; Jordan, 2005). They further argued that adult film consumers seek fantasy-like films that do not contain the realities of prophylactic measures. Moreover, both the performers and production companies considered the monthly STI test to provide sufficient protection. Other opponents included the Los Angeles Gay and Lesbian Center and AIDS Project Los Angeles. They believed that requiring HIV testing for employment would lead to discrimination and stigmatization (Abram, 2014).

Seeking to instate a condom requirement through another route, policymakers and lobbyists proposed a rule through the administrative agency Cal/OSHA (Wilken et al., 2016). By May 2015, Cal/OSHA held a public hearing on the proposal of adopting stricter statewide requirements for protective measures for AFI performers. Suggestions included consistent and correct condom use, employer-sponsored STI testing, and employer-sponsored Hepatitis A and HPV vaccinations. The proposed barrier requirements would have prohibited any potential transmission or contact of fluids, and performers would have had to use condoms, dental dams, latex gloves, and other protective gear. AFI performers and producers again lobbied against the requirements, arguing that they were adequately protected by the monthly screenings and further protective gear would harm their ability to make marketable adult films. On February 17, 2016, Cal/OSHA voted down the proposal for state-wide requirement of protective gear.

Having been defeated through the legislative and administrative processes, AIDS Healthcare Foundation, public health policymakers, and other pro-mandatory protection groups worked to get Proposition 60 on the state ballot for November 2016 (Chappell, 2016). That proposition would have required adult film performers to use condoms in the state of California along with requiring state-authorized health licenses and employer-sponsored vaccinations, testing, and examinations related to STIs. It also permitted any state resident to enforce the rule and hold the production companies liable. Voters defeated the proposition in the statewide election, 54% to 46%.

CASE STUDIES

Discussion Questions

1. One of the film industry's main arguments was that monthly testing for STIs sufficiently protects the performers. Evaluate whether this is a strong argument.
2. Within the Cal/OSHA regulation battle, the AFI argued against the prophylactic requirements by citing damages to production crew members, caterers, and other secondary or tertiary stakeholders instead of focusing on limitations against the performers' individual rights. What might have been the reasoning behind this strategy?
3. If there are only 1,200–1,500 AFI performers in the United States, why should society, as a whole, care whether they use protection when working? How do the concerns about that group of people justify the costs and effort for the public health initiatives and for the loss of tax revenue?
4. One of the key aspects of this case study is the battle between governmental interests to protect the public's health versus a person's interest in individual rights. How do the six tenets of public health law elucidate that battle in this case study (Gostin & Wiley, 2016)? The six tenets are:
   a. Government (the power and duty to protect the public's health and safety);
   b. State's police powers and limits (coercive measures to protect the public's health balanced with respect for individual rights);
   c. Populations (shared-risk large-scale interventions to protect the community's health and well-being);
   d. Communities (healthy social networks, mutual support, and civic engagement);
   e. Prevention (interventions to reduce risk or avert harm from injury and disease); and
   f. Social justice (fair and equitable treatment of groups and individuals, with particular attention to the disadvantaged).

References

Abram, S. (2014, August 14). Condom bill dies in key California committee, porn industry satisfied—For now. *Daily News*. https://www.dailynews.com/2014/08/14/condom-bill-dies-in-key-california-committee-porn-industry-satisfied-for-now/

AIDS Health. (2014). *California's condoms in porn bill (AB 1576) clears key assembly committee*. https://www.aidshealth.org/#/archives/18136

Centers for Disease Control and Prevention (CDC). (2017a). *HIV cost-effectiveness*. https://www.cdc.gov/hiv/programresources/guidance/costeffectiveness/index.html

Centers for Disease Control and Prevention (CDC). (2017b). *STDs at record high, indicating urgent need for prevention*. https://www.cdc.gov/media/releases/2017/p0926-std-prevention.html.

Centers for Disease Control and Prevention (CDC). (2018). *Sexually transmitted diseases*. https://www.cdc.gov/std/default.htm

Chappell, B. (2016, November 9). *Condom mandate for porn industry falls short in California*. NPR The Two Way. https://www.npr.org/sections/thetwo-way/2016/11/09/501405749/condom-mandate-for-porn-industry-falls-short-in-california

Gostin, L. O., & Wiley, L. F. (2016). *Public health law: Power, duty, restraint* (3rd ed.). Oakland, CA: University of California Press.

Grudzen, C. R., & Kerndt, P. R. (2007). The adult film industry: Time to regulate? *PLoS Med 4*(6), 993–996.

Jordan, C. (2005). The XXX-Files: Cal/OSHA's regulatory response to HIV in the adult film industry. *Cardozo Journal of Law & Gender, 12*, 421–444.

Robinson, M. (2016). How LA's 'Porn Valley' became the adult entertainment capital of the world. *Business Insider*. http://www.businessinsider.com/how-porn-valley-came-to-be-2016-3

The Statistic Brain Research Institute. (2016). *Adult film industry statistics & demographics*. https://www.statisticbrain.com/adult-film-industry-statistics-demographics/

U.S. Department of Health and Human Services (HHS). (2017). *HIV/AIDS: The basics*. https://aidsinfo.nih.gov/understanding-hiv-aids/fact-sheets/19/45/hiv-aids-the-basics

Verrier, R. (2014). Porn production plummets in Los Angeles. *LA Times*. http://www.latimes.com/la-et-ct-porn-economy-20140805-story.html

Vivid Entertainment, LLC v. Fielding. 774 F.3d 566 (9th Cir. 2014).

Wilken, J. A., Ried, C., Rickett, P., Arno, J. N., Mendez, Y., Harrison, R. J., Wohlfeiler, D., Bauer, H. M., Patricia Joyce, M., Switzer, W. S., Heneine, W., Shankar, A., & Mark, K. E. (2016). Occupational HIV transmission among male adult film performers—Multiple states, 2014. *Morbidity & Mortality Weekly Report,* 65,110–114.

🔍 *CASE 12-2*

Apple County Influenza Clinics: An Individual Rights Approach

Wendy M. Whitner, PhD, MPH, Marsha Davenport, MD, MS, MPH, FACPM, & Cassandra R. Henson, Dr. P.A., MBA

Apple County is a small rural county in the state of Utopia. It has a total of 47,388 residents, 40% of whom are older adults (aged 65 or older). This county is known for its beautiful retirement communities and year-round warm climate. With its large population of older adults, the county is proactive in its planning for the flu season, beginning a year in advance. The county health department has a total of three health clinics around the county, two of which specialize in geriatric medicine.

Large-Scale Influenza Vaccination Clinic Planning

You are the county administrator of Apple County's influenza program. Each of the clinics has a team that consists of managers for supplies, logistics, medical personnel, infection control, and other functions that support daily operations. You met with each clinic administrator and the Infection Control Manager about 6 months ago to go over the plans for influenza season. Your plans are based on CDC guidelines (2015, 2018b), which were both provided to each clinic for consistency in the processes and procedures across the three clinics.

You indicate that during the upcoming flu season, there must be appropriate personnel available in accordance with the CDC guidelines working from 7 a.m. to 5 p.m. Monday through Friday and 8 a.m. to 12 p.m. on Saturday, with an hour on the front end for preparation. You indicate that the flu clinic space will be in the large health education room of each facility, which is next to the clinic's entrance and near the medication storage closet. The storage closet contains a small refrigerator for open vials and other medications that require refrigeration. **TABLE 12-3** shows the Saturday schedule for all flu clinics.

Clinic Dilemmas

In accordance with this meeting, the county's marketing team posted flu clinic flyers in English all over town and released radio and television public service announcements (PSAs) regarding flu prevention and upcoming clinic hours. The flu clinics open on Saturday, which happens to be the first day for providing flu vaccines. On Friday evening, a day prior to the opening of the flu clinic, the CDC announced a flu vaccine shortage. The notification appeared on the national and local news channels. In addition, Utopia's state flu surveillance director sent out a notification on Friday evening to all county flu administrators confirming a flu epidemic in the state, particularly Apricot County, a neighboring county. The next day, the following situations occurred at Apple County's three clinics.

Apple County Clinic #1

This clinic is one of the county's clinics with a geriatrics department. The personnel (one security guard, one greeter/educator, one nurse vaccine administrator, one registration staff,

TABLE 12-3 Apple County Saturday Flu Clinics' Work Schedule

Personnel	Time to Work
Clinic administrator	7 a.m.–1 p.m.
Infection control manager	7 a.m.–1 p.m.
Supply manager	7 a.m.–1 p.m.
Greeters/educators	7 a.m.–1 p.m.
Priority client screeners	7 a.m.–1 p.m.
Registration personnel	7 a.m.–1 p.m.
Medical screeners	7 a.m.–1 p.m.
Form/payment collectors	7 a.m.–1 p.m.
Clinic flow controllers	7 a.m.–1 p.m.
Vaccination assistants	7 a.m.–1 p.m.
Nurse vaccine administrators	7 a.m.–1 p.m.
Security guards	7 a.m.–1 p.m.
EMTs	7 a.m.–1 p.m.

the logistics manager, and the clinic administrator) arrive to open the clinic at 7:00 a.m. There is a line of people that wraps around the building; it looks as if there are at least 500 people already in line. One of the people in line asks how much vaccine the clinic has on hand; the clinic has just 1,500 doses of adult flu vaccine available. One of the older adult women using a walker asked to come into the building because she needs to sit down.

Apple County Clinic #2

This clinic is the second clinic with a geriatrics department. The personnel (two security guards, two greeters/educators, two registration staff, two nurse vaccine administrators, the supply manager, the infection control manager, and the clinic administrator) arrive to open the clinic at 7:55 a.m. This clinic had just 50–100 doses of the flu vaccine on hand because the clinic administrator did not put in her request for supplemental doses of the vaccine as required last month. Around 10 a.m., there was a long line of older adults waiting to take a flu shot. One of the older adult patients asks one of the front desk staff if there are enough doses of vaccine for her to get a shot today. The staff indicates they have enough for the first 100 people. The older adult patient become upset, saying "You all are trying to kill us. This is a conspiracy to not provide us with the flu shots!" One of the security guards tries to assist the front desk staff in calming the patient down.

At 10:45 a.m., suddenly, a group of about 20 people march into the clinic demanding that they get their shots now because they live near the border of Apricot County. During the chaos, an older gentleman on his way to receive his shot fell as a result of the surge of patients to the registration desk.

Apple County Clinic #3

This clinic has 5,000 doses of flu vaccine on hand. This clinic opens on schedule at 8 a.m., but the clinic administrator, one greeter/educator, two priority client screeners, two registration personnel, three medical screeners, three form/payment collectors, one clinic flow controller, three vaccination assistants, two nurse vaccine administrators, three security guards, and three EMTs show up at 5:00 a.m. The clinic administrator calls you at 7 a.m. to let you know that there are about 100 people waiting in line to receive their flu shots. She tells you that she has had five call outs from her staff due to the flu. She also reports that one of the older adults standing in line is asking about how many vaccine doses this clinic has. She also adds that another person passed out waiting in line. A third person in line is speaking another language while waving her walking cane. She indicates that none of her staff understands what she is saying.

As the administrator, what would you do in response to each of these scenarios?

Discussion Questions

1. What are the issues present in this case?
2. What are some individual rights concerns evident in this case?
3. Describe the concerns for the healthcare providers at the clinics.
4. What is the role of the clinic administrator in these situations?
5. How could the situations that evolved in each clinic been prevented? What are the lessons learned?

References

Centers for Disease Control and Prevention (CDC). (2015). *Guidelines for large-scale influenza vaccination clinic planning.* https://www.cdc.gov/flu/professionals/vaccination/vax_clinic.htm

Centers for Disease Control and Prevention (CDC). (2018b). *seasonal influenza vaccination resources for health professionals.* https://www.cdc.gov/flu/professionals/vaccination/index.htm https://www.thinkculturalhealth.hhs.gov/assets/pdfs/EnhancedNationalCLASStandards.pdf

---

🔍 CASE 12-3

Mandatory Influenza Vaccination of Healthcare Workers: Individual Rights vs Public Health

Sharyl Kinney, DrPH, RN, CPH

Healthcare workers are at risk of exposure to influenza and spreading influenza to patients as they provide care. This results in healthcare workers who are sick and cannot come to work and patients who contract influenza during their hospitalization. The U.S. Advisory Committee on Immunization Practices has recommended influenza vaccination for healthcare workers since 1984. Despite efforts to educate healthcare workers on the importance of vaccination and the provision of free vaccination in the workplace, immunization rates among healthcare workers remain below 60% (Awali et al., 2014).

The state of Massachusetts was the first state to enact mandatory vaccination for smallpox in 1902. Henning Jacobson, who refused vaccination based on his constitutional right to individual liberty, challenged this law. The Supreme Court found in this case that the state may limit individual freedom when the public good is at stake (*Jacobson v. Massachusetts*, 1905). This case is the basis for mandatory vaccination of healthcare workers (Randall et al., 2013). Virginia Mason Hospital was the first hospital to implement mandatory influenza vaccination in 2004 (*Virginia Mason Hospital v. Washington State Nurses Association*, 2007). Eighteen states have influenza vaccination requirements for healthcare workers. These laws establish requirements for mandatory vaccination and vary widely based on healthcare facilities and required vaccinations. Many states have some type of exemption from vaccination based on medical, religious, or philosophical reasons (CDC, 2017; Field, 2009).

One state's hospital association, with the endorsement of the state health department, is circulating a draft of a mandatory influenza policy for member review. This proposal states that the current rate of influenza vaccination among healthcare workers is too low (between 35 and 55%) and is responsible for the current influenza epidemic in the state. Hospitals already have policies mandating vaccinations for rubella, measles, mumps, and Hepatitis B for all hospital employees who have contact with patients. The proposed policy includes the following provisions:

- Annual mandatory influenza vaccination is a condition of employment for all employees. Employees must provide proof of influenza vaccination upon hire and by October 1 each year. Employees who do not comply with the annual influenza vaccination requirement will be subject to termination.
- The healthcare facility will offer influenza vaccination to all employees without charge at the facility during the employee's work hours.
- Employees may request an exemption from the annual mandatory influenza vaccination based on a physician's statement that the vaccine is medically inadvisable. Healthcare workers who are exempt from vaccination must wear a surgical mask during influenza season.

The hospital association is seeking support for this policy and has identified the following stakeholders: the state medical association, the patient advocacy association, the association of hospital boards of directors, and the state nurses association. The state medical association has concerns about this policy because it may result in unequal treatment of physicians employed by hospitals compared with those who are not. The patient advocacy association supports mandatory vaccination of healthcare workers because unvaccinated workers can infect vulnerable patients. However, they do not support the provision of the policy that allows exemption for some workers and have concerns that unvaccinated healthcare workers may not wear masks. The association of hospital boards of directors have concerns that if the vaccine is mandated and a healthcare worker has an adverse reaction, such as an egg allergy or a more serious adverse effect such as Guillain-Barré Syndrome, the hospital board may assume liability for mandating the vaccine. The state nurses association opposes mandatory vaccination because it does not allow for religious or philosophical exemptions from vaccination.

Discussion Questions

1. Under what circumstances can an individual's rights be constrained for the public good? Give an example.
2. What are the arguments for and against constraining the rights of the individual healthcare worker by mandating influenza vaccination? Which arguments do you think are most compelling and why?
3. How do the stakeholders' concerns described in the case relate to the rights of individuals versus the public good?
4. How would you address these concerns related to the proposed policy?
5. Based on stakeholders' concerns, would you change the proposed policy? If you would change it, how would you change it?

References

Awali, R. A., Samuel, P. S., Marwaha, B., Ahmad, N., Gupta, P., Kumar, V., Ellsworth, J., Flanagan, E., Upfal, M., Russell, J., Kaplan, C., Kaye, K. S., & Chopra, T. (2014). Understanding health care personnel's attitudes toward mandatory influenza vaccination. *American Journal of Infection Control, 42*(6), 649–652.

Centers for Disease Control and Prevention (CDC). (2017). *Menu of state hospital influenza vaccination laws.* https://www.cdc.gov/phlp/docs/menu-shfluvacclaws.pdf

Field, R. I. (2009). Mandatory vaccination of health care workers whose rights should come first? *Pharmacy and Therapeutics, 34,* 615–618.

Jacobson v. Massachusetts, 197 U.S. 11 (1905).

Randall, L. H., Curran, E. A., & Omer, S. B. (2013). Legal considerations surrounding mandatory influenza vaccination for healthcare workers in the United States. *Vaccine, 31,* 1771–1776.

Virginia Mason Hospital v. Washington State Nurses Association, 511 F. 3d 908 (2007).

CASE STUDIES

SECTION 5

Critical Issues in Health Policy

CHAPTER 13
Medical Ethics and Healthcare Professionals

Lesley Clack, ScD

▶ Introduction

Ethics are moral principles that govern a person's behavior. Ethical behavior essentially refers to the ability to tell the difference between right and wrong (Buchbinder & Shanks, 2017). Ethical points of view also have roots in cultural and religious beliefs. In medicine and in the general healthcare community, those who provide services follow a set of principles to promote good morals and positive behaviors. Because of established medical ethics principles, healthcare professionals have the responsibility to uphold patients' healthcare decisions.

▶ Principles of Medical Ethics

There are four principles of medical ethics that were established by Beauchamp and Childress in 1979. These principles are autonomy, nonmaleficence, beneficence, and justice. The principle of autonomy, also referred to as respect for persons, is the right of the patient to make their own decision and retain control over their medical care. Providers should advise and provide recommendations to patients and should not coerce or persuade patients into making a decision. The principle of beneficence refers to the idea that healthcare providers must do everything they can to benefit each patient. Nonmaleficence means "do no harm," which means that providers must ensure that care is in the best interest of the patient, other individuals, and society (Beauchamp & Childress, 2001).

The principle of justice refers to the fact that there should be fairness in all medical decisions. Resources should be distributed in a fair and equitable manner to all patients, and providers should act in accordance with all laws and regulations. There are three main perspectives on justice: the egalitarian perspective, the libertarian perspective, and the utilitarian perspective. The egalitarian perspective favors equality and refers to the idea that fairness requires recognition of different levels of need; essentially, everyone should have equal access to the benefits and burdens arising from the pursuit of health (Longest, 2016). The libertarian perspective emphasizes freedom, individual liberty, and respect of property rights and favors the equal distribution of both benefits and burdens associated with the pursuit of health (Longest, 2016). The utilitarian perspective focuses on maximizing overall happiness and that fairness is best served when the greatest good for the greatest number are served (Longest, 2016). The American Medical Association (AMA) has set forth Principles of Medical Ethics to govern the ethical practice of physicians. The code can be obtained at https://www.ama-assn.org/delivering-care/ethics/code-medical-ethics-overview.

The governing body for each category of healthcare professionals has its own code of ethics that must be followed. For example, the American Nurses Association (ANA) provides the Code of Ethics for Nurses, available at https://homecaremissouri.org/mahc/documents/CodeofEthicswInterpretiveStatements20141.pdf. The American College of Healthcare Executives (ACHE) provides the Code of Ethics for Healthcare Executives, which is available at https://www.ache.org/about-ache/our-story/our-commitments/ethics/ache-code-of-ethics. In addition, each organization typically has its own code of ethics specified in its policies and procedures manual that must be followed by all employees.

▶ Resource Allocation

The American Medical Association's Code of Medical Ethics supports ethical resource allocation. It states that a physician's primary ethical obligation is to "promote the well-being of their patients" (AMA, 2018b). Policies for allocating healthcare resources can impede a physician's ability to fulfill that obligation. For example, physicians could advocate for policies relating to medical need, including urgency of resources, likelihood and anticipated duration of need, and change in quality of life (AMA, 2018b). Physicians have a responsibility to their profession to contribute their expertise in developing policies that are fair and equitable for all patients.

▶ Beginning-of-Life Care

Ethically, patients have the right to make their own decisions regarding beginning-of-life care. Two beginning-of-life care issues that often lead to ethical controversies are abortion and contraception. According to the U.S. Supreme Court's decision in the 1973 *Roe v. Wade* case, women have a constitutionally protected right to choose to have an abortion in the early stages of pregnancy (Planned Parenthood, 2018). Abortion is a human rights issue and is one of the most ethically charged decisions that occurs in health care.

Contraception has also been a big debate. People have the right to choose to use contraception, but a controversial debate occurred regarding whether a company can be forced to pay for it if it infringes upon their religious beliefs. The Patient Protection and Affordable Care Act included a contraceptive mandate that required employers to cover certain contraceptives for their female employees. In 2014, the

Supreme Court ruled in *Burwell v. Hobby Lobby* that the government cannot violate a person's right to exercise religion because that would be in violation of the Religious Freedom and Restoration Act (RFRA) of 1993 (573 U.S. ____ (2014)), which resulted in a reversal of this mandate.

▶ End-of-Life Care

End-of-life care decisions fall under the principle of autonomy. Patients have the right to determine the type of care they do or do not want when approaching the end-of-life. Patients should document their wishes in an advance directive. Advance directives, also known as *living wills*, are legal documents in which patients express their decisions about end-of-life care in advance. The living will specifies what treatments an individual does or does not wish to have if unconscious or dying. Living wills often address wishes regarding life-sustaining devices, resuscitation, and organ donation. Advance directives are only used in situations in which patients do not have the capacity to make decisions. In this situation, physicians must abide by the values and preferences a patient has stated in their advance directive.

▶ Ethical Challenges

Many ethical challenges can impact patients and families in the healthcare setting. Physicians and other clinical providers have moral responsibilities when providing clinical care. The questions raised in some cases do not have easy answers, and providers often must follow their own consciences, apply their own personal ethical values, or follow their organization's policies (Shi & Singh, 2017). Ten of the most common ethical challenges are:

1—Disagreement between patients/families and healthcare professionals about treatment decisions

2—Waiting lists

3—Access to needed healthcare resources for the aged, chronically ill, and mentally ill

4—Shortage of family physicians or primary care teams in both rural and urban settings

5—Medical errors

6—Withholding/withdrawing life-sustaining treatment in the context of terminal or serious illness

7—Achieving informed consent

8—Ethical issues related to participation in research

9—Substitute decision-making

10—The ethics of surgical innovation and incorporating new technologies for patient care (Breslin et al., 2005)

To address these challenges, organizations must educate healthcare professionals on how to deal with ethical issues, create policies for dealing with ethical issues, examine the patient's perspective regarding ethical issues, and report to the public the organization's measures for dealing with ethical challenges (Breslin et al., 2005).

▶ Dealing with Ethical Issues

Ethical issues and ethical compliance will continue to be priorities for healthcare organizations. Healthcare organizations, employees, and patients all expect the highest ethical conduct from healthcare professionals (Dunn, 2016). Ethical dilemmas, particularly those involving highly debated topics such as beginning- and end-of-life care, receive massive media attention and emotional public response (Dunn, 2016). The continual creation of newer, more advanced technologies will only complicate these debates. Healthcare organizations must be proactive in thinking about the impact of such actions and preparing for any potential ethical challenges that could arise.

▶ Summary

Healthcare professionals have a responsibility to uphold patients' rights when it comes to medical ethics. The principles of medical ethics were implemented to ensure patients are treated fairly and justly. Many guidelines have been established that give individuals the right to make decisions on their health.

Key Terms

Advance Directive is a written statement of a person's wishes regarding medical treatment, often including a living will, made to ensure those wishes are carried out should the person be unable to communicate them to a doctor.

Autonomy is right of the patient to make their own decision and retain control over their medical care.

Beneficence requires healthcare providers to do everything they can to benefit each patient.

Bioethics are the ethics of medical and biological research.

Egalitarian Perspective is the idea that fairness requires recognition of different levels of need, and everyone should have equal access to the benefits and burdens arising from the pursuit of health.

Justice is fairness in all medical decisions.

Libertarian Perspective emphasizes freedom, individual liberty, and respect of property rights and favors the equal distribution of both benefits and burdens associated with the pursuit of health.

Nonmaleficence means to "do no harm." Care is in the best interest of the patient.

Utilitarian Perspective focuses on maximizing overall happiness and that fairness is best served when the greatest good for the greatest number are served.

References

American College of Healthcare Executives (ACHE). (2018). *ACHE Code of Ethics.* https://www.ache.org/about-ache/our-story/our-commitments/ethics/ache-code-of-ethics

American Medical Association (AMA). (2018a). *AMA Principles of Medical Ethics.* https://www.ama-assn.org/sites/default/files/media-browser/principles-of-medical-ethics.pdf

American Medical Association (AMA). (2018b). *Code of Medical Ethics.* https://www.ama-assn.org/delivering-care/ama-code-medical-ethics

American Nurses Association (ANA). (2018). *Code of Ethics for Nurses.* https://www.nursingworld.org/coe-view-only

Beauchamp, T. L., & Childress, J. F. (2001). *Principles of biomedical ethics* (5th ed.). New York: Oxford University Press.

Breslin, J. M., MacRae, S. K., Bell, J., Singer, P. A., & the University of Toronto Joint Centre for Bioethics Clinical Ethics Group. (2005). Top 10 health care ethics challenges facing the public: Views of Toronto bioethicists. *BMC Medical Ethics, 6*(5), 1–8.

Buchbinder, S. B., & Shanks, N. H. (2017). *Introduction to health care management* (3rd ed.). Burlington, MA: Jones & Bartlett Learning.

Burwell v. Hobby Lobby. 573 U.S. _____ (2014). https://www.supremecourt.gov/opinions/13pdf /13-354_olp1.pd

Dunn, R. T. (2016). *Dunn & Haimann's healthcare management* (10th ed.). Chicago, IL: Health Administration Press.

Longest, B. B. (2016). *Health policymaking in the United States* (6th ed.). Chicago, IL: Health Administration Press.

Planned Parenthood. (2018). *Roe v. Wade.* https://www.plannedparenthoodaction.org/issues/abortion /roe-v-wade

Shi, L., & Singh, D. A. (2017). *Essentials of the U.S. health care system.* Burlington, MA: Jones & Bartlett Learning.

$\mathcal{P}$ *CASE 13-1*

A Problem of Epidemic Proportions: Ethical Concerns in the Opioid Crisis

Lynne Walker MSN, RNC-NIC, CNE & Alice Colwell MSN, RNC-NIC

It is a typical summer weekend night in a small rural town outside of Baltimore. Riley and Donnie are the first responder crew on the 3–11 p.m. shift on this particular night. Because of their years of experience, the team have some idea of what the night might bring. Perhaps a call from an elderly gentleman who fell, maybe a call from someone who thought they were having a heart attack, but most likely, Riley and Donnie will be called again to respond to an opioid overdose. Sadly, this scenario is becoming the norm.

As expected, the first responders take a call about a suspected heroin overdose. Riley and Donnie quickly respond as expected but do so with a sense of apathy. The first responders are acutely aware of the scenario they are about to see—it happens all the time.

Riley and Donnie drive to a familiar location to find the victim, Heather. They know her by name and can assume what happened on this particular night. Riley and Donnie have helped Heather six times before and have provided lifesaving medications for her addiction each time.

Everyone involved knows what has happened and what needs to be done to effectively and successfully reverse the heroin overdose. However, tonight may play out differently. The use of Narcan (an opioid antagonist) is taxing supplies so much that demand is far exceeding availability. This is what Riley and Donnie experience tonight. The first responders have only one dose left and are debating whether Heather deserves the last available dose. The first responders feel that Heather has been privileged to receive Narcan but has continually reverted to her old ways and is taking advantage of the limited resources currently available.

The opioid crisis in the United States is currently a public health emergency. According to the CDC, in 2016, 42,249 individuals died from an opioid overdose, a 27.9% increase from 2015. Many of the opioid deaths were attributed to overdoses involving synthetic opioids. On average, 116 Americans die each day from an opioid overdose. These statistics continue to rise each year (Seth et al., 2018).

Many cities across the United States are seeing the effects of an alarming number of opioid overdoses. First responders continue to rely upon Narcan to save the lives of individuals experiencing an opioid overdose. Like Heather, many overdose victims require multiple doses of Narcan to revive them after each overdose, and many have experienced repeated episodes of opioid overdoses. After overdosing and being revived, many are again using opioids within a short period of time. This not only places a strain on medical responders but communities are also faced with a financial quandary of how to pay for Narcan doses.

Every week first responders make decisions about who will receive the Narcan and who will not. Communities across the nation must decide how much money to spend on Narcan and face fact that the current funding for Narcan may not be sustainable.

Communities have postulated several potential ways to address the dilemma—none of which seem ideal. One possible solution discussed is limiting the number of times a first responder can administer Narcan to an overdose victim. Other possible solutions include having the overdose victim pay for the doses or raising taxes on the general population to spread the burden (Wootsen, 2017). Most recently, states are seeking to impose taxes on the manufacturers and distributors of opioid medications in order to generate funding for addiction services (S. 523, 115th Cong., 2017).

One law that directly addresses the allocation of funding to states for the opioid crisis is the Comprehensive Addiction and Recovery Act (CARA), which was signed into law by President Barack Obama in July 2016. This law awards grants to states to fund the purchasing of Narcan along with many other measures to address the crisis (ASAM, 2018). In 2018, the bipartisan CARA 2.0 was introduced, which asks for additional dollars to expand first responder training and access to Narcan (S. 2456, 115th Cong., 2018).

Along with the resource problem, another issue troubling Riley and Donnie is the requirement that 1–2 doses of Narcan are to be withheld per shift to be used in the case of an accidental nonuser exposure to an opioid, such as in the case of a first responder exposure, or if a child is exposed to a family member or friend's opioids. In these cases, not having the Narcan needed can mean the difference between life and death of an innocent victim. Riley especially is struggling with the fact that an individual may not be saved based on the need to "hold back" a few doses for possible cases of accidental exposure, although she understands the rationale.

Riley and Donnie struggle with other dilemmas as well. Both feel an immense obligation to care for not only a great number of overdose victims in any one day but also the burden of making decisions about who may live or die. Riley often lies awake at night pondering whether she is enabling overdose victims in their addiction by repeatedly administering doses of Narcan.

Riley starts to think back to an Ethics in Public Health course she took in her undergraduate studies. She remembers that the ethical principle of beneficence could apply in these situations. She recalls that beneficence is an ethical principle in which actions are used to benefit others and promote the good of others. Social justice was also an important concept in public health ethics and included the premise that benefits and burdens should be distributed fairly among members of a society. This also can include decisions about how society determines the allocation of their resources and provides for the health and welfare of citizens (Butts & Rich, 2016). Riley ponders the question of whether resources are being distributed fairly and how first responders make these decisions.

Utilitarianism is another principle to take into consideration in these cases and is an underlying principle of public health ethics. Utilitarianism is the principle in which we provide the greatest good for the greatest number of people (Butts & Rich, 2016). If Riley and Donnie administer repeated doses of Narcan to one individual, what are the consequences for the next person who overdoses after all the doses are depleted?

Equipped with this knowledge, Riley and Donnie must now face the decision that will change the course of Heather's life.

Discussion Questions

1. A small percentage of society as a whole are recipients of Narcan. Explain how social justice plays a role in distributing resources. What are the limits of the obligation that society has in distributing their resources in order to help others?
2. Identify an ethical principle you espouse and describe how it can be applied to the scenario should Riley and Donnie administer a dose of Narcan to Heather. Identify a violation of an ethical principle should Riley and Donnie withhold the dose.
3. What interventions can be implemented to combat the opioid crisis?
4. As major stakeholders, describe how the pharmaceutical industry is impacting the opioid crisis. What role can the pharmaceutical companies play in fighting the opioid epidemic?

References

American Society of Addiction Medicine (ASAM). (2018). *Summary of the Comprehensive Addiction and Recovery Act.* https://www.asam.org/advocacy/issues/opioids/summary-of-the-comprehensive -addiction-and-recovery-act
Budgeting for Opioid Addiction Treatment Act. S. 523, 115th Cong. (2017–2018). https://www.congress.gov /bill/115th-congress/senate-bill/523?q=%7B%22search%22%3A%5B%22opioid+tax%22%5D%7D

Butts, J. B., & Rich, K. L. (2016). *Nursing ethics: Across the curriculum & into practice* (4th ed.). Burlington, MA: Jones & Bartlett Learning.

Comprehensive Addiction and Recovery Act 2.0. S. 2456, 115th Cong. (2017–2018).

Seth, P., Scholl, L., Rudd, R., & Bacon, S. (2018). Overdose deaths involving opioids, cocaine and psychostimulants—United States 2015–2016. *Morbidity and Mortality Weekly Report, 67,* 349–358. https://www.cdc.gov/mmwr/volumes/67/wr/mm6712a1.htm?s_cid=mm6712a1_w

Wootsen, C. (2017, June 17). One politician's solution to the overdose problem: Let them die. *The Washington Post.* https://www.washingtonpost.com/news/to-your-health/wp/2017/06/28/a-council-members-solution-to-his-ohio-towns-overdose-problem-let-addicts-die/?utm_term=.066fcc343ef3

🔍 *CASE 13-2*

Direct-to-Consumer Genetic Testing: Pandora's Box?

Catherine E. Tymkow, EdD, DNP, MS(N), RN, APN, WHNP-BC

Over-the-counter and direct-to-consumer genetic testing have become a burgeoning enterprise since the sequencing of the human genome. In many ways, genetics has become the "designer science" of the 21st century. However, as science progresses and the public become more aware of the possibilities of DNA testing for an array of health and other uses, genetics will continue to grow in importance as a public health and policy concern. One need only look at Internet or television advertising to see the daunting number of testing services and self-diagnostic products. The fact that direct-to-consumer testing has advanced beyond policy governing marketing, access, and distribution of these products raises complex and perplexing ethical–legal issues for providers and the need for education about these offerings to the public. Consider the following case:

Joan is a 46-year-old divorced mother of four, who recently heard an advertisement for a new "simple, at-home genetic test" to determine her risk for developing breast or ovarian cancer. The TV ad states that the test is effective in predicting cancer risk in families with histories of breast or ovarian cancer. The ad also states that medical interventions have been shown to be effective in lowering the risk of cancer even in individuals with a family history of the disease. Because Joan's maternal grandmother died of colon cancer and her maternal aunt died of breast cancer at age 50, Joan feels her risk and her children's risk for developing these and other types of cancer are high.

Joan also sees a recent article on the Internet that the Federal Drug Administration (FDA) has approved direct-to-consumer testing for the BRCA breast cancer mutation (Begley, 2018). She feels comforted by this article and the reassuring nature of the advertisements about BRCA testing. She notes that the price for testing by some companies seems very reasonable. She selects one of the many vendors who provide the test, charges the $99 fee to her credit card, and sends her saliva sample in for examination. A few weeks later, she receives her results, which indicate she does not have BRCA 1 or BRCA 2 mutations. Relieved, Joan informs her children about her results and that they do not need to worry about getting cancer.

Joan knows that she should still continue her monthly self-breast exams, but after her negative test results she performs self-breast exams only sporadically. She sees her primary healthcare provider (PHCP) every year for a routine exam. Her last exam after her negative BRCA test was negative. The following year she was traveling and did not schedule her yearly exam, and the year after that her mother (who lives in another state) was quite ill, requiring Joan to travel frequently, so yet again Joan did not have time to schedule her yearly exam. In the third year, she does schedule an exam, and her PHCP discovers a moderately sized lump on her right breast, which upon biopsy is found to be malignant.

When Joan's oncologist suggests that she might want to consider BRCA analysis because she has two daughters and other cancer history, Joan tearfully reveals to the oncologist the results of her earlier BRCA analysis. She feels that she has been misled by the results and the advertising surrounding the test. She tells her oncologist that if she had not had the test, she would have been more diligent in keeping her yearly appointments and in doing her own self-breast exam.

Interestingly, Joan's primary healthcare provider (PHCP) informs her, after she told him that she had ordered the test herself because she didn't want the results in her medical record, that most breast cancer is not inherited and that the BRCA test can only identify three of the more than 1,000 genetic mutations associated with the BRCA 1 and 2 susceptibility gene (Begley, 2018). He also told her that her negative result was not a guarantee that she would never develop breast or uterine cancer.

Nevertheless, Joan is angry. She thinks the company should not have been able to offer a test with such limited use and she feels she was poorly informed by the company. Some recent professional articles seem to mirror this concern (Covolo et al., 2018). She is also very depressed and worried. Joan informs her daughters about her newfound knowledge and is consumed with guilt that she provided poor information to her family.

Discussion Questions

1. Are there factors in Joan's history that would or should have led her PHCP to counsel her about genetic testing? If yes, what are they?
2. What information should Joan's PHCP have told her about BRCA 1 and 2 testing had she asked before submitting her sample?
3. There is no mention in this case of what information or counsel was given to Joan before she sent her sample for testing. What information would be crucial for her to know and affirm before submitting her sample for testing? What should healthcare providers advise patients about direct-to-consumer testing?
4. Although direct-to-consumer testing for BRCA has recently been approved by the FDA, what concerns should consumers have about testing?
5. What policy concerns should providers and patients have about DTC testing?

References

Begley, S. (2018). *FDA approves first direct-to-consumer test for breast cancer risk.* STAT. https://www.statnews.com/2018/03/06/fda-approves-test-breast-cancer/

Covolo, L., Rubinelli, S. Ceretti, E., & Gelatti, U. (2015). Internet-based direct-to-consumer genetic testing: A systematic review. *Journal of Medical Internet Research, 17*(2), e279.

🔍 *CASE 13-3*

Alzheimer's Disease: An Ethical Dilemma

Catherine E. Tymkow, EdD, DNP, MS(N), RN, APN, WHNP-BC

James is a 58-year-old married man with three adult children. His mother has recently died as a result of Alzheimer's disease. James was distressed by the deterioration of his mother and burdened by his responsibilities for her care. James has recently heard of a direct-to-consumer genetic test for Alzheimer's disease. He has read that Alzheimer's has a strong familial tendency and wishes to know if he is at risk for developing the disease. James doesn't want to contact a healthcare professional because he is afraid his life insurance company will cancel his coverage and leave his wife unprotected should he die as a result of the disease.

James easily obtains a direct-to-consumer genetic testing kit for Alzheimer's disease online. He reads the information booklet that comes with the kit but finds it confusing. He follows the directions carefully and sends in his sample for testing.

A few weeks later, the results arrive in the mail and state that James has tested positive for Apoliopoprotien E, indicating a mutation on chromosome 19. Because James did not understand the information presented in the testing kit's booklet or that this positive test does not mean he will develop Alzheimer's disease with 100% certainty (U.S. National Library of Medicine, 2018). He assumes that the finding means he will eventually develop the disease just as his mother did.

James is devastated by the results of his test. He sees no need to consult his healthcare provider because he knows from caring for his mother that nothing can be done to cure the disease. He does not discuss the results with his family because he is afraid of burdening them with the findings. He believes that keeping the findings to himself is the best way to protect his family. Tragically, James becomes profoundly depressed and makes the decision to end his own life at age 70, which is when his mother's symptoms first manifested, to prevent suffering the effects of the disease and to spare his family from the burden of his care.

Discussion Questions

1. The ethical principle of autonomy, which seeks to allow the individual as much independence in discussion making as possible (Westrick, 2014), is a driving principle that affects healthcare professionals' interaction with their patients. Identify the role adherence to autonomy played in James' situation. Does James have the ethical right to obtain this information on his own?

2. The ethical principle of nonmaleficence is also a driving principle affecting healthcare professionals. Identify how the ethical principle of nonmaleficence might be used to limit the harm James has suffered.

3. Can the ethical principles of autonomy and nonmaleficence be reconciled to allow James to obtain the information he needs without causing harm in the process? If so, describe what this process might look like.

4. Title II of the Genetic Information Nondiscrimination Act of 2008 (GINA), which prohibits genetic information discrimination in employment, took effect on November 21, 2009. GINA prohibits health insurers from discrimination based on the genetic information of enrollees. Specifically, health insurers may not use genetic information to make eligibility, coverage, underwriting or premium-setting decisions. Furthermore, health insurers may not request or require individuals or their family members to undergo genetic testing or to provide genetic information. As defined in the law, genetic information includes family medical history, manifest disease in family members, and information regarding individuals' and family members' genetic tests (U.S. Equal Opportunity Commission, 2017).

    Are James' concerns regarding his health and life insurance valid? How would GINA address James' concerns?

5. As his healthcare provider, James confides in you the results of his genetic profile for Alzheimer's disease. James reveals his deep distress over the findings and his wish to keep the results from his wife and grown children, who are also patients of yours.

    What duty of confidentiality do you owe to James in this situation?

    What can be done if James refuses to consult with a genetic counselor?

    What duty do you owe his children who may share his genetic propensity for developing the disease? Do they have a right to know? Can you violate your duty of confidentiality to tell them?

References

U.S. Equal Employment Opportunity Commission. (2017). *Genetic information discrimination*. https://www.eeoc.gov/laws/types/genetic.cfm

U.S. National Library of Medicine (2018). *APOE Gene*. https://ghr.nlm.nih.gov/gene/APOE#conditions

Westrick, S. J. (2014). *Essentials of nursing law and ethics*. Jones & Bartlett, Learning: Burlington, MA.

CHAPTER 14

The Changing Dynamics of Health Policy and the Healthcare Delivery System

Lesley Clack, ScD

▶ Introduction

The healthcare system in the United States is a constantly changing environment in the midst of transformation. With the uncertainty of healthcare reform, future changes will likely rely on comparative effectiveness research (CER) (KFF, 2009). CER has been discussed as part of the national health reform debate as a way to improve the quality of healthcare in the United States and curb healthcare spending. Title VIII of the American Recovery and Reinvestment Act (ARRA) of 2009 authorized $1.1 billion for conducting CER (Weinstein & Skinner, 2010). CER develops and disseminates information regarding best practices to patients and providers with a goal of improving health outcomes. By using evidence to identify the best treatments and interventions, this may in turn assist with lowering costs to the healthcare system.

▶ Comparative Effectiveness Systems

The Institute of Medicine (IOM) defines CER as the "generation and synthesis of evidence that compares the benefits and harms of alternative methods to prevent, diagnose, treat, and monitor a clinical condition to improve the delivery of care" (Sox & Greenfield, p. 203, 2009). CER compares technologies, products, and procedures of two or more healthcare interventions to set the standard of care. Essentially, CER determines how well a healthcare treatment will work using the highest standards of clinical evidence. However, simply providing information on the best treatments and procedures to use is not by itself sufficient to improve a healthcare system (Kovner & Knickman, 2015). In the United States, CER is primarily used in research settings. In other countries, CER has a more prevalent role in the healthcare system through generating guidelines for care and reimbursement. With a recent push in the United States to improve quality while reducing costs, the benefits of CER and systems in other countries warrant consideration.

Quality Improvement

One of the primary goals of CER is to enable healthcare providers to choose the option with the best health outcome. IOM identified CER as a priority in its 2009 report, *Initial National Priorities for Comparative Effectiveness Research*, in response to the ARRA calling upon the IOM to recommend a list of topics to be the priority of CER investment (IOM, 2009). Improving patient outcomes relies on receiving information from patients regarding symptoms and effects of treatment (Weldring & Smith, 2013). IOM has identified patient-centeredness as one of the six dimensions of quality care (2001), which has resulted in a renewed focus on involving patients in care. A patient-reported outcome (PRO) is a patient's response regarding their health, quality of life, or functional status without interpretation of the patient's response by a provider (Weldring & Smith, 2013). An example of a PRO would be asking a patient to rate the severity of their pain on a scale of 0 to 10, with 0 being no pain and 10 being most severe. PROs are very useful for assessing outcomes as a part of CER (Segal et al., 2013). The use of PROs in CER has grown, and this base of research has the potential to "improve the efficiency of data collection and analysis, and to also provide new opportunities to bring meaningful evidence back to decision makers and patients in meaningful ways" (Segal et al., 2013, p. 2). In IOM's *100 Initial Priority Topics for Comparative Effectiveness Research*, 22 priorities are related to improve the quality of life and health outcomes (**BOX 14-1**).

Cost Savings

Another significant benefit of using CER in the healthcare system is to control costs. CER can help healthcare systems to control costs without compromising PROs (Kovner & Knickman, 2011). While implementing CER is costly, the benefits of cost reduction to the system may outweigh the cost of implementing CER. Relying more heavily on CER allows healthcare systems to identify the costs and effectiveness of treatments and technologies to justify that spending money on them will improve PROs (Chandra et al., 2011). In IOM's *100 Initial Priority Topics for Comparative Effectiveness Research*, 11 priorities are related to controlling costs (**BOX 14-2**).

Systems in Other Countries

The U.S. healthcare system is different from other countries in that it is decentralized. Many industrialized countries, such as the United Kingdom (UK), Canada, Germany, and Australia, have centralized healthcare systems (Benson & Lyerly, 2010). Although the ARRA did allocate $1.1 billion in 2009 to advance CER in the

BOX 14-1 IOM CER Priority Topics for Quality of Life and Health Outcomes

Compare the effectiveness of upper endoscopy utilization and the frequency for patients with gastroesophageal reflux disease on morbidity, quality of life, and diagnosis of esophageal adenocarcinoma.

Compare the effectiveness of management strategies for localized prostate cancer (e.g., active surveillance, radical prostatectomy [conventional, robotic, and laparoscopic], and radiotherapy [conformal, brachytherapy, proton-beam, and intensity-modulated radiotherapy]) on survival, recurrence, side effects, quality of life, and costs.

Compare the effectiveness (including survival, hospitalization, quality of life, and costs) of renal replacement therapies (e.g., daily home hemodialysis, intermittent home hemodialysis, conventional in-center dialysis, continuous ambulatory peritoneal dialysis, renal transplantation) for patients of different ages, races, and ethnicities.

Compare the effectiveness (including effects on quality of life) of treatment strategies (e.g., topical steroids, ultraviolet light, methotrexate, biologic response modifiers) for psoriasis.

Compare the effectiveness of different quality improvement strategies in disease prevention, acute care, chronic disease care, and rehabilitation services for diverse populations of children and adults.

Compare the effectiveness of different benefit design, utilization management, and cost-sharing strategies in improving healthcare access and quality in patients with chronic diseases (e.g., cancer, diabetes, heart disease).

Compare the effectiveness of monotherapy and polytherapy (i.e., use of two or more drugs) on seizure frequency, adverse events, quality of life, and cost in patients with intractable epilepsy.

Compare the effectiveness of surgical resection, observation, or ablative techniques on disease-free and overall survival, tumor recurrence, quality of life, and toxicity in patients with liver metastases.

Compare the effectiveness of interventions (e.g., community-based multi-level interventions, simple health education, usual care) to reduce health disparities in cardiovascular disease, diabetes, cancer, musculoskeletal diseases, and birth outcomes.

Compare the effectiveness of shared decision making and usual care on decision outcomes (treatment choice, knowledge, treatment-preference concordance, and decisional conflict) in children and adults with chronic disease such as stable angina and asthma.

Compare the effectiveness of accountable care systems and usual care on costs, processes of care, and outcomes for geographically defined populations of patients with one or more chronic diseases.

Compare the effectiveness and outcomes of care with obstetric ultrasound studies and care without the use of ultrasound in normal pregnancies.

Compare the effectiveness of traditional risk stratification for coronary heart disease (CHD) and noninvasive imaging (using coronary artery calcium, carotid intima media thickness, and other approaches) on CHD outcomes.

Compare the effectiveness of treatment strategies for primary open-angle glaucoma (e.g., initial laser surgery, new surgical techniques, new medical treatments) particularly in minority populations to assess clinical and patient-reported outcomes.

(continues)

BOX 14-1 IOM CER Priority Topics for Quality of Life and Health Outcomes *(continued)*

Compare the effectiveness of adding information about new biomarkers (including genetic information) with standard care in motivating behavior change and improving clinical outcomes.

Establish a prospective registry to compare the effectiveness of surgical and nonsurgical strategies for treating cervical spondylotic myelopathy (CSM) in patients with different characteristics to delineate predictors of improved outcomes.

Compare the effectiveness of comprehensive, coordinated care and usual care on objective measures of clinical status, patient-reported outcomes, and costs of care for people with multiple sclerosis.

Compare the effectiveness of treatment strategies for obesity (e.g., bariatric surgery, behavioral interventions, and pharmacologic treatment) on the resolution of obesity-related outcomes, such as diabetes, hypertension, and musculoskeletal disorders.

Compare the effectiveness of care coordination with and without clinical decision supports (e.g., electronic health records) in producing good health outcomes in chronically ill patients, including children with special healthcare needs.

Compare the effectiveness (e.g., pain relief, functional outcomes) of different surgical strategies for symptomatic cervical disc herniation in patients for whom appropriate nonsurgical care has failed.

Compare the effectiveness of hospital-based palliative care and usual care on patient-reported outcomes and cost.

Compare the effectiveness of traditional training of primary care physicians in primary care mental health and colocation systems of primary care and mental health care on outcomes including depression, anxiety, physical symptoms, physical disability, prescription substance use, mental and physical function, satisfaction with the provider, and cost.

Institute of Medicine. (2009). *Initial National Priorities for Comparative Effectiveness Research*. Washington, DC: The National Academies Press. https://doi.org/10.17226/12648.

BOX 14-2 IOM CER Priority Topics for Cost Savings

Compare the effectiveness of management strategies for localized prostate cancer (e.g., active surveillance, radical prostatectomy [conventional, robotic, and laparoscopic], and radiotherapy [conformal, brachytherapy, proton-beam, and intensity-modulated radiotherapy]) on survival, recurrence, side effects, quality of life, and costs.

Compare the effectiveness and costs of alternative detection and management strategies (e.g., pharmacologic treatment, social/family support, combined pharmacologic and social/family support) for dementia in community-dwelling individuals and their caregivers.

Compare the effectiveness of accountable care systems and usual care on costs, processes of care, and outcomes for geographically defined populations of patients with one or more chronic diseases.

Compare the effectiveness (including survival, hospitalization, quality of life, and costs) of renal replacement therapies (e.g., daily home hemodialysis, intermittent home hemodialysis, conventional in-center dialysis, continuous ambulatory peritoneal dialysis, renal transplantation) for patients of different ages, races, and ethnicities.

Compare the effectiveness and cost-effectiveness of conventional medical management of type 2 diabetes in adolescents and adults versus conventional therapy plus intensive educational programs or programs incorporating support groups and educational resources.

Compare the effectiveness of different benefit design, utilization management, and cost-sharing strategies in improving healthcare access and quality in patients with chronic diseases (e.g., cancer, diabetes, heart disease).

Compare the effectiveness of comprehensive, coordinated care and usual care on objective measures of clinical status, patient-reported outcomes, and costs of care for people with multiple sclerosis.

Compare the clinical and cost-effectiveness of surgical care and a medical model of prevention and care in managing periodontal disease to increase tooth longevity and reduce systemic secondary effects in other organ systems.

Compare the effectiveness of monotherapy and polytherapy (i.e., use of two or more drugs) on seizure frequency, adverse events, quality of life, and cost in patients with intractable epilepsy.

Compare the effectiveness of hospital-based palliative care and usual care on patient-reported outcomes and cost.

Compare the effectiveness of traditional training of primary care physicians in primary care mental health and colocation systems of primary care and mental health care on outcomes including depression, anxiety, physical symptoms, physical disability, prescription substance use, mental and physical function, satisfaction with the provider, and cost.

Institute of Medicine. (2009). *Initial National Priorities for Comparative Effectiveness Research*. Washington, DC: The National Academies Press. https://doi.org/10.17226/12648.

United States, the United States has not historically been known as a leader in CER (Shafrin, 2012). While there has been a recent push and investment in CER in the United States, there has traditionally been a lack of publicly available CER, which impedes providers in making informed decisions (Sorenson, 2010). In other countries, government agencies typically make nationwide decisions on medical therapies and whether they will be covered based on CER regarding cost and benefit of treatments (Chandra et al., 2011). European countries have been using CER systems for 20 to 30 years to inform pricing and coverage decisions and to develop evidence-based practices (Sorenson, 2010). In the UK, health care is publicly financed through a universal healthcare system called the National Health Service (NHS) (Kovner & Knickman, 2015). In the UK, the National Institute for Health & Clinical Excellence (NICE) decides which treatments are reimbursed by NHS based upon CER (Chandra et al., 2011). As evidenced by other countries' success, expanding CER in the United States is essential for improving health outcomes and controlling costs.

▶ Forecasting

Although the future of healthcare in the United States is unpredictable, forecasting is still important. Forecasting is simply a method by which healthcare companies can prepare and plan for future possible occurrences. Forecasting is critical to strategic planning, and healthcare facilities should use it to determine where they should focus their attention in their short- and long-range planning (Kovner & Knickman, 2015). Both the Centers for Medicare and Medicaid Services (CMS) and the Congressional Budget Office (CBO) publish reports that can be used as a basis for predicting future trends and changes in healthcare. There are a variety of different forecasting methods (Kovner & Knickman, 2015):

- Quantitative forecasting methods analyze past data to predict future events. A time-series analysis that looks at changes and trends over time is an example of a quantitative forecasting technique.
- The Delphi method is a qualitative forecasting method that relies on expert opinions to make a prediction. The Delphi method involves polling experts about their predictions in order to reach a consensus.
- Another approach is to rely on nationally recognized leaders in the field to make predictions based upon their past experience. For example, media channels often report predictions and forecasts by calling upon nationally recognized leaders for their opinions.

Although forecasting is not an exact science, it is important in providing a reference point upon which to make predictions regarding future events.

▶ Dynamics of Future Change

Sociodemographic and Economic Changes

Certain changes, such as sociodemographic and economic changes, will influence the healthcare system in the United States. The ever-increasing population of older adults will put strains on Medicare and Social Security (Shi & Singh, 2017). The CMS *2017 Annual Report of the Board of Trustees of the Federal Hospital Insurance and Federal Supplementary Medical Insurance Trust Funds* states that legislation is needed to address the substantial financial shortfall that the Medicare program is facing. Funding legislation could include borrowing money from the Federal Reserve or cutting other programs such as Social Security benefits. Current projections show that the Medicare program will be completely depleted by 2026 (Board of Trustees of the Federal Hospital Insurance and Federal Supplementary Medical Insurance Trust Funds, 2018). This shortfall is due in part to rising healthcare expenditures. Healthcare expenditures have increased, on average, by 2.1% annually over the past 5 years (Board of Trustees of the Federal Hospital Insurance and Federal Supplementary Medical Insurance Trust Funds, 2018). The other issue with the increase of healthcare expenditures is that it affects the affordability of healthcare services. Over the 15-year period from 2000 to 2015, the average annual household income decreased by 4% (Shi & Singh, 2017). Health policy research, such as CER and other data-driven collection strategies, is needed to examine affordability of health care in the age of decreasing income and rising costs.

Technological and Workforce Changes

The emergence of new technology is important for the advancement of healthcare (Knickman & Kovner, 2015). However, new medical technology does increase costs to the system (Shi & Singh, 2017). Future technologies should focus on those that can enhance accessibility and affordability of healthcare services. It is likely that we will see even more integration of telehealth applications used in the delivery of patient care. Telehealth and telemedicine applications are also useful for dealing with healthcare workforce shortages. The Association of American Medical Colleges predicts a shortage of as many as 90,000 physicians by 2025 (Bernstein, 2015). In addition, it is projected that the greatest shortfall will be in specialists who treat diseases more common in the older adult population. Policies are needed to address the physician shortage through initiatives geared toward providing funds for students in medical schools and ensuring there is an adequate supply of physicians in rural areas.

Changes in Healthcare Reform

There will continue to be dissenting opinions about the best system for healthcare in the United States. Over the past decade, how healthcare is paid for and the role and organization of health insurance has been at the forefront (Kovner & Knickman, 2015) of political debate. The political forces at play have a significant impact on health reform. For example, the Patient Protection and Affordable Care Act (PPACA) of 2010 included the individual mandate as one of its major provisions. The individual mandate required all individuals (with a few exceptions) to purchase health insurance or pay a penalty on their income taxes. On December 20, 2017, under the Trump administration, the individual mandate was repealed as of January 2019 through the passage of the Tax Cuts and Jobs Act of 2017 (Public Law No. 115-97, 2017). In 2019, President Trump stated that the priorities are on lowering the cost of prescription drugs, boosting funding to end childhood cancer and HIV/AIDS, and securing the passage of legislation to ban "late-term" abortion (Ault, 2019). These priorities will likely shift, and health reform will continue as a heavily debated topic in 2020 and beyond.

Changes in Models of Care Delivery

Although there are many opinions regarding what type of healthcare system would work best in the United States, there is widespread consensus that the existing model of healthcare delivery must change (Shi & Singh, 2017). Over the past decade, spearheaded by the PPACA, the United States has continued to move from a volume-oriented to a value-based healthcare system (Kovner & Knickman, 2015). Some of the current models, such as Accountable Care Organizations (ACOs) and Patient-Centered Medical Homes (PCMHs), are value-based systems that focus on quality and achieving the desired healthcare outcomes rather than the volume of services produced. Due to many of the factors previously discussed, such as the aging of the population and the desire to reduce costs to the system, we will likely continue to see the emergence of new models of care delivery.

▶ Summary

The U.S. healthcare system constantly changes and evolves because of the implementation of new healthcare policy such as the PPACA. Among the constant changes there are common goals. A common goal discussed in this chapter is that quality services must be provided at a reasonable cost. In order to determine if this goal is met, CER is developed and disseminated. Ensuring health outcomes have been met is a data-driven endeavor. Future changes in the U.S. healthcare system may take into consideration successes of other countries.

Key Terms

Comparative Effectiveness Research (CER) involves generation and synthesis of evidence that compares the benefits and harms of alternative methods to prevent, diagnose, treat, and monitor a clinical condition to improve the delivery of care.

Data Driven is determined by or dependent on the collection or analysis of data.

Delphi Method is a qualitative forecasting technique that looks at changes and trends over time.

Forecasting is a method by which healthcare companies can prepare and plan for future possible occurrences.

Healthcare Data Analytics applies statistical techniques to allow informed decisions to be made based on the data.

Quantitative Forecasting is a method for analyzing past data to predict future events.

Strategic Planning is used to set the priorities of organizational management activity, focus energy and resources, strengthen operations, ensure that employees and other stakeholders are working toward common goals, and establish agreement around intended outcomes/results.

Time-Series Analysis is a quantitative forecasting technique that looks at changes and trends over time.

References

Ault, A. (2019). *Trump tackles drug costs, HIV, cancer, abortion in State of the Union*. https://www.medscape.com/viewarticle/908731

Benson, A., & Lyerly, K. (2010). *Improving medical decisions through comparative effectiveness research: cancer as a case study*. Friends of Cancer Research. http://www.focr.org/sites/default/files/CER%20REPORT%20FINAL.pdf

Bernstein, L. (2015). U.S. faces 90,000 doctor shortages by 2025, Medical School Association warns. *The Washington Post*. https://www.washingtonpost.com/news/to-your-health/wp/2015/03/03/u-s-faces-90000-doctor-shortage-by-2025-medical-school-association-warns/?noredirect=on&utm_term=.41719ed5a5d3

Boards of Trustees of the Federal Hospital Insurance and Federal Supplementary Medical Insurance Trust Funds. (June 5, 2018.) *2017 Annual Report*. https://www.cms.gov/Research-Statistics-Data-and-Systems/Statistics-Trends-and-Reports/ReportsTrustFunds/Downloads/TR2018.pdf

Chandra, A., Jena, A. B., & Skinner, J. S. (2011). The pragmatist's guide to comparative effectiveness research. *Journal of Economic Perspectives*, 25(2), 27–46.

Institute for Medicine (IOM). (2001). *Crossing the quality chasm: A new health system for the 21st century*. Washington, D.C.: National Academy Press.

Institute of Medicine (IOM). (2009). Initial priorities for comparative effectiveness research. http://www.chi.org/uploadedFiles/Industry_at_a_glance/Institute%20of%20Medicine%20Report%20on%20CER%20063009.pdf

Kaiser Family Foundation (KFF). (2009). Explaining health reform: What is comparative effectiveness research? https://kaiserfamilyfoundation.files.wordpress.com/2013/01/7946.pdf

Kovner, A. R., & Knickman, J. R. (Eds.) (2015). *Jonas & Kovner's health care delivery in the United States* (11th ed.). New York: Springer Publishing.

Segal, C., Holve, E., & Sabharwal, R. (2013*). Collecting and using patient-reported outcomes (PRO) for comparative effectiveness research (CER) and patient-centered outcomes research (PCOR): Challenges and opportunities*. Academy Health. https://www.academyhealth.org/sites/default/files/Collecting%20and%20Using%20PRO%20for%20CER%20and%20PCOR.pdf

Shafrin, J. (2012). *International approaches to comparative effectiveness research.* Healthcare Economist. https://www.healthcare-economist.com/2012/06/18/international-approaches-to-comparative -effectiveness-research/

Shi, L., & Singh, D. (2017). *Essentials of the U.S. health care system* (4th ed.). Burlington, MA: Jones & Bartlett Learning.

Sorenson, C. (2010). *Use of CER in drug coverage and pricing decisions: A six-country comparison.* The Commonwealth Fund. https://www.commonwealthfund.org/publications/issue-briefs /2010/jul/use-comparative-effectiveness-research-drug-coverage-and-pricing

Sox, H. C., & Greenfield, S. (2009). Comparative effectiveness research: A report from the IOM. *Annals of Internal Medicine, 151*(3), 203–205.

Weinstein, M. C., & Skinner, J. A. (2010). Comparative effectiveness and health care spending— Implications for reform. *New England Journal of Medicine, 362,* 460–465.

Weldring, T., & Smith, S. M. S. (2013). Patient-Reported Outcomes (PROs) and Patient-Reported Outcomes Measures (PROMs). *Health Services Insights, 6,* 61–68.

🔎 *CASE 14-1*

Where Might We Go? International Comparisons

Raymond J. Higbea, PhD & Gregory A. Cline, PhD

When scholars, professionals, and government officials seek to gain an understanding of the United States health system, they frequently revert to comparing the U.S. health system to those of the Organization of Economic Cooperation and Development (OECD) countries. Although this is the best comparison we have, its weakness is its inability to include the cultural and historic or contextual aspects of these countries. The United States was settled by immigrant groups or clans from European countries and around the world. Most of these settlers arrived in groups and settled in distinct areas, with some members venturing out to conquer more land. Thus, the American individual was born who connected to his or her heritage group but not to the point of feeling inhibited from venturing out to find his or her own way in the world. This stands in contrast to how other areas of the world were settled, where over a number of centuries clan groups were organized into nation states. These clan tendencies remain in some OECD countries today, resulting in a communitarian view of government and social responsibility.

In the United States, the provision of health services that ultimately resulted in employer-sponsored health insurance is first a byproduct of the Industrial Revolution and then post–WWII wage and price freeze. Following two world wars, the American public did not tolerate anything that resembled socialism or communism and thus had no desire to follow the lead of their European peers in developing a universal healthcare system. In contrast, the European states implemented national health coverage in Germany and England as governmental means to appease unruly labor groups. Government-sponsored health insurance became prevalent throughout Europe as Europeans rebuilt their countries and governments following the devastating destruction from WWII. From the mid-20th century through the 21st century, Americans have considered the federal government the healthcare provider of last resort or safety net provider (or payer) for the vulnerable and low-income members of society, whereas in European and other OECD countries, government-provided health services have become an assumed provision of federal governmental services.

As national health insurance programs have developed, four types of systems have emerged: national health system, national health insurance, statutory health insurance, and free market. A national health system is where the federal government owns everything and pays for everything. All hospitals, physician offices, and other providers are owned by or employed by the federal government. All services are paid for by the government, although they are funded by some type of direct taxation. Although everyone has unlimited access, timely access for nonemergent care may be rare. Citizens tend to have a very favorable view of the system and care is often rated as some of the best quality care in the world. The cost of providing this model of healthcare delivery is around 10% of GDP. The country best known for this system is the United Kingdom; the United States uses this system for Military Health Services (except TriCare) and Indian Health Services.

National health insurance is a system where the government functions as the payer or insurer with services delivered through the private sector. Within this system, everyone has access to healthcare services through a private provider, and all services are paid for by the government. The cost of care within this system runs around 9% of GDP, citizens view this system favorably, and the quality of care is rated very highly. As with all national health plans funded by global budgets, individuals are not responsible for payment, often implying their access is free, although they pay for these services through taxes. Access for nonemergent health needs can result in a substantial wait, but emergent health needs are treated in a timely manner. Two countries best known for this system are Australia and Canada; the U.S. equivalent is traditional Medicare.

Statutory health insurance is a system where the government requires all citizens to have health insurance coverage purchased on the private market with government provided funds. In this system, the only role of the government is to require everyone have a health insurance plan and pay the insurance premiums. All healthcare delivery and insurance functions are carried out in the private sector. Again, the perception is often that the care is free when in reality all citizens pay for this universal access through taxes. The public satisfaction with this system is moderate to low, and the public expenditures are in line with the previous two systems at 10% of GDP. Switzerland and the Netherlands are representative countries. In the United States this system is equivalent to Medicare Advantage, the Health Exchanges, and employer-sponsored insurance.

A free market is a system where all services, providers, and payment occur in the private market with government involvement occurring in aspects such as safety, quality, and licensure. In this system, individuals get whatever they can afford to purchase. Quality, satisfaction, and access are low, whereas cost varies from very low (less than 10%) to high (greater than 15% of GDP). The one term that best describes this system is *fragmented*, with representative countries ranging from the United States on the high end to developing countries on the low end.

Over the past half century in the United States, most of the population recognizes that the cost of providing healthcare services has increased at a consistent rate generally twice that of Consumer Price Index (CPI) inflation. However, what most citizens do not realize is that the federal government's involvement in healthcare services has increased at a pace at least equal to cost inflation. Since 2000, 36% of all bills introduced and passed at the federal level have had something to do with healthcare. Viewed from another lens, most policy issues have long periods of stability punctuated by short spurts of increased activity that returns to the previous baseline. In contrast, healthcare legislation follows this same pattern, with the exception of each period of heightened activity resulting in a new, higher baseline.

Discussion Questions

1. Describe how the delivery of and payment for healthcare services in the United States compares with the delivery of and payment for healthcare services in other developed nations.
2. Based on the above discussion, provide an argument for either increased or decreased federal government involvement in healthcare delivery and payment.
3. Using the above models and discussion, make your own argument for how much the U.S. healthcare system could evolve within the next 10 years.

✩ CASE 14-2

Forecasting Patient Demand for Improved Resource Allocation

Raymond J. Higbea, PhD & Jeffery Skinner, MHA, RN

Over several decades, demand for emergency department (ED) services has increased. Concomitantly, the number of operational EDs has decreased (AHA, 2016). As a result, this has created a resource challenge for administrations as they seek to meet increased demand with limited assets. Multiple solutions have been employed, such as redirecting less acutely ill patients to lower levels of care and providing clinical areas for patients waiting for inpatient beds (boarding) or prolonged assessments (clinical decision units). Several process improvement solutions have been employed to enhance key performance indicators, such as monitoring arrival to provider times and decision to disposition times. Other methods rely on tools to document how busy the ED is at any given time. Although these tools are accurate, they are not predictive and provide little value in resource allocation and adjustment. Finally, several EDs have found some utility in staffing to the day and shift to better meet historic resource needs; however, even these imprecise attempts fall short of expectations.

The concept of value-based care began in the early 1990s as large employers, insurance companies, and the federal government attempted to rectify an imbalance between escalating healthcare costs and poor-quality outcomes as documented in reports such as *To Err is Human* by the Institute of Medicine (IOM, 1999). Providers were generally receptive to quality initiatives that allowed them to earn an extra 1% to 3% from payers and quality organizational certifications. Prior to these efforts, providers had begun working on improving process efficiency and patient quality. As the process and quality improvement activities matured over the next two decades, they proved themselves reckless and ineffective at improving quality or decreasing costs. With the implementation of the PPACA, the federal government began a process of paying providers for quality outcomes on a revenue-neutral basis (value-based payments)—if you improved from your established base, you could earn more; if you did not improve, you earned less.

As the manager of Continuum Health's metro emergency department in Majestic Falls, Michigan—a 100,000 plus visit per year ED—pondered the current milieu, he wondered how he could better align resources with variable needs (patient volumes), while at the same time creating an ED visit of increased value (value = quality / cost) (Skinner & Higbea, 2015). The manager identified the need for variable staffing schedules that better aligned staffing resources with fluctuating patient demand. Data analysis revealed variation in patient arrival patterns by month, leading to natural 3-month groupings, creating seasonal patterns. Once these seasons were identified, they were divided by the day of the week to create four groupings of similar volumes. An existing labor forecasting tool was enhanced to create an anticipated forecast of patient arrivals, more closely aligned with typical patient arrival patterns. The original 4-hour forecast was enhanced to a 2-hour average forecast that provided the best result. Creation of a variable staffing model and the use of an enhanced labor forecasting tool allowed charge nurses to adjust staffing by 2-hour intervals, which provided significant improvements to operational effectiveness and efficiencies including:

- confidence in the planning and implementation of resources,
- an annual 55% reduction in overtime pay (approximately $132,000),
- decreased quality scores variability,
- decreased staff turnover, and
- stabilized patient experience scores (Higbea et al., 2018).

Discussion Questions

1. Based on the above scenario, explain how the deployment of this forecasting approach affected the value of an ED visit.
2. If the above forecasting model provides an ED visit of increased value, how does this increased value correlate with health policy?
3. How could policymakers use this example as encouragement for providers to seek similar management approaches?

References

American Hospital Association (AHA). (2016). *Trendwatch chartbook 2016: Trends affecting hospitals and health systems*. http://www.aha.org/research/reports/tw/chartbook/ch3.shtml

Institute of Medicine (IOM). (1999). *To err is human: Building a safer health system.* http://www.national academies.org/hmd/~/media/Files/Report%20Files/1999/To-Err-is-Human/To%20Err%20is%20 Human%201999%20%20report%20brief.pdf

Skinner, J., & Higbea, R. J. (2015). *Forecasting the potential for emergency department overcrowding.* Transactions from the International Conference on Health Information Technology Advancement. Paper 52. https://scholarworks.wmich.edu/cgi/viewcontent.cgi?referer=https://search.yahoo .com/&httpsredir=1&article=1048&context=ichita_transactions

Higbea, R. J., Skinner J., Buer, D., & Horvath, C. (2018). Utilizing predictive analytics to align emergency department staffing resources with patient demand. *Healthcare Financial Management, 72*(2). http://www.hfma.org/Content.aspx?id=59165

ꗏ CASE 14-3

Ethically Delivering Care

Raymond J. Higbea, PhD, Lara Jaskiewicz, PhD, Gregory A. Cline, PhD, & Alyssa Luboff, PhD

The study of ethics in Western cultures begins with Aristotle (384–322 BC), one of the fathers of Western philosophy and Plato's most successful student. From 423–348 BC, Aristotle wrote prolifically on multiple topics, from physics and zoology to ethics. Aristotle's ethical writings focused on virtue, or the excellence of character. He believed that virtue is cultivated in the same way as a skill such as carpentry: through practice and following the model of accomplished masters. Virtue, according to Aristotle, is the ability to work skillfully with our natural drives and emotions. It is a mean, a middle path of wise action that neither constrains too much nor gives into excess. For example, fear is a natural emotion. If we constrain our fear too much, we fail to notice real dangers and are rash. However, if we give in to an excess of fear, we fail to act when necessary and are cowardly. Courage, Aristotle explains, is the ability to act wisely with fear, avoiding the extremes of rashness (deficiency) and cowardice (excess).

Aristotle divided virtuous actions into just and noble acts. Just acts are those actions that society expects from its members, such as paying our bills and obeying the laws. From the lens of leadership and economics, just acts are transactional. Noble acts are those actions beyond what society expects of its members, such as placing ourselves in physical danger to assist a stranger in distress. From the lens of leadership and economics, noble acts are transformational. It was in this context that the Greek physician Hippocrates (460–320 BC) developed the Hippocratic Oath describing the physician's duty to each patient. This included the just virtues of confidentiality and nonmaleficence (NLM, 2002).

During the years between Hippocrates and the 19th century, philosophers from the Jewish, Islamic, and Christian traditions published multiple works that coalesced around the virtuous duty of the physician to the patient. Finally, in 1803, physician and author Thomas Percival coined the term "medical ethics," which included four core virtues, or "values": autonomy, beneficence, nonmaleficence, and justice (Pellegrino, 1986). These virtues served medical ethics well until the 1930s and 1940s, which saw the rise of totalitarianism and WWII. Doctors in Nazi Germany and the Japanese Empire experimented on individuals they deemed "undesirable" or beneath the threshold of human dignity. Even in the United States, similar experiments were performed within the same time frame. In the Tuskegee University syphilis study, African Americans were purposefully not given the identified cure, penicillin, in order to observe the disease's progression and impact (CDC, 2017). Following WWII, the Nuremberg Code (1947) and Declaration of Helsinki (1964) were drafted to address the Nazi and Japanese atrocities (Alliance for Human Research Protection, 2018). These international agreements established the importance of patient autonomy and informed consent when participating in medical research. Meanwhile, the Tuskegee Study continued in the United States.

The next set of medical ethics challenges came during the 1970s and 1980s through legal cases regarding elective abortions, the right to die (Cruzan and Quinlan cases), and Baby Doe cases (treatment of disabled or ill newborns regardless of parent preference). In the early 1970s, the Tuskegee Study became a focus of congressional investigation. These cases focused on patient autonomy, respect of persons, and advance directives. More recently, these same concerns have been directed toward medical infertility and genomic medical advancements.

In the late 1990s and early 2000s, the collapse of several large financial firms ushered in increased statutory financial requirements for organizations. These new statutory requirements resulted in the addition of business ethics and compliance with medical ethics. As a result of these environmental and legal challenges, medical ethics expanded from the original four values to include veracity, conflict of interest, and compliance. Throughout the 20th and 21st centuries, medical ethics has shifted to become healthcare ethics; unfortunately, this transformation has been a reaction rather than a proactive consideration of the ethical consequences of emerging activities.

This shift from medical to healthcare ethics occurred as the healthcare delivery model transitioned from individual to third-party payment and from a transformational, relational model to a transactional, productivity model. Prior to the introduction of medical insurance, physicians and patients had established relationships that included discussion of treatment plans and payment. As medical insurance and other third-party payers emerged throughout the 20th and 21st centuries, physicians and patients were excluded from payment and risk discussions. This resulted in a weakening, if not fracturing, of the physician–patient relationship. All healthcare providers enter their profession to care for people, but over the past century these relationships have lost context, communication, and trust—all elements of a relational ethic, or what ethicist and psychologist Carol Gilligan first described as "the ethics of care."

Table 14-1 below suggests an expansion of current medical (MED) and business (BUS) ethics to respond to the current healthcare environment and include the ethics of care. The model is relational and patient focused. The value this reorganization brings to healthcare

TABLE 14-1 Expanded Values for Health Care	
Compassion	**Justice**
How we direct ourselves toward others	*How we protect others*
Beneficence (MED/Care)	Autonomy (MED/Care)
Nonmaleficence (MED/Care)	Rights (BUS)
Respect for dignity (BUS/Care)	Confidentiality (BUS)
Spirit of service (BUS)	Consent (MED)
How we relate to others	*What we promise others*
Love (Care)	Veracity (MED)
Communication (BUS/Care)	Honesty (BUS)

Compassion	Justice
Relationships (Care)	Transparency (BUS)
Emotion (Care)	Conflict of interest (BUS)
	How we situate others
Preservation and Empowerment	Context (Care)
Professional competence (BUS)	Diversity/Cultural sensitivity (MED/BUS/Care)
Stewardship (BUS)	*How we prepare ourselves for others*
Personal vitality (BUS)	Virtue (BUS)
Organizational vitality (BUS)	Integrity (BUS)
	Fidelity (MED)
	Resilience (Care)

ethics is at least twofold. First, it recognizes and uplifts the professional agency and responsibility of the provider; and, second, it preserves the dignity and principal concerns of the patient.

Discussion Questions

1. Given past abuses, what role should government play in the development and practice of medical ethics?
2. Could this reorganization of ethical virtues (why we do what we do) rebalance the provider/patient relationship?
3. Because payment for healthcare services is linked to the delivery of care, how could payment models be used to rebalance current healthcare ethics to include the ethics of care?
4. How could the above model be used to influence transformation of the delivery of healthcare services?
5. How could the above model be correlated with public policy?

References

Alliance for Human Research Protection (AHRP). (2018). *1964: Declaration of Helsinki diverges from the Nuremberg Code*. http://ahrp.org/1964-wma-assembly-approves-the-declaration-of-helsinki/

Centers for Disease Control and Prevention (CDC). (2017). *U.S. Public Health Service Syphilis study at Tuskegee*. https://www.cdc.gov/tuskegee/timeline.htm

National Library of Medicine (NLM). (2002). *Greek medicine: The Hippocratic Oath*. https://www.nlm.nih .gov/hmd/greek/greek_oath.html

Pellegrino, E. D. (1986). Percival's medical ethics: The moral philosophy of an 18th-century English gentleman. *Journal of the American Medical Association, 146*(11), 2265–2269.

Appendix

▶ A Guide to Case Study Teaching

Case studies are used in classrooms as an active learning method that allow students to apply knowledge they have learned in a real-world context. Case studies help students develop skills in essential areas, such as problem solving, critical thinking, and decision-making. Case studies are valuable assets for instructors and may be used in various ways, such as to enhance in-class discussion, individual analysis, or group work.

Health policy management and related fields are ideal for case study use. First, the number and types of people who study health policy are expansive—from legal and policy experts to clinicians. Case studies provide a method for analyzing within an individual's own experience and perspective. Secondly, with the ever-changing landscape of health policy, case studies apply current laws and trends in health policy through a case approach.

▶ A Guide to Case Study Analysis for Students

This text uses a collection of case studies so students can critically analyze health policy management concepts. Each case study includes a set of questions for critical evaluation, although students should also go beyond the questions provided in their analysis of each case.

The benefit of case study analysis is that it allows for real-world examples that may be encountered in health policy management and related fields. The purpose of case study analysis is to identify key concepts and issues, identify alternative solutions to the problem, and form relevant conclusions.

Steps in Case Study Analysis

1. Read the syllabus or instructions for case study analysis provided by your instructor to learn the goal of the analysis. In addition, read any questions provided that you will need to answer in advance so that you know which pieces of the case study require your focus.
2. Thoroughly read the case study, as many times as needed, highlighting the key issues in the case.

3. Identify the most important facts surrounding the case.
4. Use the textbook and/or other resources to research the issues in the case.

Writing the Case Study Analysis

1. Begin with an introduction that identifies the key concepts and issues and provides a brief summary of the case.
2. The second section should cover background information and research on key issues.
3. In the body of the paper, provide answers to the questions given within the case in paragraph form—one paragraph per question. Use outside research to support answers where needed.
4. Discuss any additional alternatives to the problem and propose solution/recommendations.

Glossary

A

Abuse occurs if an activity abuses the healthcare system, such as charging outrageous fees or using billing codes that are related to, but pay higher than, the service actually provided.

Accountable Care Organization (ACO) a set of providers who are jointly held accountable for achieving measured improvements in quality and reductions in the rate of spending growth.

Advance Directives a written statement of a person's wishes regarding medical treatment, often including a living will, made to ensure those wishes are carried out should the person be unable to communicate them to a doctor.

Affordable Care Act (ACA) a healthcare law passed by Congress in 2010 during the administration of President Barack Obama.

Agency for Healthcare Research and Quality (AHRQ) a U.S. government agency that functions as a part of the Department of Health & Human Services (HHS) to support research to help improve the quality of health care.

Agenda Setting the longest and most complex of the policy process. Categories include: definition of a problem, germination of a policy, and ideas to legislation development.

Alternative Payment Models (APMs) created under the Quality Payment Program, rewards providers who outperform others in delivering high-quality, coordinated, and efficient care.

Autonomy right of the patient to make their own decision and retain control over their medical care.

B

Beneficence healthcare providers must do everything they can to benefit each patient.

Bioethics the ethics of medical and biological research.

C

Center for Medicaid & Medicare Services (CMS) a federal agency within the United States Department of Health and Human Services (HHS) that administers the Medicare program and works in partnership with state governments to administer Medicaid, the Children's Health Insurance Program (CHIP), and health insurance portability standards.

Children's Health Insurance Program (CHIP) provides medical coverage for individuals under age 19 whose parents earn too much income to qualify for Medicaid, but not enough to pay for private coverage.

Children's Health Insurance Program Reauthorization Act (CHIPRA) provided states with significant new funding, new programmatic options, and a range of new incentives for covering children through Medicaid and CHIP.

Civic Participation promoting the quality of life in a community, through both political and non-political processes.

Comparative Effectiveness Research (CER) generation and synthesis of evidence that compares the benefits and harms of alternative methods to prevent, diagnose, treat, and monitor a clinical condition to improve the delivery of care.

Cost Sharing the share of costs covered by insurance that individuals pay out of their own pocket.

Covered Entities defined in the HIPAA rules as (1) health plans, (2) healthcare clearinghouses, and (3) healthcare providers who electronically transmit any health information in connection with transactions for which HHS has adopted standards.

D

Data driven determined by or dependent on the collection or analysis of data.

Delphi Method a qualitative forecasting technique that looks at changes and trends over time.

Department of Health & Human Services (HHS) the U.S. government's principal agency for protecting the health of all Americans and providing essential human services, especially for those who are least able to help themselves.

E

Effective providing services based on scientific knowledge to all who could benefit, and refraining from providing services to those not likely to benefit.

Efficient avoiding waste, including waste of equipment, supplies, ideas, and energy.

Egalitarian perspective the idea that fairness requires recognition of different levels of need, and everyone should have equal access to the benefits and burdens arising from the pursuit of health.

Electronic Health Records (EHR) an Electronic Health record (EHR) is a digital version of a patient's paper chart.

Emergency Medical Treatment and Labor Act (EMTALA) federal law to protect patients from being "dumped" from hospitals for not having the necessary coverage to pay for services rendered.

Emergency preparedness plan a course of action developed to mitigate the damage of potential events that could endanger an organization's ability to function. The plan should include measures that provide for the safety of personnel and, if possible, property and facilities.

Enforcement Rule a decree from HIPAA that sets out the rules that govern the responsibilities and requirements of Covered Entities and Business Associates about how it expects them to cooperate in the enforcement process.

Episode of care (EOC) one or more healthcare services given by a provider during a specific period of relatively continuous care in relation to a particular health, medical problem, or situation.

Equitable providing care that does not vary in quality because of personal characteristics such as gender, ethnicity, geographic location, and socioeconomic status.

Executive Branch the president is responsible for implementing and enforcing the laws.

F

Federal poverty level (FPL) a measure of income used by the U.S. government to determine who is eligible for subsidies, programs, and benefits.

Federally Qualified Health Center (FQHC) located in medically underserved areas and provide essential access to comprehensive primary care in underserved communities and are a key component of our healthcare system.

Fee-for-service (FFS) a payment model where services are unbundled and paid for separately.

Financial Statements written records of a businesses' financial situation. There are three reports that depict the financial activities: balance sheet, income statement, and statement of cash flows.

Forecasting a method by which healthcare companies can prepare and plan for future possible occurrences.

Fraud when someone misrepresents or falsifies a fact related to healthcare services to receive payment for a health plan or the government.

H

Health Professional Shortage Area (HPSA) designated as having a shortage of either primary medical care, dental care, or mental health providers, and may be urban or rural areas.

Healthcare data analytics application of statistical techniques to allow informed decisions to be made based on the data.

Health Insurance can reimburse the insured for expenses incurred from illness or injury, or pay the care provider directly.

Health Literacy degree to which individuals have the capacity to obtain, process, and understand basic health information and services needed to make appropriate health decisions.

Health Insurance Portability and Accountability Act (HIPAA) a U.S. law designed to provide privacy standards to protect patients' medical records and other health information provided to health plans, doctors, hospitals and other healthcare providers.

I

Individual Rights guarantee individuals the rights to certain freedoms without interference from the government or other individuals.

Informed Consent the requirement that healthcare providers must provide patients with all of the information that they need to make an informed decision about their care.

J

Judicial Branch the main duty of the judicial branch when is to interpret the law and determine if the law is constitutional or unconstitutional.

Justice fairness in all medical decisions.

K

Key Performance Indicators (KPI) a measurable value that demonstrates how effectively a company is achieving key business objectives. Organizations use KPIs to evaluate their success at reaching targets.

Key Stakeholder a person, group, or organization that has interest or concern in an organization. Stakeholders can affect or be affected by the organization's actions, objectives, and policies.

L

Legislative Branch consists of the two houses of Congress—the Senate and the House of Representatives. Congress is granted all legislative powers, meaning Congress decides which laws are passed.

Legislative Process includes development and submission of legislation to one of the legislative chambers by a policy entrepreneur.

Libertarian Perspective emphasizes freedom, individual liberty, and respect of property rights and favors the equal distribution of both benefits and burdens associated with the pursuit of health.

M

Medicare Access and CHIP Reauthorization Act (MACRA) created a new provider incentive structure through the Quality Payment Program.

Medicaid a healthcare program that assists low-income families or individuals in paying

for doctor visits, hospital stays, long-term medical, custodial care costs, and more.

Medicaid Expansion a provision in the ACA called for expanding Medicaid eligibility in order to cover more low-income people.

Medical errors preventable adverse effects of *medical* care whether or not evident or harmful to the patient.

Medically Underserved Area (MUA) consist of an entire county or group of counties where residents have a shortage of health services.

Medicare Part A is managed by Medicare and provides Medicare benefits and coverage for inpatient hospital care.

Medicare Part B covers medical services and supplies that are medically necessary to treat your health condition.

Medicare Part C plans offer Medicare-covered benefits through private health plans instead of through Original Medicare.

Medicare Part D a voluntary outpatient prescription drug benefit for people on Medicare.

Medicare Physician Fee Schedule (MPFS) a complete listing of fees used by Medicare to pay doctors or other providers/suppliers.

Merit-based Incentive Payment System (MIPS) is one of two tracks under the Quality Payment Program, which moves Medicare Part B providers to a performance-based payment system.

Modification Process the last phase of the policy process. This is the review and refinement phase.

N

Nonmaleficence "do no harm." Care is in the best interest of the patient.

O

Office for Civil Rights (OCR) enforces laws against discrimination based on race, color, national origin, disability, age, sex, and religion.

Office of Inspector General (OIG) has been at the forefront of the Nation's efforts to fight waste, fraud and abuse in Medicare, Medicaid, and more than 100 other Health and Human Services programs. OIG develops and distributes resources to assist the healthcare industry in its efforts to comply with the Nation's fraud and abuse laws and to educate the public about fraudulent schemes so they can protect themselves and report suspicious activities.

Operations Process begins once the bill is signed into law by the executive and becomes the duty of the executive.

P

Patient Bill of Rights a list of guarantees for those receiving medical care. It may take the form of a law or a non-binding declaration.

Patient-centered providing care that is respectful of and responsive to individual patient preferences, needs, and values, and ensuring that patient values guide all clinical decisions.

Patient-Centered Medical Home (PCMH) seeks to meet the healthcare needs of patients and to improve patient and staff experiences, safety, outcomes, and system efficiency.

Patient Rights include the right to make decisions regarding medical care, the right to accept or refuse treatment, and the right to formulate advance directives.

Pay-for-performance (P4P) any type of payment arrangement for reimbursing providers that includes incentives aligned with performance.

Policy a rule to guide decisions based on good intent and societal values, dealing with a matter of public concern.

Policymakers private actors, government entities, and authoritative decision makers.

Policymaking Process a decision-making process including policy formulation, policy implementation, and policy modification. Policy formulation includes agenda setting, policy implementation includes rulemaking, and policy modification includes revisiting prior decisions.

Privacy Officer a person designated by an organization that routinely handles protected health information, to develop, implement, and oversee the organization's compliance with the U.S. Health Insurance Portability and Accountability Act (HIPAA) privacy rules.

Privacy Rule establishes national standards to protect individuals' medical records and other personal health information and applies to health plans, healthcare clearinghouses, and those healthcare providers that conduct certain healthcare transactions electronically.

Prospective Payment System (PPS) type of episode-of-care reimbursement in which the third-party payer established the payment rates for the healthcare services in advance for a specific time period.

Protected Health Information (PHI) any information in a medical record that can be used to identify an individual, and that was created, used, or disclosed in the course of providing a healthcare service, such as a diagnosis or treatment.

Provider Rights include the right to be treated with fairness and dignity by employers, to be protected from harassment, and to be able to excuse themselves from patient care with which they disagree.

Q

Quality Care the degree to which healthcare services for individuals and populations increase the likelihood of desired health outcomes and are consistent with current professional knowledge.

Quality Payment Program (QPP) improves Medicare by helping eligible clinicians focus on care quality and making patients healthier.

R

Reimbursement the action of repaying a person who has spent or lost money.

Resource Based Relative Value Scale (RBRVS) is the physician payment system used by the Centers for Medicare & Medicaid Services (CMS) and most other payers.

Retrospective Payment Method fee-for-service reimbursement in which providers receive compensation after health services have been rendered.

Right to Health a legal obligation on states to ensure appropriate health, including access to timely, acceptable, and affordable health care for all people without discrimination.

S

Safe avoiding injuries to patients from the care that is intended to help them.

Security Rule requires appropriate administrative, physical, and technical safeguards to ensure the confidentiality, integrity, and security of electronic protected health information.

Social Cohesion willingness of members of a society to cooperate with each other in order to survive and prosper.

Social Determinants of Health (SDOH) conditions in which people are born, grow, live, work and age. These circumstances are shaped by the distribution of money, power and resources at global, national and local levels.

Social Security Act (SSA) enacted in 1935 by Franklin Delano Roosevelt, America's foremost social welfare law, designed to counteract the dangers of old age, poverty, disability, and unemployment through a range of government programs and benefits.

Stark Laws federal regulation governing physicians referring patients to medical facilities in which there is a financial interest, be it ownership, investment, or a structured compensation arrangement. There are three Stark Law provisions.

Strategic planning organizational management activity that is used to set priorities, focus energy and resources, strengthen operations, ensure that employees and other stakeholders are working toward common goals, establish agreement around intended outcomes/results.

T

Time-Series Analysis a quantitative forecasting technique that looks at changes and trends over time.

Timely reducing waits and sometimes harmful delays for both those who receive and those who give care.

U

Underinsured Population citizens who have inadequate healthcare coverage.

Uninsured Population citizens who lack health insurance coverage.

Utilitarian perspective focuses on maximizing overall happiness, and that fairness is best served when the greatest good for the greatest number are served.

V

Value-based purchasing (VBP) a system in which purchasers hold providers of healthcare accountable for both the quality and costs of health care.

Vulnerable Populations include the economically disadvantaged, racial and ethnic minorities, the uninsured, low-income children, the elderly, the homeless, those with human immunodeficiency virus (HIV), and those with other chronic health conditions, including severe mental illness.

W

Waste unnecessary costs and use of resources, such as spending on services that lack evidence of producing better outcomes than less expensive alternatives.

World Health Organization (WHO) primary role is to direct and coordinate international health within the U.N. system.

Index